INTERNATIONAL BANK CRISIS MANAGEMENT

A TRANSATLANTIC PERSPECTIVE

At the international level, bank crisis management has become a key part of banking and banking regulation. Accordingly, *International Bank Crisis Management – A Transatlantic Perspective* analyses the legal regimes governing bank crisis management in the EU, UK and US, discussing the different procedures and tools available as well as the regulatory architecture and the authorities involved.

Building on a broad working definition of 'bank crisis management' and referring to several cases, this book explores the techniques and approaches employed by the authorities to deal with troubled banks on both sides of the Atlantic. The legal analysis distinguishes between procedures and tools aimed at liquidating the bank in crisis vis-à-vis those aimed at restructuring. In this regard, attention is paid to the rules allowing for the use of public money in handling banks in trouble as well as to the role that deposit insurance schemes can play. Considerations on the impact on banks of the current crisis provoked by the COVID-19 pandemic are advanced, primarily focusing on the expected surge of non-performing loans as well as on ways to effectively manage these assets.

These issues are approached from a comparative law perspective, providing law and economics considerations and focusing on strengths and drawbacks of the rules currently in force. On these grounds, this work advances some policy considerations as well as reform proposals aiming at enhancing the legal regimes in force.

Hart Studies in Commercial and Financial Law: Volume 9

Hart Studies in Commercial and Financial Law

Series Editors: John Linarelli and Teresa Rodríguez de las Heras Ballell

This series offers a venue for publishing works on commercial law as well as on the regulation of banking and finance and the law on insolvency and bankruptcy. It publishes works on the law on secured credit, the regulatory and transactional aspects of banking and finance, the transactional and regulatory institutions for financial markets, legal and policy aspects associated with access to commercial and consumer credit, new generation subjects having to do with the institutional architecture associated with innovation and the digital economy including works on blockchain technology, work on the relationship of law to economic growth, the harmonisation or unification of commercial law, transnational commercial law, and the global financial order. The series promotes interdisciplinary work. It publishes research on the law using the methods of empirical legal studies, behavioural economics, political economy, normative welfare economics, law and society inquiry, socio-legal studies, political theory, and historical methods. Its coverage includes international and comparative investigations of areas of law within its remit.

Volume 1: The Financialisation of the Citizen: Social and Financial Inclusion through European Private Law
Guido Comparato

Volume 2: MiFID II and Private Law: Enforcing EU Conduct of Business Rules
Federico Della Negra

Volume 3: Reforming Corporate Retail Investor Protection: Regulating to Avert Mis-Selling
Diane Bugeja

Volume 4: The Future of Commercial Law: Ways Forward for Change and Reform
Edited by Orkun Akseli and John Linarelli

Volume 5: The Cape Town Convention: A Documentary History
Anton Didenko

Volume 6: Regulating the Crypto Economy: Business Transformations and Financialisation
Iris H-Y Chiu

Volume 7: The Future of High-Cost Credit: Rethinking Payday Lending
Jodi Gardner

Volume 8: The Enforcement of EU Financial Law
Edited by Jan Crijns, Matthias Haentjens and Rjnhard Haentjens

Volume 9: International Bank Crisis Management: A Transatlantic Perspective
Marco Bodellini

International Bank Crisis Management

A Transatlantic Perspective

Marco Bodellini

• HART •
OXFORD • LONDON • NEW YORK • NEW DELHI • SYDNEY

HART PUBLISHING

Bloomsbury Publishing Plc

Kemp House, Chawley Park, Cumnor Hill, Oxford, OX2 9PH, UK

1385 Broadway, New York, NY 10018, USA

29 Earlsfort Terrace, Dublin 2, Ireland

HART PUBLISHING, the Hart/Stag logo, BLOOMSBURY and the Diana logo are trademarks of Bloomsbury Publishing Plc

First published in Great Britain 2022

A catalogue record for this book is available from the British Library.

A catalogue record for this book is available from the Library of Congress.

ISBN: HB: 978-1-50996-130-6
ePDF: 978-1-50996-132-0
ePub: 978-1-50996-131-3

Typeset by Compuscript Ltd, Shannon

PREFACE

At the international level, bank crisis management – the procedures, tools, techniques and strategies to manage bank crises and the legal regimes governing them – has become over time a key part of banking. Bank crisis management is relevant both from the perspective of the banking activity and the internal organisation of banks and from the perspective of the public controls exercised by the authorities over them.

The global financial crisis has brought bank crisis management under the spotlight, clearly showing the key importance of specific and efficient crisis management regimes to handle ailing institutions. In the aftermath of the global financial crisis of 2007–09, several jurisdictions introduced new crisis management regimes which apply to banks or reformed the ones previously developed. In this regard, the Financial Stability Board (FSB) Key Attributes of Effective Resolution Regimes for Financial Institutions, adopted in 2011 and revised in 2014, have been crucial in helping legislators and regulators navigate towards the adoption of specific bank crisis management frameworks. Similarly, the International Association of Deposit Insurers (IADI) Core Principles for Effective Deposit Insurance Systems, adopted in 2009 and then amended in 2014, also played a very important function in ensuring that countries developed legal frameworks on deposit insurance and accordingly set up deposit guarantee schemes which are adequately involved in bank crisis management.

However, the FSB Key Attributes mostly target institutions that are systemically significant or critical in failure, with the vast majority of small and medium-sized banks, often non-systemically significant in the event of failure, thus falling outside their primary scope of application. The lack of special regimes for small and medium-sized banks (*rectius* non-systemic banks or banks non-systemically significant in case of failure) in many jurisdictions has been regarded as a critical issue, possibly further exacerbated by the expected serious economic consequences which will arise from the COVID-19 pandemic. The pandemic-provoked crisis is bound to also harm banks in the near future by causing a relevant surge of non-performing loans, which in turn will lead institutions to have to record losses. Such losses will negatively affect bank capital, potentially causing institutions to fail. Effective bank crisis management regimes will be therefore key to tackling all those issues, thereby limiting spill-over effects.

On these grounds, beside systemic bank resolution regimes, an increasing interest exists at the international level on the insolvency proceedings to initiate in the event of crises involving non-systemic banks (typically small and medium-sized institutions). These proceedings are commonly understood as alternative to the ones used to handle the crisis of systemic banks, often referred to as resolution regimes. At European level, there exists such distinction between resolution for systemic banks (rectius banks which have passed the public interest test) and other insolvency proceedings for non-systemic banks (rectius banks which have not passed the public interest test). While the former is now harmonised as a result of the adoption and transposition of the Bank Recovery and Resolution Directive (BRRD), the latter diverge from Member State to Member State. The lack of harmonisation in this area is deemed able to negatively affect also the resolution procedure as such. To tackle this issue, in 2021, the European Commission launched a consultation focused on these insolvency regimes as well as on the role that deposit guarantee schemes could (and possibly should) play to contribute to effectively manage bank crises, with a view to advancing a reform proposal in due course. The objective of the Commission's initiative is thus to harmonise at least the key features of bank insolvency regimes at European level.

Similarly, UNIDROIT is leading a global initiative, involving a number of international organisations and bank supervisors, with a view to drafting general principles, guidelines and standards to be used to develop special legal regimes to handle banks which are not systemically significant or critical in the event of failure. Such banks are those that would in principle fall outside the scope of application of the FSB Key Attributes. These guidelines and standards are expected to help countries all over the world design effective legal frameworks concerning the management of crises affecting such banks.

***

Based on these considerations, in dealing with international bank crisis management, this work contributes to the debate ongoing among policy-makers, scholars and law practitioners, with a view to critically discussing some of the most controversial issues at stake, while advancing policy remarks and exploring ideas for reform proposals. The study takes an analytical and comparative, yet critical approach, which goes beyond the simple discussion of the law of resolution, as bank crisis management in its entirety is the subject of the analysis. Thus, from a holistic perspective, emphasis is placed on the institutional architecture, the situation in which the banking system finds itself as a consequence of the COVID-19-provoked crisis and the related need to adopt and implement effective regimes to enable authorities to handle problem banks. Attention is also paid to how public money can be used to prevent bank crises as well as in the context of an already ongoing crisis. With regard to dual-track regimes, the resolution procedure is discussed vis-a-vis insolvency proceedings to initiate when resolution is not considered to be needed in the public interest. In single-track regimes, the whole crisis management procedure is explored, focusing on the different available tools. The role of deposit guarantee schemes in bank crises is also analysed. The non-performing loan problem is tackled based on the expected outcomes generated by the COVID-19-provoked economic crisis. Against this backdrop, different ways to deal with banks in crisis are confronted, by looking, from a comparative law perspective, at the European Union (EU) (with special attention paid to the Banking Union and to Italy), the United Kingdom (UK) and the United States (US). The international dimension of this analysis is thus covered by focusing on the legal frameworks and past experience of some of the most advanced and developed jurisdictions around the world.

***

In tackling these issues, this work is divided into eight chapters, as follows.

Chapter one provides a useful working definition of the concept of bank crisis management, along with a number of other key definitions which are applied throughout the work. The definition of bank crisis management is necessarily broad and aims at encompassing the most common and effective tools and procedures employed and initiated in some of the most developed jurisdictions around the world (namely the EU – Banking Union, US and UK).

Chapter two focuses on the supervisory and crisis management architecture designed in the EU, UK and US in response to the global financial crisis of 2007–09. In this regard, the establishment of the Banking Union is discussed, mostly focusing on the Single Supervisory Mechanism (first pillar), the Single Resolution Mechanism (second pillar) and the European Deposit Insurance Scheme (third missing pillar). On the other hand, the reform passed in the UK through the adoption of the Financial Services Act 2012 is explored, focusing on the key functions assigned to the Bank of England for overseeing the financial system as a whole. In the US, the interaction between federal and state authorities in supervising banks and managing bank crises is analysed, also looking at the innovations introduced by the Dodd-Frank Act in 2010. The key role of the FDIC is also explored and discussed.

Chapter three deals with what can be defined as a bank's first lines of defence when facing a crisis, namely capital and early intervention measures. The concept of capital is discussed looking at the rationale behind bank capital regulation. Capital requirements and the role of the Basel Committee on Banking Supervision in shaping bank capital regulation at the international level, through the adoption of soft law principles, are analysed. Along with capital, the so-called early intervention measures are discussed; these are tools and procedures at the authorities' disposal to adopt and initiate when the crisis is still at the early stages. Accordingly, early intervention measures aim to ensure that banks address their weaknesses promptly when the triggers for their submission to a crisis management procedure have not been met yet. References to the Italian special administration and the US prompt and corrective action are made to point to the importance of acting timely.

Chapter four is devoted to bank insolvency regimes looking at the EU non-harmonised frameworks (paying special attention to the Italian compulsory administrative liquidation), the UK statutory modified insolvency regimes for banks, and receivership in the US. The main critical issues of bank insolvency regimes and their inappropriateness for the crisis of banks which are systemically significant or critical in failure are analysed. Against this background, the so-called compulsory administrative liquidation under Italian law, which has been in force for decades, is examined as a possible model for EU harmonisation of bank insolvency proceedings. In particular, the application of the transfer of assets and liabilities tool and of other resolution-like tools in the context of liquidation is discussed on the grounds that they would provide resolution authorities with alternatives to the so-called atomistic liquidation which is often regarded as inappropriate for banks. Bank liquidation and the impact of the limits resulting from the State Aid Framework as to the use of public money in liquidation are explored by referring to the cases of Veneto Banca and Banca Popolare di Vicenza. The US regime with the so-called receivership administered by the Federal Deposit Insurance Corporation is explored, being commonly regarded as one of the most important international benchmarks for bank crisis management, particularly in light of the experience gained by the American authority over the last 70 years.

Chapter five is entirely dedicated to systemic institution crisis management with the analysis of bank resolution in the EU and UK, on one hand, and, the Orderly Liquidation Authority in the US, on the other. The different legal definitions provided in those three jurisdictions are taken into account. The chapter looks at the new resolution administrative procedure as regulated in the EU under the Bank Recovery and Resolution Directive. Against this background, the different resolution tools regulated by the Bank Recovery and Resolution Directive are confronted. Special attention is placed on the controversial features of the bail-in tool, considering the arguments both for and against it. Resolution financing arrangements and their main shortcomings are analysed, referring to the resolution of four small-sized Italian banks in 2015. The resolution of Banco Popular in Spain conducted in 2017 by the Single Resolution Board in cooperation with the Spanish Resolution authority is also analysed. The interaction between the Bank Recovery and Resolution Directive and the State Aid Framework as to the so-called government financial stabilisation tools is explored, with special attention paid to the European Commission's Crisis Communications. The UK and US frameworks to deal with systemic institutions in crisis are also discussed.

Chapter six deals with the role of deposit guarantee schemes in bank crises. Their different functions, moving from the so-called pay-box function, are analysed with reference to both the EU and US frameworks. After a discussion on the legislation currently in force on both sides of the Atlantic, the Italian experience and the impact of the State Aid Framework on the interventions of deposit guarantee schemes (other than depositors' pay-out) are analysed and compared with the US regime and experience. Against this background, the position of the European Commission as to the qualification of such interventions as State Aid provision is discussed along with the recent judgments of the General Court of the European Union and of the Court of Justice of the

European Union in the *Banca Tercas* case. A discussion on the current legal constraints to deposit guarantee schemes optional interventions is provided with a view to advancing some reform proposals concerning the adoption of a European harmonised deposit guarantee scheme-based special administrative regime for failing banks.

Chapter seven discusses the possible impact that the COVID-19 crisis will have on banks. This impact is expected to determine over time a significant surge in the stock of non-performing loans accounted in the banks' balance sheets. A discussion on non-performing loans and their legal treatment is provided, before moving on to an analysis of ways and strategies to effectively tackle such issue. In this regard, asset management companies established to manage non-performing loans with a long-term view are examined by looking at some past experiences. The EU legal framework governing the creation of asset management companies is then discussed along with the impact of the State Aid regime. Some policy considerations are put forward also looking at the Temporary Framework of the European Commission on State Aid to face the COVID-19 emergency.

Chapter eight concludes by providing some policy considerations on the importance of bank crisis management in the next future.

***

My academic and policy-related works in the area of bank crisis management have given me the opportunity over time to discuss a number of issues explored in this book with staff at the IMF, World Bank, IADI, EFDI, Unidroit, EBRD, ECB, ESRB, European Commission, European Parliament, SRB, Bank of Italy and Bank of England, to whom I am extremely grateful.

A warm thank you goes to Roberta Bassi and Rosemarie Mearns at Hart Publishing for their support and encouragement of the project, and help with the publication.

Finally, I would like to thank my family for the ever-present support. To them I dedicate this work.

All errors are my own responsibility.

CONTENTS

LIST OF ABBREVIATIONS

A-IRB	Advanced internal ratings-based
AIG	American International Group
AMC	Asset management company
AQR	Asset quality review
AT1	Additional Tier 1
BAP	Bank administration procedure
BBVA	Banco Bilbao Vizcaya Argentaria
BCBS	Basel Committee on Banking Supervision
BHC	Banking holding company
BIP	Bank insolvency procedure
BIS	Bank for International Settlements
BPER	Banca Popolare dell'Emilia Romagna
BRRD	Bank Recovery and Resolution Directive
CET1	Common Equity Tier 1
CJEU	Court of Justice of the European Union
CoCos	Contingent convertibles
CRD	Capital Requirements Directive
CRP	Capital restoration plan
CRR	Capital Requirements Regulation
D-SIBs	Domestic systemically important banks
DBS	Dunfermline Building Society
DGSD	Deposit Guarantee Schemes Directive
DGS	Deposit guarantee scheme

DIF	Deposit insurance fund
EBA	European Banking Authority
EC	European Commission
ECA	European Court of Auditors
ECB	European Central Bank
ECHR	European Convention on Human Rights
ECSC	European Coal and Steel Community
EDIS	European Deposit Insurance Scheme
EFDI	European Forum of Deposit Insurers
ESM	European Stability Mechanism
EU	European Union
FDIA	Federal Deposit Insurance Act
FDIC	Federal Deposit Insurance Corporation
FDICIA	Federal Deposit Insurance Corporation Improvement Act
FIDT	Fondo Interbancario di Tutela dei Depositi
FOLF	Failing or likely to fail
FPC	Financial Policy Committee
FSA	Financial Services Authority
FSB	Financial Stability Board
FSCS	Financial Services Compensation Scheme
FSMA	2000 Financial Services and Markets Act 2000
G-SIB	Global systemically important bank
G-SIFI	Global Systemically Important Financial Institution
G10	Group of 10
G20	Group of 20
GAO	Government Accountability Office
IADI	International Association of Deposit Insurers
IAS	International Accounting Standards
ICSID	International Centre for the Settlement of Investment Disputes

IDI	Insured depository institution
IFRS	International Financial Reporting Standards
IGA	Intergovernmental Agreement
IMF	International Monetary Fund
IST	Implementing Technical Standard
IPS	Institutional protection scheme
IRB	Internal ratings-based
IRTs	Information resources and technology
JSTs	Joint Supervisory Team
LGD	Loss given default
MEP	Member of the European Parliament
MPC	Monetary Policy Committee
MREL	Minimum requirement for own funds and eligible liabilities
NCA	National Competent Authority
NPL	Non-performing loan
NRA	National Resolution Authority
O-SIIs	Other systemically important institutions
OCC	Office of the Comptroller of the Currency
OECD	Organisation for Economic Co-operation and Development
OLA	Orderly Liquidation Authority
OLF	Orderly Liquidation Fund
P&A	Purchase and Assumption
PCA	Prompt corrective action
PD	Probabilities of default
PIA	Public interest assessment
PRA	Prudential Regulation Authority
PRC	Prudential Regulatory Committee
QFCs	Qualified financial contracts
RTS	Regulatory Technical Standards

RWA	Risk-weighted asset
SGA	Società di Gestione Attivi
SMEs	Small and medium-sized enterprises
SPOE	Single point of entry
SRB	Single Resolution Board
SREP	Supervisory review and evaluation process
SRF	Single Resolution Fund
SRM	Single Resolution Mechanism
SRMR	Single Resolution Mechanism Regulation
SSM	Single Supervisory Mechanism
TBTF	Too big to fail
TFEU	Treaty on the Functioning of the European Union
TLAC	Total loss-absorbing capacity
UK	United Kingdom
UNCITRAL	United Nations Commission on International Trade Law
UNCTD	United Nations Conference on Trade and Development
UNIDROIT	International Institute for the Unification of Private Law
US	United States
VaR	Value-at-risk
WHO	World Health Organization

1

International Bank Crisis Management

Framing the Key Definitions and Drawing the Perimeter of the Analysis

I. Introduction

The global financial crisis of 2007–09 showed that effective bank crisis management is crucial to handling failing banks whilst ensuring that their crisis is not transmitted to other connected institutions, thereby potentially triggering a system-wide crisis. This conclusion has been reached as during the global financial crisis several jurisdictions lacked specific tools and procedures to handle failing banks. As a consequence, most failing institutions were either submitted to normal corporate insolvency proceedings or rescued with public funds. However, both approaches were (and still are) far from being efficient since, as a result, they gave rise to a number of negative consequences, ranging from value destruction to public finance deterioration, and sometimes negative systemic repercussions as well.

On these grounds, in the aftermath of the global financial crisis a host of policy-driven initiatives have been taken with a view to enabling jurisdictions to adopt bank-specific crisis management regimes. Prominent among such initiatives have been the Financial Stability Board's (FSB) Key Attributes of Effective Resolution Regimes for Financial Institutions,[1] on one side, and the International Association of Deposit Insurers (IADI) Core Principles for Effective Deposit Insurance Systems,[2] on the other. However, while the IADI Core Principles are centred on the role of deposit insurance systems, the FSB Key Attributes focus on the crisis of banks which are systemically significant or critical in failure, thus leaving aside non-systemic banks, such as small and medium-sized institutions, which are the vast majority. With a view to designing special regimes for non-systemic (often small and medium-sized) bank crises, some initiatives have been recently

[1] See Financial Stability Board, 'Key Attributes of Effective Resolution Regimes for Financial Institutions' (15 October 2014).

[2] See International Association of Deposit Insurers, 'IADI Core Principles for Effective Deposit Insurance Systems' (November 2014).

launched. The most important ones are the consultation conducted in 2021 by the European Commission aiming to adopt a harmonised small and medium-sized bank crisis management regime in the EU[3] and the UNIDROIT's project to develop guidelines to help countries design an effective small and medium-sized non-systemic bank crisis management framework.[4] Such efforts are of great relevance as there are no international standards or guidance concerning crisis management regimes dealing with non-systemic banks. The lack of such standards and principles has caused the effectiveness of small and medium-sized bank crisis management regimes to significantly differ from country to country, with negative repercussions, inter alia, for institutions and groups operating on a cross-border basis.

Yet, before analysing both the bank crisis management regimes currently in force in some of the most important jurisdictions around the world, and such initiatives which are ongoing, some key definitions need to be provided in order to establish a common language and precisely draw the perimeter of the analysis undertaken in this work. Also, despite the importance of effective crisis management regimes for every financial institution, this study focuses exclusively on banks, irrespective of their corporate legal structure.[5] Banks in this context are understood as those institutions that, regardless of how they are defined in their home jurisdiction, engage in the business of taking deposits from the public and extending loans on their own account. Such institutions are referred to as 'credit institutions' in the EU framework and 'depository institutions' in the US framework.

II. Bank Crisis Management: Framing the Key Definitions

In this work, 'bank crisis management' is used as an umbrella term to broadly refer to every procedure and/or legal tool available in a given jurisdiction to handle banks in crisis. Irrespective of the systemic or non-systemic nature of the institutions concerned, such procedures and tools include those which are activated and used in the early stages of a crisis to prevent its escalation, as well as procedures and tools aimed at restructuring (or at least keeping some functions working), and procedures and tools applied with a view to dissolving the failing entity and making it exit the market.

[3] See European Commission, 'Targeted Consultation Review of the Crisis Management and Deposit Insurance Framework', available at ec.europa.eu/info/consultations/finance-2021-crisis-management-deposit-insurance-review-targeted_en.

[4] See UNIDROIT, 'Project on Bank Liquidation Work Programme 2020–2022', available at www.unidroit.org/work-in-progress/bank-insolvency/#1631778452950-20a21187-49af.

[5] Obviously, the legal structure of a bank can affect the way in which it is to be handled in the context of a crisis; with regard to cooperatives, see International Association of Deposit Insurers, 'Ways to resolve a financial cooperative while keeping the cooperative structure – Guidance paper' (2021).

Closely connected to 'bank crisis management' is 'bank crisis management regime(s)' or 'bank crisis management framework(s)'. These terms are used interchangeably in this work and refer to the rules and provisions, irrespective of their nature and source, in force in a given jurisdiction governing bank crisis management procedures and legal tools.

On these grounds, bank crisis management procedures are the different procedures available in a given jurisdiction which can be initiated to handle a bank in crisis, ranging from procedures activated at the early stages of a crisis, to resolution procedures aimed at keeping the bank's critical functions work and winding-up procedures intended to dissolve the bank in crisis thereby making it exit the market. With regard to the latter, the exit of the failing bank from the market can take place either through a so-called atomistic liquidation (also known as 'piecemeal liquidation') under which the activities are interrupted and the assets are sold piece by piece to repay creditors, or by transferring some assets and liabilities to other institutions, through the application of special tools, such as the transfer tool, the asset management company or the bridge bank. Bank crisis management legal tools are, in turn, those instruments that the authorities in charge of handling the crisis are empowered to adopt with a view to making the procedure as effective and smooth as possible. Different legal tools will be available depending on the procedure that has been initiated as well as on the jurisdiction concerned.

'Bank insolvency proceedings/regimes/procedures' refers to those proceedings/regimes/procedures specifically dedicated to non-systemic banks in crisis, hence typically small and medium-sized institutions, which are available in some jurisdictions and usually aimed at making the institution concerned exit the market. They might differ in a number of ways from normal corporate insolvency proceedings applicable to non-financial firms as they are tailored to the peculiarities of banks. They also differ from the resolution procedure that, according to the FSB's Key Attributes, is typically activated to handle the crisis of banks which are systemically significant or critical in failure and aims at keeping the critical functions working with a view to preserving financial stability while avoiding the use of public money.

III. Other Relevant Definitions

Beside the working definitions above, which allow proper analysis in this work, a number of other definitions will also be referred to throughout this study. These have been provided primarily by international organisations and/or included in some key legislative acts.

'Insolvency proceeding' has been defined in a number of international soft law instruments as well as in some EU legislative acts. According to UNCITRAL and UNIDROIT, an insolvency proceeding is

> a collective judicial or administrative proceeding, including an interim proceeding, pursuant to a law relating to insolvency in which the assets and affairs of a debtor are or

> were subject to control or supervision by a court or other competent authority for the purpose of reorganization or liquidation.[6]

In the EU, while the Settlement Finality Directive defines an insolvency proceeding as

> any collective measure provided for in the law of a Member State, or a third country, either to wind up the participant or to reorganise it, where such measure involves the suspending of, or imposing limitations on, transfers or payments,

the Bank Recovery and Resolution Directive (BRRD) refers to normal insolvency proceedings as

> collective insolvency proceedings which entail the partial or total divestment of a debtor and the appointment of a liquidator or an administrator normally applicable to institutions under national law and either specific to those institutions or generally applicable to any natural or legal person.

The more general term 'insolvency' is defined by UNCITRAL, on one hand, as 'collective proceedings commenced with respect to debtors that are in severe financial distress or insolvent'[7] and, on the other, as the situation 'when a debtor is generally unable to pay its debts as they mature or when its liabilities exceed the value of its assets'.[8]

Both UNCITRAL and UNIDROIT provide the same definition of 'liquidation', ie 'proceedings to sell and dispose of assets for distribution to creditors in accordance with the insolvency law'.[9]

'Reorganisation' is defined by UNCITRAL and UNIDROIT as

> the process by which the financial well-being and viability of a debtor's business can be restored and the business continue to operate, using various means possibly including debt forgiveness, debt rescheduling, debt-equity conversions and sale of the business (or parts of it) as a going concern.[10]

Similarly, at EU level, 'reorganisation measures' are defined by the Winding-up Directive as

> measures which are intended to preserve or restore the financial situation of a credit institution and which could affect third parties' pre-existing rights, including measures involving the possibility of a suspension of payments, suspension of enforcement (measures or reduction of claims)

[6] Such a definition is used in the UNCITRAL Model Law on Recognition and Enforcement of Insolvency-Related Judgments (2018) and the UNCITRAL Model Law on Enterprise Group Insolvency (2019); UNIDROIT, 'Principles on the Operation of Close-out Netting Provisions' (2013) and 'Convention on Substantive Rules for Intermediated Securities' (2009). The UNCITRAL Legislative Guide on Insolvency Law defines insolvency proceedings as 'collective proceedings, subject to court supervision, either for reorganization or liquidation'; see 'The UNICTRAL Legislative Guide on Insolvency Law' (2005).

[7] UNCITRAL, 'United Nations Model Law on Cross-border Insolvency' (1997).

[8] UNCITRAL, 'Legislative Guide on Insolvency Law' (2005, n 6).

[9] ibid; UNIDROIT (2013, n 6).

[10] ibid.

and by the Financial Collateral Directive as

> measures which involve any intervention by administrative or judicial authorities which are intended to preserve or restore the financial situation and which affect pre-existing rights of third parties, including but not limited to measures involving a suspension of payments, suspension of enforcement measures or reduction of claims.

In a similar vein, the World Bank defines 'restructuring activities' as 'Measures that restructure the debtor's business (operational restructuring) and measures that restructure the debtor's finances (financial restructuring)'.[11]

The IMF also provided a definition of 'pre-insolvency', which refers to 'procedures that are a hybrid of out-of-court rehabilitation and formal rehabilitation procedures'.[12]

It is worth noting that most of these definitions were drafted having in mind non-financial companies. Thus, while they are helpful to identify and clarify some basic common grounds as to terminology, wording and key features, which can also be relevant in the area of bank crisis management, the special nature of banks, directly resulting from their peculiar business model, might make such definitions sometimes inadequate and therefore inapplicable to them. In this vein, whereas the definition of 'insolvency proceedings' drafted by UNIDROIT and UNCITRAL, as well as the ones contained in the EU framework, provide an effective description of the liquidation process that insolvent companies typically go through, obviously they do not refer to the special treatment that bank deposits need in order to avoid situations of panic potentially resulting from a number of depositors being unable to withdraw money from their accounts. Similarly, the definition of 'insolvency' provided by UNCITRAL, referring to the inability to pay debts as they mature or to the situation when liabilities exceed the value of assets, might be inappropriate as a ground to initiate bank crisis management procedures in that when those conditions are met, it might be too late to successfully handle the crisis of a bank. That is the reason why typically the triggers to initiate a bank crisis management procedure have a forward-looking approach and usually are met before the bank concerned is balance-sheet insolvent, namely when liabilities exceed the assets or when it is no longer able to pay debts as they fall due.

However, the definition of 'insolvency proceedings' developed by the International Monetary Fund and World Bank in the context of bank insolvency is highly relevant, describing them as

> all types of official action involving the removal of management and/or the imposition of limits on, or suspension of, the rights of shareholders and the assumption of direct control by a banking authority or other officially-appointed person over a bank that has crossed a 'threshold' for the commencement of insolvency proceedings.[13]

[11] World Bank, 'Out-of-Court Debt Restructuring' (2012).

[12] International Monetary Fund, 'Orderly and Effective Insolvency Procedures: Key Issues' (1999).

[13] International Monetary Fund and World Bank, 'An overview of the legal, institutional, and regulatory framework for bank insolvency' (2009).

IV. Jurisdiction-Specific Definitions

In addition to these general definitions, there are also a number of other definitions which, to a certain extent, diverge from each other, being more jurisdiction-specific. This is the case with the term 'resolution', which in the EU legal framework refers to the administrative procedure defined under the BRRD as the application of resolution tools by a resolution authority in order to achieve one or more resolution objectives,[14] whereas in the US it is used as an umbrella term referring to every method used to handle a failing bank, through liquidation with depositor pay-out, purchase and assumption of the bank's franchise by another bank and disposition of the residual assets and any liabilities under Federal Deposit Insurance Corporation (FDIC) receivership, or even through orderly liquidation of large financial firms under the Dodd-Frank Act.

Interestingly, despite the general definition of liquidation provided by UNCITRAL and UNIDROIT,[15] such term has a specific meaning in the context of banking which is different in the US as compared to its meaning in the EU. Thus, while in the US, liquidation is one of the resolution methods typically employed by the FDIC in the context of a receivership, in the EU, pursuant to the BRRD, liquidation refers to the process of selling assets in the context of normal insolvency proceedings.

Moreover, in the EU, winding-up proceedings are defined by the Winding-up Directive as

> collective proceedings opened and monitored by the administrative or judicial authorities of a Member State with the aim of realising assets under the supervision of those authorities, including where the proceedings are terminated by a composition or other, similar measure,

while under the BRRD, winding-up is the 'realisation of assets of an entity'.

V. The Perimeter of the Analysis

Building on the definitions above, this work discusses a host of key issues in the area of bank crisis management, focusing on the legal framework and past experience of some key jurisdictions, namely the EU (with special attention paid to the Banking Union and Italy), the UK and the US.

The study moves from the analysis, in chapter two, of the bank supervisory and crisis management architecture in place in the EU, the UK and the US, and focuses on the reforms passed in the aftermath of the global financial crisis of 2007–09 as a legislative and regulatory response to that event. Against this background, the Banking Union is explored with the analysis of its three pillars, namely the Single

[14] Art 2(1)(1) of the BRRD.

[15] UNIDROIT, 'Legislative Guide on Insolvency Law' (2005, n 6); UNIDROIT (2013, n 6).

Supervisory Mechanism (SSM), the Single Resolution Mechanism (SRM) and the European Deposit Insurance Scheme (EDIS). In the same vein, the UK and US bank supervisory and crisis management architectural structures are discussed, exploring the roles of the main authorities, namely the Bank of England in the UK and the FDIC in the US.

The so-called first lines of defence are analysed in chapter three. In this vein, the concept of capital and the rationale behind minimum capital requirements are examined, also looking at the work of the Basel Committee on Banking Supervision and at the capital standards (namely Basel I, Basel II, Basel III and Basel IV) that it has developed over time. Also, early intervention measures are dealt with, particularly focusing on temporary administration in the EU, special administration in Italy and prompt and corrective action in the US.

The crisis of non-systemic (often small and medium-sized) banks and the related bank insolvency regimes are explored in chapter four, moving from a discussion on their main drawbacks, with a view to providing some recommendations for the creation of an EU harmonised regime. Against this backdrop, the Italian, UK and US frameworks and past experiences are discussed to ascertain whether some of their features can be imported in an EU harmonised regime to be developed. In this context, special attention is paid to the tools that the authorities involved in those jurisdictions are empowered to apply, the objectives that they are expected to achieve as well as their decision-making process. The role of law courts is also tackled along with the criticalities arising in the EU from the interplay between the state aid regime and the crisis management framework. A number of cases from Italy, UK and US are also discussed to substantiate the arguments advanced. The main characteristics that such an EU harmonised regime for small and medium-sized non-systemic bank crises should have are also sketched out.

The crisis management of systemic institutions, with resolution in the EU and UK and orderly liquidation authority in the US, is the subject of chapter five. In this regard, the discussion moves from the analysis of the FSB's Key Attributes of Effective Resolution Regimes for Financial Institutions as they have shaped the regimes of all the main jurisdictions across the world. Accordingly, the resolution tools are discussed, paying special attention to the most controversial one (bail-in), along with the available sources of funding and their shortcomings. The interplay between the state aid regime and the crisis management framework in the EU is explored, again focusing on the critical issues resulting from some serious inconsistencies between the two. Impediments to resolvability, the process to remove them and the interaction among the authorities involved are also dealt with. A number of recent resolution cases are referred to as well.

The key role of deposit guarantee schemes (DGSs) in bank crises is addressed in chapter six, moving from the mechanics of their functioning and the advantages they bring in terms of providing an effective safety net to the benefit of the whole system. The interplay between the legislation on DGSs and the state aid regime, which characterises the EU framework, is carefully explored as several limitations arise from it. In this regard, the position of the European Commission is analysed along with some Italian cases which represent milestones as to the application of the state aid regime restrictions. The other constraints refraining DGSs in the EU from playing an even more important role are analysed vis-à-vis the US framework and experience. A limited-scope reform proposal to allow DGSs to play a leading role in bank crises in the EU is also advanced.

The COVID-19-provoked crisis and the expected inherent surge of non-performing loans (NPLs) are dealt with in chapter seven. NPLs are discussed along with their accounting and regulatory treatment, and then one of the major ways to tackle them – asset management companies – is explored building on previous experiences across the globe.

Some final remarks and policy considerations are put forward in chapter eight.

On this basis, in dealing with international bank crisis management, this work contributes to the debate ongoing among policy-makers, scholars and law practitioners, with a view to critically discuss the main issues at stake, while advancing policy remarks and exploring ideas for reform proposals.

2

The Bank Supervisory and Crisis Management Architecture in the EU, UK and US

I. Introduction

Following the global financial crisis of 2007–09, the bank supervisory and crisis management architecture has been significantly revised in the European Union (EU), United Kingdom (UK) and United States (US), with a view to making the domestic frameworks, and thereby their systems, more reactive and effective in the event of shocks affecting also banks.

In the EU, the Banking Union has been established with the aim of facilitating the integration and enhancement of the European banking system, while eradicating the vicious link between sovereigns and their national banking systems.

In the UK, the Financial Services Act 2012 has given to the Bank of England responsibility for overseeing the financial system as a whole. Accordingly, the Financial Policy Committee has been established and a new regulator, the Prudential Regulation Authority, set up; while the latter was initially a subsidiary of the Bank of England, it was later incorporated by the Bank of England.

In the US, the bankruptcy of Lehman Brothers along with the government rescue of American International Group (AIG), prompted Congress to introduce the Orderly Liquidation Authority (OLA) under the Dodd-Frank Act for non-bank firms whose bankruptcy would pose a systemic risk. The stated objective of the OLA is to avoid the binary choice between disruptive bankruptcy and taxpayer bail-out and to create an incentive-compatible process suited to large financial conglomerates.

This chapter focuses on the main characteristics featuring the bank supervisory and crisis management architecture in the EU, UK and US.

II. The European Banking Union

The Banking Union is often regarded as one of the most ambitious and important European projects after the creation of the single market and the introduction of the single currency (euro).[1] Its main innovations are the centralisation of bank supervision and crisis management, and the mutualisation of deposit insurance at European level. The key concept underlying the decision to centralise these functions is what has been labelled as the financial 'trilemma': in a complex jurisdictional domain, such as the EU, financial stability, an integrated banking and financial market and national supervision cannot co-exist.[2] Since financial stability is considered a public good of primary importance, and an integrated banking and financial market is one of the most significant achievements of the creation of the EU, the decision has been made to centralise bank supervision (and crisis management) at European level. In other words, centralisation of bank supervision, crisis management and deposit insurance is expected to deliver on the objective of maintaining financial stability within an integrated European banking and financial market.

The new institutional architecture, in turn, rests upon the so-called Single Rulebook, a set of harmonised rules applying to every credit institution[3] established in the EU Member States.[4] In this regard, the most relevant legislative acts, which form the Single Rulebook, are the Capital Requirements Directive (CRD)[5] and Capital Requirements Regulation (CRR)[6] package, the Bank Recovery and Resolution Directive (BRRD)[7] and the Deposit Guarantee Schemes Directive (DGSD).[8]

[1] On the Banking Union see R Lastra, 'Banking Union and Single Market: Conflict or Companionship?' (2013) 36 *Fordham International Law Journal* 5; N Moloney, 'European Banking Union: Assessing its Risks and resilience' (2014) 51 *Common Market Law Review* 1609; JH Binder, 'The Banking Union and the Governance of Credit Institutions: A Legal Perspective' (2015) 16 *European Business Organization Law Review* 467; BS Nielsen, 'Main Features of the European Banking Union' (2015) 26 *European Business Law Review* 805; M Nieto, 'Banking on Single Supervision in the Eurozone: Scepticism and a Reform Proposal' (2015) 16 *European Business Organization Law Review* 539; G Ferrarini, 'Single Supervision and the Governance of Banking Markets: Will the SSM Deliver the Expected Benefits?' (2015) 16 *European Business Organization Law Review* 513.

[2] See D Schoenmaker, 'The financial trilemma' (2011) 111 *Economics Letters* 57, 59, where it is said that 'the financial trilemma states that financial stability, financial integration and national financial policies are incompatible. Any two of the three objectives can be combined but not all three; one has to give'.

[3] The terms 'credit institutions' and 'banks' are used interchangeably across the book when referring to EU institutions.

[4] This means that the scope of application of these rules goes beyond the jurisdictional domain of the Banking Union, as they are in force in every EU Member State.

[5] Directive 2013/36/EU of the European Parliament and of the Council of 26 June 2013 on access to the activity of credit institutions and the prudential supervision of credit institutions and investment firms, amending Directive 2002/87/EC and repealing Directives 2006/48/EC and 2006/49/EC (Capital Requirements Directive) [2013] OJ L 176/338.

[6] Regulation (EU) No 575/2013 of the European Parliament and of the Council of 26 June 2013 on prudential requirements for credit institutions and investment firms and amending Regulation (EU) No 648/2012 (Capital Requirements Regulation) [2013] OJ L 176/1.

[7] Directive 2014/59/EU of the European Parliament and of the Council of 15 May 2014 establishing a framework for the recovery and resolution of credit institutions and investment firms (Bank Recovery and Resolution Directive) [2014] OJ L173/190.

[8] Directive 2014/49/EU of the European Parliament and of the Council of 16 April 2014 on deposit guarantee schemes (Deposit Guarantee Scheme Directive) [2014] OJ L 173/149.

The Banking Union is clearly a key component of the Economic and Monetary Union and has been created as a response to the global financial crisis of 2007–09 as well as to the ensuing Euro Area sovereign debt crisis of 2010–12. The Banking Union seeks to ensure that the banking sector of the participating countries (and the wider EU banking sector) is stable, safe and reliable, thus contributing to financial stability. Through the Banking Union, banks are expected to become more robust and able to withstand future financial crises, while non-viable banks are meant to be resolved or liquidated without using taxpayers' money and with minimal impact on the real economy and the banking system. Further, harmonised rules and centralised supervision are intended to reduce market fragmentation.[9]

Every Euro Area Member State has been part of the Banking Union since the outset, while non-Euro Area EU Member States can join the Banking Union by entering into close cooperation agreement with the European Central Bank (ECB). So far, Bulgaria and Croatia have joined the Banking Union in this way, in 2020.

In the original project, the three pillars of the Banking Union were: the Single Supervisory Mechanism (SSM),[10] the Single Resolution Mechanism (SRM)[11] and the European Deposit Insurance Scheme (EDIS).

The SSM is a new system of banking supervision that comprises the ECB and the national supervisors, so-called National Competent Authorities (NCAs) of the participating countries.

The SRM is a new system of bank crisis management that comprises the Single Resolution Board (SRB) and the National Resolution Authorities (NRAs) of the participating countries.

The EDIS was meant to be the centralised deposit guarantee scheme financed by the banks established in the participating countries and charged to provide equivalent protection to every depositor regardless of the country where their bank is located. However, a political agreement has not yet been reached as to the creation of the EDIS, which is therefore often referred to as 'the missing pillar of the Banking Union'.

[9] Among the main reasons for the creation of the Banking Union were: a relevant amount of cross-border activities within both Euro-Area and non Euro-Area countries performed by large banks; integrity of the euro and internal market threatened by the fragmentation of the financial sector; the need for supervisors able to oversee highly complex and interconnected institutions; the need to replace the home country control principle as it was no longer sufficient; the need to cut the link between sovereign debts and domestic banking systems; and an awareness that the coordination among supervisors brought by European System of Financial Supervision, even if positive, was not enough.

[10] The legal foundations of the SSM are the Council Regulation (EU) No 1024/2013 of 15 October 2013 conferring specific tasks on the European Central Bank concerning policies relating to the prudential supervision of credit institutions [2013] OJ L 287/63 and Regulation (EU) No 468/2014 of the European Central Bank of 16 April 2014 establishing the framework for cooperation within the Single Supervisory Mechanism between the European Central Bank and national competent authorities and with national designated authorities (SSM Framework Regulation) (ECB/2014/17) [2014] OJ L 141/1.

[11] The legal basis of the SRM is Regulation (EU) No 806/2014 of the European Parliament and of the Council of 15 July 2014 establishing uniform rules and a uniform procedure for the resolution of credit institutions and certain investment firms in the framework of a Single Resolution Mechanism and a Single Resolution Fund and amending Regulation (EU) No 1093/2010 (SRM Regulation) [2014] OJ L 225/1.

A. The Single Supervisory Mechanism (First Pillar)

Through the establishment of a new system of supervision (the SSM) based on the close cooperation between the ECB and NCAs, the goal is to ensure consistent oversight of every bank in the Banking Union and tackle the issue of supervisory forbearance ontologically embedded in domestic supervision. At the same time, the involvement of NCAs is expected to enable the SSM to take advantage of the skills they own and the experience they have gained over the years in supervising banks in their jurisdiction. This aspect was considered crucial because when the SSM was created the ECB had no track record nor specific competences in the area of banking supervision since it had acted thus far only as the central bank of the Euro Area countries. The role of NCAs within the SSM was, therefore, regarded as of paramount importance.

Under the new regime, the ECB carries out banking supervision with a common European approach, taking actions, implementing corrective measures and ensuring the consistent application of regulations and policies. This means that the ECB, in cooperation with NCAs, is responsible for ensuring that banking supervision is effective and consistent across the Banking Union. The ECB has the authority to: conduct supervisory reviews, on-site inspections and investigations; grant and withdraw banking licences; assess banks' acquisitions and disposal of qualifying holdings; ensure compliance with EU prudential rules; and set higher capital requirements in order to counter any financial risks.[12]

[12] The choice to confer these tasks upon the ECB was influenced by the so-called Meroni doctrine. In the *Meroni* judgment of 1958 (Case C -9/56 and 10/56, *Meroni v High Authority* [1957/1958] ECR 133), the Court of Justice of the European Union (CJEU) declared inadmissible under EU law the delegation of discretionary powers to bodies that are not established under the (now defunct) European Coal and Steel Community (ECSC) Treaty. New bodies with discretionary powers can only be established by the Member States by a transfer of competences in the way of a Treaty amendment but not by normal secondary legislation. Therefore, the Meroni doctrine requires a basis in primary law for authorities with discretionary powers. In other words, the CJEU's two main concerns were the attribution of discretionary powers to an entity not foreseen in the Treaty and the absence of judicial review of its acts. To tackle these issues, the decision was made to confer these tasks, entailing the exercise of discretionary powers, to an already existing EU institution such as the ECB. The legal basis for the conferment of supervisory responsibilities to the ECB is Art 127(6) of the TFEU (Consolidated Version of the Treaty on the Functioning of the European Union [2021] OJ C 326/47), which allows the Council to confer 'specific tasks concerning policies relating to the prudential supervision of credit institutions and other financial institutions with the exception of insurance undertakings' and requires for its adoption unanimity by the Council, after consulting with the Parliament and the ECB. Similar issues were faced with the creation of the supervisory board and have been tackled through the non-objection procedure, which according to Art 26(8) SSM Framework Regulation (Regulation (EU) No 468/2014 of the European Central Bank of 16 April 2014 establishing the framework for cooperation within the Single Supervisory Mechanism between the European Central Bank and national competent authorities and with national designated authorities), gives the Governing Council the upper hand as it can reject (object to) a decision prepared by the Supervisory Board; on these issues see R Lastra, *International Financial and Monetary Law* (Oxford, Oxford University Press, 2015) *passim*.

On the other hand, NCAs are responsible for assisting the ECB with the preparation and implementation of any acts relating to the tasks conferred on the ECB by the SSM Regulation and carry out supervision of less significant banks under the coordination of ECB.

To make supervision more effective and efficient, credit institutions have been grouped into two categories: significant institutions; and less significant institutions.[13] While the former, which currently number 115 and hold almost 82 per cent of banking assets in the participating countries, are directly supervised by the ECB, the latter remain supervised by their NCAs in close cooperation with the ECB. The ECB in turn can decide at any time to draw less significant institutions under its direct remit to ensure that supervisory standards are applied consistently.

One of the most effective forms of collaboration between the ECB and NCAs within the SSM are the so-called joint supervisory teams (JSTs). The SSM Framework Regulation governs their tasks and composition. They actively foster a common supervisory culture and promote consistent supervisory practices and approaches.

The JSTs carry out ongoing supervision of the significant banks. Accordingly, they: perform the Supervisory Review and Evaluation Process (SREP); propose the supervisory examination programme, including a plan of on-site inspections; implement the approved supervisory examination programme and any supervisory decisions; and ensure coordination with the on-site inspection teams and liaise with the national supervisors.

A JST is established for each significant institution. JSTs are formed of staff of the ECB and the relevant NCAs, including the ones of the countries in which credit institutions, banking subsidiaries or significant cross-border branches of a given banking group are established. The size, overall composition and organisation of a JST are tailored to the size, business model and risk profile of the bank it supervises.

The new role of the ECB as the main prudential supervisor for significant credit institutions should reduce the risk of forbearance, which was embedded in the previous system based on national supervision. Nevertheless, the goal of further integrating the European banking sector has not been achieved. Integration and consolidation of the banking sector still takes place mainly at national level also because protectionist approaches are sometimes adopted in certain countries

[13] The criteria to qualify institutions as significant are: total value of assets exceeding €30 billion; economic importance for the specific country or the EU economy as a whole; total value of assets exceeding €5 billion and ratio of cross-border assets/liabilities in more than one other participating Member State to total assets/liabilities above 20%; institution has requested or received funding from the European Stability Mechanism or the European Financial Stability Facility; an institution can also be considered significant if it is one of the three most significant banks established in a particular country.

aiming at discouraging cross-border mergers and takeovers. This in turn also makes it more complicated to remove the twofold interdependence between banks and sovereigns.

B. The Single Resolution Mechanism (Second Pillar)

The SRM is a system of cooperation between the SRB and the NRAs of participating countries whose main purpose is to ensure the efficient resolution of failing or likely to fail (FOLF)[14] banks with minimal costs for taxpayers and to the real economy. The SRB sits at the top of the system and has powers allegedly allowing it to resolve a bank over a weekend. A Single Resolution Fund (SRF), financed through contributions paid by banks, has been created with a view to having available resources to use for the implementation of resolution measures. The scope of application of the SRM mirrors the one of the SSM and also the criteria for the distribution of tasks between the SRB and NRAs are rather similar to the ones which apply in the SSM. Accordingly, the SRB is in charge of handling the crisis of significant, as well as cross-border, institutions, and NRAs are in charge of less significant institutions.

The creation of the SRM is closely connected with the adoption of the BRRD, which, by implementing the Financial Stability Board Key Attributes of Effective Resolution Regimes for Financial Institutions,[15] has introduced a new administrative procedure, called resolution, which should be initiated to successfully handle a bank crisis when a number of requirements are met, particularly when this is considered to be in the public interest.[16]

[14] According to Art 32(4) of the Directive 2014/59/EU, 'an institution shall be deemed to be failing or likely to fail in one or more of the following circumstances: (a) the institution infringes or there are objective elements to support a determination that the institution will, in the near future, infringe the requirements for continuing authorisation in a way that would justify the withdrawal of the authorisation by the competent authority including but not limited to because the institution has incurred or is likely to incur losses that will deplete all or a significant amount of its own funds; (b) the assets of the institution are or there are objective elements to support a determination that the assets of the institution will, in the near future, be less than its liabilities; (c) the institution is or there are objective elements to support a determination that the institution will, in the near future, be unable to pay its debts or other liabilities as they fall due; (d) extraordinary public financial support is required except' in a few cases.

[15] FSB, 'Key Attributes of Effective Resolution Regimes for Financial Institutions' (2014), *passim*.

[16] According to Art 32 of the BRRD, 'Member States shall ensure that resolution authorities shall take a resolution action in relation to an institution referred to in point (a) of Article 1(1) only if the resolution authority considers that all of the following conditions are met: (a) the determination that the institution is failing or is likely to fail has been made by the competent authority, after consulting the resolution authority or; subject to the conditions laid down in paragraph 2, by the resolution authority after consulting the competent authority; (b) having regard to timing and other relevant circumstances, there is no reasonable prospect that any alternative private sector measures, including measures by an IPS, or supervisory action, including early intervention measures or the write down or conversion of

Still, in this regard, the lack of a harmonised regime for bank insolvency proceedings represents a major issue, further exacerbated by the fact that the majority of banks in the event of becoming FOLF will likely be submitted to such proceedings and not to resolution.[17] This is further discussed in chapters four and five.

C. The Incomplete Banking Union

Almost 10 years after the establishment of its first component – the SSM – the Banking Union project is still incomplete and some important parts are missing. While centralisation of bank supervision has been fully achieved with the conferral of relevant tasks upon the ECB within the SSM along with the NCAs, crisis management functions have been assigned to a new European agency, the SRB, placed within the SRM along with the NRAs. However, the SRB is only in charge of the resolution of institutions under its remit to be then executed by the NRAs.[18] Thus, FOLF credit institutions that do not meet the so-called public interest assessment (PIA)[19] for their submission to resolution will be placed into insolvency proceedings under national laws, which are not harmonised at European level and are administered by domestic (either administrative or judicial) authorities depending on the national rules of the jurisdiction concerned.[20] In a similar vein, mutualisation of deposit insurance through the establishment of the EDIS has not yet been reached due to different positions and views among Member States. Therefore, deposit insurance works only at national level on the grounds of the (different) domestic provisions transposing the DGSD.

The incompleteness of the Banking Union is a major issue as it causes the reliability of credit institutions, and thus the safety of deposits, to still depend on the public finance of the Member States where they are established. As a consequence, the goal of removing the vicious link between sovereigns and national banking systems has not been achieved and will not be achieved until

relevant capital instruments and eligible liabilities in accordance with Article 59(2) taken in respect of the institution, would prevent the failure of the institution within a reasonable timeframe; (c) a resolution action is necessary in the public interest pursuant to paragraph 5'.

[17] See M Bodellini, 'Alternative forms of deposit insurance and the quest for European harmonized deposit guarantee scheme-centred special administrative regimes to handle troubled banks' (2020) 2–3 *Uniform Law Review* 212.

[18] According to Art 2(1)(1) of the BRRD, 'resolution means the application of a resolution tool or a tool referred to in Article 37(9) in order to achieve one or more of the resolution objectives referred to in Article 31(2)'.

[19] See M Bodellini, 'Impediments to resolvability: critical issues and challenges ahead' (2019) 5 *Open Review of Management, Banking and Finance* 48, where it is underlined that the PIA aims at ascertaining whether the resolution of a failing or likely to fail institution is considered to be needed in the public interest.

[20] See M Bodellini, 'The Optional Measures of Deposit Guarantee Schemes: Towards a New Bank Crisis Management Paradigm?' (2021) 13 *European Journal of Legal Studies* 341.

a fully fledged mutualised EDIS is operational and bank insolvency regimes are harmonised.

This critical situation is likely to be further exacerbated by the impact of the COVID-19-provoked economic crisis, which is expected to also affect credit institutions (and more generally, the financial system) when the massive relief measures introduced by many Member States will necessarily be lifted.[21]

Despite its incompleteness, the Banking Union project should be positively assessed. However, for the Banking Union to deliver on the original goals, its completion, through the creation of a fully fledged EDIS, is needed. Additionally, the harmonisation of bank insolvency regimes will be key as the majority of EU banks in the event of being FOLF will likely be liquidated under national laws rather than resolved. Currently, there are also discrepancies between the resolution regime and the state aid framework in relation to the provision of public support that incentivise the preference of national bank insolvency proceedings over resolution.[22] With a view to avoiding distortions, such incentives should be removed by aligning the requirements to meet for the provision of public support in both regimes. Against this background, despite its catastrophic impact on the economy (and on the society at large), the COVID-19-provoked crisis should be treasured and leveraged with a view to reaching a political agreement on the establishment of the EDIS and the harmonisation of national bank insolvency regimes. In this regard, at the beginning of 2021 the Commission launched a consultation seeking to collect views and feedback on the revision of the Crisis Management and Deposit Insurance Regime.[23] The ECB and the SRB, in participating to the Commission's consultation, have already pointed to the importance of setting up a fully fledged EDIS and harmonising national bank insolvency regimes.[24] This is certainly the right moment to make the last step and complete the original project. After all, only through these legislative actions can a real Banking Union be established to the benefit of the European banking system and ultimately for the good of the European people.

[21] See M Bodellini and P Lintner, 'The impact of the Covid-19 pandemic on credit institutions and the importance of effective bank crisis management regimes' (2020) 9 *Law and Economics Yearly Review* 182.

[22] R Lastra, C Russo and M Bodellini, 'Stock Take of the SRB's activities over the past years: What to Improve and Focus On?' (2019) Study Requested by the ECON Committee of the European Parliament, 1–40.

[23] See European Commission, 'Targeted Consultation Review of the Crisis Management and Deposit Insurance Framework' (2021), available at ec.europa.eu/info/consultations/finance-2021-crisis-management-deposit-insurance-review-targeted_en.

[24] See European Central Bank, 'ECB contribution to the European Commission's targeted consultation on the review of the crisis management and deposit insurance framework', (2021), available at www.ecb.europa.eu/pub/pdf/other/ecb.consultation_on_crisis_management_deposit_insurance_202105~98c4301b09.en.pdf; see Single Resolution Board, 'SRB replies to consultation on Review of the Crisis Management and Deposit Insurance Framework', (2021), available at srb.europa.eu/sites/default/files/2021-04-20_srb_replies_consultation_cmdi_review.pdf.

III. The UK Bank Supervisory and Crisis Management Architecture

Over the last two decades, the legal framework governing the Bank of England and its operations has been reformed a number of times with a view to introducing structural changes improving its functioning and internal organisation and extending its tasks and powers.[25] Accordingly, its functions have been significantly expanded by including bank prudential supervision and bank crisis management, in addition to monetary policy, thereby transforming the UK system in a central-bank-based system.[26]

As a result, the Bank of England is today the British independent authority in charge of: *micro* and *macro* prudential supervision; supervision of market infrastructures; resolution and crisis management; monetary policy and central banking; issuance of bank notes; and emergency liquidity assistance provision.[27]

Against this backdrop, the Bank of England has been given a dual mandate (also referred to as the 'twin mandate') that encompasses the objective of maintaining both price stability and financial stability. It also has as a secondary objective to support the Government's economic policy, including growth and employment.[28] The Bank of England dual mandate is reflected in its internal organisation, which relies on a number of committees: the Monetary Policy Committee (MPC), established in 1998, in charge of monetary policy; the Financial Policy Committee (FPC), established in 2012, with the task of identifying, monitoring and removing or reducing systemic risks to protect the financial system; and the Prudential Regulatory Committee (PRC), established in 2016, in charge of taking the most relevant decisions of the Prudential Regulation Authority (PRA).[29]

[25] The Bank was in private hands for the first 252 years of its existence and then nationalised with its capital stock transferred to HM Treasury in 1946. The shares are held by the Treasury Solicitor on behalf of HM Treasury; see Bank of England, 'Who Owns the Bank of England?', available at www.bankofengland.co.uk/knowledgebank/who-owns-the-bank-of-england.

[26] See UK Government, 'Bank of England and Financial Services Bill given royal assent and Parliament passes the Bank of England and Financial Services Act 2016' (4 May 2016), available at www.gov.uk/government/organisations/hm-treasury, stating that 'The Financial Services Act 2012 dismantled the failed tripartite system, putting the Bank of England at the centre of a new framework of financial regulation'. In other words, the Financial Services Act 2012, which came into force on 1 April 2013, created two new statutory regulators, the Prudential Regulation Authority (PRA), and the Financial Conduct Authority (FCA). The Financial Services Authority (FSA), created under the Financial Services and Markets Act (FSMA) 2000, ceased to exist. The FSA was previously responsible for the regulation of both the 'prudential' and 'conduct' aspects of financial institutions, on the assumption that combining conduct and prudential regulation would have lowered the risk of missing something important.

[27] M Bodellini and D Singh, 'Monetary policy in the face of the covid-19 crisis: the interesting case of the United Kingdom' (2020) 6 *Open Review of Management, Banking and Finance* 48.

[28] See R Lastra and K Alexander, 'The ECB Mandate: Perspectives on Sustainability and Solidarity' (2020), In-depth analysis requested by the ECON Committee of the European Parliament, Monetary Dialogue Papers, 8, arguing that 'In the UK, financial stability is a statutory objective of the Bank of England on a par with price stability (twin mandate)'.

[29] See S Goulding and R Abley, *Relationship management in banking: Principles and practice* (London, Kogan Page, 2018) 137.

All this means that through the legislative reforms passed in the aftermath of the global financial crisis of 2007–09, the Bank of England has been given a much broader set of functions, and consequently of powers, than was previously the case.[30] The Bank is the monetary authority, the lender of last resort, the macro-prudential supervisor, the micro-prudential supervisor, the financial markets infrastructure regulator and the resolution authority.[31] The objective of this institutional reform has mainly been to strengthen the role and function of the Bank of England at the centre of the UK financial system. These changes were considered necessary to better monitor and manage the financial system as whole against the build-up of any exposure that could create contagious threats and consequent systemic instability. In this regard, a central bank-based macro-prudential model was regarded as the most effective way to reach those goals.

As to the oversight over the banking system, the PRA, now part of the Bank of England, is responsible for day-to-day (regulation and) supervision of approximately 1,500 financial institutions (around 950 banks, 550 insurers, and some complex investment firms) that carry significant risk on their balance sheet. The PRA is competent to authorise the firms under its remit, which are dual-regulated (in prudential terms by the PRA and in conduct of business terms by the FCA). In this regard, the PRA is tasked with making judgements about the prudential safety and soundness of individual firms, having specific regard to their capital, liquidity and leverage. The PRA is expected to take a more judgemental approach and to challenge the business models of financial institutions. All this means that the PRA is the UK bank micro-prudential supervisor. The PRA has two main objectives: to promote the safety and soundness of PRA authorised firms; and to contribute towards securing an appropriate degree of protection for those who are or may become insurance policy-holders. It also has a secondary objective, which is to facilitate effective competition. The PRA's objective to facilitate competition is subordinate to its general objective to promote the safety and soundness of the firms that it supervises and regulates (and to its insurance objective). However, such secondary objective requires the PRA to take a more proactive approach on competition than was the case in the past when it only had to have regard to the need to minimise the adverse effects on competition resulting from the exercise of its general functions. This means that in taking action which advances its general and/or insurance objective, the PRA is expected to act in a way which advances its secondary objective as well.

As to the resolution process, the framework in force provides that the PRA must determine that the firm is FOLF. Similar to the provisions under the BRRD, a UK bank is determined as FOLF if: there has been a failure to meet asset or management requirements that would justify the PRA withdrawing the bank's permission

[30] n 27.

[31] See R Lastra, 'Accountability mechanisms of the Bank of England and of the European Central Bank', Study for the Committee on Economic and Monetary Affairs (2020) Policy Department for Economic, Scientific and Quality of Life Policies, European Parliament, 15.

to carry out regulated activities; the firm's assets are less than its liabilities; the bank is unable to pay its liabilities; or extraordinary public financial support is required, but other than to remedy a serious disturbance in the economy of the UK.

The second condition for the initiation of resolution is that the Bank of England must decide that it is not reasonably likely that action other than resolution will prevent the failure of the firm.[32] In making this decision, the Bank of England must consult with the PRA, the FCA and the Treasury.

The third condition is that the Bank of England must decide that using a stabilisation option (ie a resolution tool, according to the BRRD terminology) is in the public interest in the advancement of a special resolution objective. In making that decision, the Bank must consult with the PRA, the FCA and the Treasury.

The fourth and last condition is that the Bank of England must decide that the special resolution objectives will not be met to the same extent through the winding up of the bank. In making that decision, the Bank of England must consult with the PRA, the FCA and the Treasury.

IV. The US Bank Supervisory and Crisis Management Architecture

The US bank supervisory and crisis management architecture is based on a complex and sophisticated interaction between federal and state authorities. Depending on the nature and size of banks, the latter will indeed be under the remit of either federal or state authorities, or both. Such a complex framework somehow has been developed to take into account the peculiarities of the US banking sector, where most groups have at the top a banking holding company (BHC).[33] The BHC is not authorised to perform the banking activity, but still it controls one or more subsidiaries, which in turn are authorised as banks. Banks – also referred to as insured depository institutions (IDIs)[34] – are state or federally chartered institutions that take deposits, which are insured by the Federal Deposit Insurance Corporation (FDIC), and extend loans.[35] In the US, a bank has a special legal form and can

[32] Possible alternative actions include supervisory measures such as suspending dividends or management bonuses, financial restructuring or partial sale.

[33] See D Avraham, P Selvaggi and J Veckery, 'A Structural View of U.S. Bank Holding Companies' (2021) 7 *FRBNY Economic Policy Review* 65, available at www.newyorkfed.org/medialibrary/media/research/epr/12v18n2/1207avra.pdf.

[34] The terms 'banks' and 'insured depositary institutions' (IDIs) are used interchangeably across the book with regard to US institutions.

[35] See A Gelpern and N Véron, 'An Effective Regime for Non-viable Banks: US Experience and Considerations for EU Reform' (2012) Requested by the ECON committee of the European Parliament, Economic Governance Support Unit (EGOV) – Directorate-General for Internal Policies of the Union, 12, pointing out that saving and loans associations (also referred to as 'thrifts') and credit unions, on the contrary, are not included in that category.

be established either by state charter or by federal charter. The charter, in turn, represents both the institution's constitutive document and the banking licence.[36]

Federally chartered institutions are granted their charter by the Office of the Comptroller of the Currency (OCC), while state regulatory agencies issue state bank charters under individual state laws.[37] Federally chartered institutions must also obtain FDIC insurance to take deposits and become members of the Federal Reserve System, whereas state-chartered banks are not required to become Federal Reserve members.[38] However, they still need to obtain FDIC insurance, which in turn triggers federal supervision. It follows that every US bank has a primary federal regulator/supervisor responsible for its prudential regulation and supervision.[39]

Depending on the federal agency that is in charge to regulate and supervise them, US IDIs can be grouped into three categories:

- Federally chartered banks. These must be members of the Federal Reserve System and are chartered, regulated and supervised by the OCC.
- State-chartered banks that are members of the Federal Reserve System. These are supervised by one of the 12 Federal Reserve Banks that compose the Federal Reserve System on the basis of the Federal Reserve District where they are established.
- State-chartered banks that are not members of the Federal Reserve System. These are supervised by the FDIC.[40]

BHCs are supervised by the Federal Reserve Board on a consolidated basis and the authority to do so is usually delegated to the Federal Reserve Bank that is geographically competent.[41]

[36] On the structure of the US banking system see A Gelpern and N Véron, 'The Long Road to a US Banking Union: Lessons for Europe' in JF Kirkegaard and AS Posen (eds) *Lessons for EU Integration from US History* (Washington DC, Peterson Institute for International Economics), available at www.piie.com/system/files/documents/kirkegaard-posen_ec-report2018-01.pdf.

[37] See M Bodellini, 'Old Ways and New Ways to Handle Failing Banks across the Atlantic' (2021) 2 *Journal of Comparative Law* 581.

[38] See Federal Financial Institutions Examination Council, 'Annual Report 2018', available at www.ffiec.gov/PDF/annrpt18.pdf, according to which federally chartered banks hold the bulk of US bank assets. At the end of 2018, 866 federally chartered banks held US $11.3 trillion in assets, while 793 state-chartered Federal Reserve member banks held US $2.9 trillion in assets and 3,140 state-chartered non-member banks held US $2.6 trillion in assets.

[39] See n 35, 14.

[40] On the supervisory functions performed by the FDIC with regard to state-chartered banks that are not members of the Federal Reserve System, see J Deslandes, C Dias and M Magnus, 'Liquidation of Banks: Towards an "FDIC" for the Banking Union?' (2019), In-depth analysis, European Parliament, Economic Governance Support Unit, Directorate-General for Internal Policies, 10.

[41] See n 35, 14, highlighting that financial holding companies are a subset of BHCs that meet more stringent criteria allowing them to perform a broader range of financial activities. They also underscore that the Federal Reserve Board is responsible for approving foreign banks' entry in the US and for supervising foreign banking organisations as well.

Thus, while many large banks and all BHCs fall entirely under federal oversight, small banks are typically state-chartered, and therefore supervised by both state and federal authorities.[42]

Based on these characteristics, the US bank crisis management framework provides specific rules for IDIs, which are different from those that apply to BHCs. In the event of a crisis, while IDIs are always subject to a special regime ('receivership'), BHCs are to reorganise or liquidate pursuant to the Bankruptcy Code, like any non-financial firm, unless they are deemed systemically important. When that is the case, the so-called OLA will apply according to the Dodd-Frank Act.[43]

Structurally, the US regime for failing banks is centralised in one institution, the FDIC, and has been tested more than any other system in the world since its creation in 1933.[44]

One of the most peculiar features of the US framework is that during the crisis management process ('resolution'),[45] the FDIC acts both as deposit insurer and as receiver (and sometimes also as supervisor).[46] Despite concerns about conflicts of interest potentially resulting from such a multiple mandate,[47] this setting has over time remained unchallenged and is often regarded as one of the main reasons for the effectiveness of the US system.[48]

Over its almost 90-year existence, the FDIC has developed a range of methods to successfully deal with failing banks.[49] The FDIC uses a broad array of transaction structures to transfer assets and liabilities of failing banks to other private players with a view to reducing as much as possible the costs of the crisis for taxpayers.

Interestingly, during the period 2008–13, the FDIC managed to close down almost 500 IDIs, including some very large banks, without destabilising the market.[50]

[42] See Conference of State Bank Supervisors, 'Annual Report 2018', available at www.csbs.org/system/files/2019-03/CSBS_AR2018_FINALproof.pdf.

[43] Dodd-Frank Act, Sec 203(b)(2).

[44] See Federal Deposit Insurance Corporation, 'Insured Bank Deposits are Safe; Beware of Potential Scams Using the Agency's Name' Press release (2017), available at www.fdic.gov/about/learn/symbol; see n 35, 8, underscoring that the FDIC was established in 1934 after a number of bank failures and decades of unsuccessful attempts to establish a deposit insurance system at federal level.

[45] The term 'resolution' has in the US context a different meaning to the European context. In the US, 'resolution' is an umbrella term that refers to every method used to handle a failing bank (through liquidation with depositor pay-out, purchase and assumption of the bank's franchise by another bank and disposition of the residual assets and any liabilities under FDIC receivership; or 'orderly liquidation' of large financial firms under the Dodd Frank Act). In the EU, on the other hand, 'resolution' is an administrative procedure regulated by BRRD, which applies to 'failing or likely to fail' banks that meet the so-called public interest test.

[46] See n 40, 1.

[47] See JL Douglas and RD Guynn, 'Restructuring and Liquidation of US Financial Institutions' in E Bruno (ed) *Global Financial Crisis: Navigating and Understanding the Legal and Regulatory Aspects* (London, Globe Law and Business, 2009) *passim*.

[48] n 35, 20.

[49] See n 37, 583.

[50] See Federal Deposit Insurance Corporation, 'Crisis and Response: An FDIC History, 2008–2013' (2017), available at www.fdic.gov/bank/historical/crisis (*passim*).

As deposit insurer, the FDIC is meant to pay out insured depositors using the resources of the Deposit Insurance Fund (DIF). After paying out insured depositors, the FDIC is entitled to subrogate to their rights in the liquidation process. In this way, the FDIC typically becomes the largest and one of the most senior creditors of the receivership.[51]

The FDIC manages the DIF that is funded in advance with risk-based contributions provided by IDIs. Additionally, the DIF has a borrowing authority of US $100 billion from the US Treasury and there is also in place a note purchase agreement for US $100 billion with the Federal Financing Bank, which is a specialised government corporation under the control of the Treasury.[52]

[51] See n 35, 19.

[52] See Federal Deposit Insurance Corporation, 'Annual Report 2018' (2018), available at www.fdic.gov/about/strategic/report/2018annualreport/2018ar-final.pdf.

3

The First Lines of Defence

Bank Capital and Early Intervention Measures

I. Introduction

Since the late 1980s, capital has acquired an increasingly important function in banking regulation. Often, the essence of banking regulation is identified in the rules on capital requirements. The reason for this is that the more capital banks hold, the safer and more robust they are considered to be. From a more general perspective, this leads to the consideration that the safety and soundness of the banking system are somehow expected to be achieved by requesting banks to hold a higher level of capital.[1] Building on these premises, both the amount and the quality of capital that credit institutions must hold have significantly risen over the last 30 years.

This objective has been reached primarily through the numerous efforts of the Basel Committee on Banking Supervision (BCBS) which, starting in 1988, has developed a series of soft-law principles and standards on capital requirements which have been then converted into hard-law provisions in the main jurisdictions around the world. Capital is therefore considered the first line of defence to ensure a bank's soundness and thereby the banking system's stability.

Relatedly, the so-called early intervention measures are meant to play an equivalently important preventive function, that is to ensure that bank's soundness and viability are restored after a shock, thereby preventing these difficulties from escalating and turning into an unresolvable crisis.

Moving on from these assumptions, this chapter analyses, on one hand, bank capital, focusing on its function(s), the rationale behind its regulations and the main provisions adopted at the international level and, on the other, the so-called early intervention measures, also referring to some recent cases where such measures have been adopted.

[1] M Bodellini, 'The long "journey" of banks from Basel I to Basel IV: has the banking system become more sound and resilient than it used to be?' (2019) 20 *ERA Forum* 81.

II. The Concept of Capital and the Rationale behind Minimum Bank Capital Requirements

Unlike in the case of non-financial institutions, for banks economic capital and regulatory capital are different concepts. Economic capital is the amount of capital that shareholders would provide their company with in the theoretical scenario of missing special mandatory provisions on minimum bank capital requirements. Typically, firms choose to issue a mix of equity and debt instruments that meets the risk appetite of both equity-holders and debt-holders. On the other hand, regulatory capital is the amount of capital that banks are requested to hold by the special rules that apply to them, whereby minimum capital requirements are laid down. Thus, it is a compulsory amount that banks must hold in order to be allowed to perform the banking activity; if they do not comply with such rules, the authorities are empowered to withdraw their licence (as well as to reject the authorisation application in the first place). Yet, regulatory capital includes a larger set of items than economic capital as it encompasses not only equity instruments but also hybrid instruments as well as long-term, typically subordinated, debt instruments.

From a practical perspective, the capital's way of working is relatively straightforward and simple. First of all, in general terms capital is a means to fund the ongoing operations of a firm, and this holds true even for special entities like banks. But more importantly for the latter, moving from the assumption that, as any other firm, they can incur losses, capital acts as a buffer which is expected to absorb unexpected losses and thereby limit their impact on the company's health in the first place; in turn this also limits their impact on its counterparties as well as on the whole system, should such institution be systemic.[2] It is clear that, on one hand, counterparties would be damaged by the firm's default and, on the other, the system as a whole could be harmed should the institution in crisis be very large or particularly interconnected with other financial firms. The consideration that in the event of a crisis, knock-on effects might be rather severe even in the case of a medium-sized bank failure makes capital requirements even more crucial. Thus, regulatory capital has been designed as a form of protection against risks. But what renders capital even more significant is that it is meant to absorb unexpected losses, being a 'cushion' for rainy days,[3] whereas reserves are commonly used to cover expected losses.[4]

Leverage, by contrast, is a different concept, as it refers to the value of a bank's exposures divided by its own capital. Typically, banks buy sovereign bonds and

[2] See K Alexander, *Principles of Banking Regulation* (Cambridge, Cambridge University Press, 2019) 87, arguing that bank capital has four main purposes: absorbing losses; providing start-up funding; reducing losses to deposit insurance schemes; and creating incentives to shareholders, directors and managers to exercise more prudence in overseeing the bank's operations.

[3] R Lastra, *International Financial and Monetary Law* (Oxford, Oxford University Press, 2015) *passim*.

[4] G Walker and R Purves, *Financial Services Law* (Oxford, Oxford University Press, 2018) *passim*.

other securities and make loans as well. These are the most common items accounted in the assets side of a bank's balance sheet. Banks buy assets usually by issuing debt instruments, such as deposits, bonds and notes. Before the global financial crisis there were no internationally agreed limits to the amount of leverage that banks were allowed to carry.[5] After the global financial crisis, banks have been pressured to deleverage due to the introduction of new rules and limits in this regard. Deleveraging might be the result of either the banks increasing their capital or the banks selling their assets and repaying some of their debts.[6]

The rationale behind capital regulation lies in the peculiarities of the bank's business model. Commercial banks mainly collect deposits from the public and use them to extend loans. Hence, deposits are the most relevant form of financing for commercial banking institutions. This means that banks rely extensively upon liabilities (as opposed to equity) to buy assets.[7] As a consequence, they are by nature highly leveraged institutions, and this represents a source of regulatory concern.[8]

Also, the main feature of deposits is that they are withdrawable on demand, which makes them short-term liabilities.[9] Banks hold (as reserves at the central bank and other liquid assets) only a tiny fraction of the total amount of deposits they have taken and use the remaining part to extend loans. They act in this way with view to making profits, which arise from charging higher interests on their borrowers than the interests paid to depositors. However, the short-term nature of deposits and the longer-term maturity of loans might create an issue, known as maturity mismatch. While such a business model functions efficiently in good times, this is not necessarily the case in bad times, since the fractional reserves, namely the part of deposits that the bank has not used to extend loans and has invested in liquid – and typically less profitable – assets, might not suffice to meet the depositors' withdrawals. Such a situation can in turn deteriorate very quickly, leading to a phenomenon called 'bank run', whereby many depositors, concerned about the solidity and solvency of their bank, withdraw their deposits at the same time. This phenomenon is very difficult to handle as banks do not have the deposits readily available and so have to sell their assets to satisfy the withdrawals. Such sales might have to take place at discounted prices, thereby causing losses, which capital is expected to absorb.

Capital is meant to address these issues, because when a bank is undercapitalised it is more vulnerable to the maturity mismatch. This results from the

[5] n 2, 86. Many large global banking groups from early 2000s to around 2010 operated with less than 3% equity capital as a percentage of their total assets. As a consequence, losses of only 3% on their assets would have made them insolvent

[6] n 1, 83.

[7] See S Heffernan, *Modern Banking* (New York, Wiley, 2005) 2.

[8] n 2, 86.

[9] n 1, 83.

share capital being able to absorb losses much more effectively than any other instrument.[10] In other words, significant losses can cause a bank run, but if the bank concerned holds a proportionally adequate amount of capital, the latter will likely absorb the losses. If the losses are effectively absorbed, depositors should be less prone to run on their bank to withdraw their deposits since the bank's health is ensured by the protection provided by capital. Therefore, given the importance of deposits to the public and the role of banks in maintaining financial stability, banking institutions are subject to minimum capital requirements.[11]

Against this background, while deposit guarantee schemes, which are also considered a safety net, operate reactively (as shown in chapter six), capital requirements are a preventive measure. Also, while deposit guarantee schemes might increase moral hazard,[12] capital requirements do not, being regarded as capable of creating incentives for shareholders, directors and managers to exercise more prudence in overseeing the bank's operations.[13] This does not mean that capital should be seen as a panacea to solve every problem, but is certainly a very important and effective tool to increase a bank's soundness and robustness. Therefore, banks (as well as other financial firms) are not free to choose the amount of capital to hold, since this could place depositors, other creditors and stakeholders at undue risk. By contrast, they must meet minimum capital requirements and ratios.

It is also worth noting that widespread banking failures have the potential to inflict heavy social costs, including reduction in credit availability. Adequate bank capital levels, as required by the regulation, can prevent these issues allowing banks to keep on financing their borrowers.

As to the economic rationale for bank capital regulation, there are typically information asymmetries between depositors and banks on one side, and between banks and borrowers on the other. Capital regulation is meant to reduce such

[10] See R Cranston, E Avgouleas, K Van Zwieten, C Hare and T Van Sante, *Principles of Banking Law* (Oxford, Oxford University Press, 2017) 28, underlining that this arises from the fact that common equity is perpetual and irredeemable and ranks last in the event of insolvency.

[11] n 1, 84.

[12] However, in this regard see International Association of Deposit Insurers (IADI), 'Enhanced Guidance for Effective Deposit Insurance Systems: Deposit Insurance Coverage – Guidance Paper' (2013) 8, arguing that 'Traditionally, coverage limits in deposit insurance systems have been set to balance the protection of small-scale depositors who are less able to monitor and evaluate the strength of a bank against the incentives such protection creates for greater risk taking by banks. The concern raised by both practitioners and researchers was that making depositors insensitive to risk (because they were protected) increased moral hazard. Depositors with balances exceeding the (relatively low) coverage level were exposed to risk of a bank failure and expected to exercise market disciple to limit bank risk taking. Deposit insurance systems, therefore, balanced the conflicting goals of protecting the largest number of depositors while keeping the total value of deposits fully protected low'. It is also emphasised that after the global financial crisis, 'It became clear that the objective of promoting financial stability outweighed concerns about limiting moral hazard'. This is also grounded in the consideration that despite the expectation being 'that uninsured depositors would monitor their banks' risk profile and exercise market discipline by shifting to less risky banks as warranted', in fact, 'the ability of most depositors and all but the largest creditors to do so is now recognized as limited and ineffective in a crisis'.

[13] n 2, 87.

information asymmetries between the bank's management and key stakeholders, including depositors, creditors and investors, by providing them all with precise information on the financial condition of the bank.[14]

Additionally, banks are very interconnected among each other, and within the financial and economic systems. As a consequence, negative externalities can be easily transmitted to other players, such as other banks, financial and non-financial institutions, and depositors, generating so-called knock-on effects.[15] Against this backdrop, regulation, including capital regulation, is regarded as necessary because markets, by nature, fail. Thus, since markets are imperfect structures, it is highly unlikely that private players would be able to set themselves the adequate amount of capital to hold and therefore capital requirements rules are needed. All this means that bank capital regulation is also important to promote the stability of the financial system, which could be harmed in the event of widespread bank failures due to the so-called 'domino effect'.[16]

These considerations have to be linked to the fact that financial stability is a public good, and as such has to be kept at any cost. And in this respect, capital is regarded as a very effective tool.[17]

Lastly, the recently introduced rules on resolution can properly function (ie a failing bank can be effectively resolved) only if there are enough capital (as well as debt) instruments to write down and convert.[18] In other words, the write-down and bail-in tool can be successfully applied when resolving a bank only if such bank has issued a sufficient amount of bail-in-able liabilities. When meeting some specific requirements, the latter can be accounted for as part of the regulatory capital.

III. Capital Requirements and the Role of the Basel Committee on Banking Supervision

The most important standard-setter in the field of bank capital is the Basel Committee on Banking Supervision (BCBS).

[14] n 1, 84.

[15] See M Bodellini, 'From Systemic Risk to Financial Scandals: the Shortcomings of US Regulation on Hedge Funds' (2017) 11 *Brooklyn Journal of Corporate, Financial & Commercial Law* 417.

[16] n 1, 84.

[17] See n 10, 28, underlining that 'the risk of individual institution failure and of a systemic collapse is mostly addressed through prudential regulation in the guise of capital and liquidity requirements'.

[18] See M Bodellini, 'To Bail-in, or To Bail-out, That Is the Question' (2018) 19 *European Business Organization Law Review* 365; M Bodellini, 'Greek and Italian "Lessons" on Bank Restructuring: Is Precautionary Recapitalisation the Way Forward?' (2017) 19 *Cambridge Yearbook of European Legal Studies* 144; P Brierley, 'Ending Too-Big-To-Fail: Progress Since the Crisis, the Importance of Loss-Absorbing Capacity and the UK Approach to Resolution' (2017) 18 *European Business Organization Law Review* 457.

The BCBS was established in 1974 by the central banks and the supervisory authorities of the G10 countries under the aegis of the Bank for International Settlements (BIS), which is based in Basel, Switzerland. The Committee does not have any supranational status, being simply a forum of experts who meet periodically with the aim of enhancing the effectiveness of banking regulation. The BCBS mainly creates standards (ie soft-law principles) that are then transposed into domestic legislation and/or regulation through the adoption of laws and/or regulations thereby becoming binding and enforceable rules.

Despite the lack of a direct legal binding force of its standards, the BCBS has become a de facto international regulatory body.[19] Many argue that the informality and independence of the BCBS have served well in the design of international banking rules, as it has acted with a fair degree of 'depoliticisation' and a considerable amount of technical expertise and competence in banking-related matters.[20]

Even though there is no international legal obligation to implement the BCBS capital standards, for most countries incentives and sanctions are stronger than generally recognised. This is why the most important jurisdictions across the world have always transposed into their domestic banking regulations the soft-law principles designed over time by BCBS.[21]

The BCBS is committed to the promotion of best practices in banking supervision. The most significant examples of this are certainly the Basel Capital Accords, the first of which was published in 1988 ('Basel I'). Importantly, capital regulation before this initiative was often informal and adopted only at the domestic level. Some countries did not even have specific rules on bank capital since they were not deemed necessary. The underlying assumption was that banks were able to set their own adequate amount of capital without the need for rules laying down minimum requirements to comply with. However, at the end of the 1980s this perception radically changed, and the BCBS issued Basel I.

IV. The Adoption of Basel I

The BCBS adopted Basel I in 1988. Basel I played a prominent role as there had previously been no international standards on bank capital to apply to internationally active institutions.[22] This represented a major problem, since diverse rules

[19] Since January 2013, the Basel Committee on Banking Supervision has its own 'charter' available at www.bis.org/bcbs/charter.html. As stated in the Charter, the internal organisational structure of the BCBS comprises: the Committee; working groups and task forces; the Chairman; and the Secretariat. The Committee's Secretariat is provided by the Bank for International Settlements (BIS) in Basel.

[20] See R Lastra and M Bodellini, 'Soft Law and Sovereign Debt' (2018), Intergovernmental Group of Experts on Financing for Development, United Nations, 7.

[21] See E Jones and A Zeitz, 'The Limits of Globalizing Basel Banking Standards' (2017) 3 *Journal of Financial Regulation* 89, 124.

[22] Basel Committee on Banking Supervision, 'International Convergence of Capital Measurement and Capital Standards' (1988), available at www.bis.org.

in different jurisdictions made it difficult for banks operating at the international level to comply with the provisions of every country in which they were active.[23] Additionally, the lack of internationally accepted standards typically tends to encourage a race to the bottom, whereby jurisdictions might feel tempted to attract institutions by offering them a more business-friendly environment, for example, by introducing a legal framework that does not require banks to hold capital at all (or where capital requirements are very low). Yet, arguably this is not a desirable outcome, since, even though capital can be expensive for banks,[24] there is no doubt that its adequate amount is an effective instrument to help face idiosyncratic crises in the first place and systemic crises subsequently. Against this backdrop, the effort of putting in place some basic standards to harmonise capital requirements rules for internationally active banks was therefore a significant step forward compared to the regime previously in place.

Basel I had a very simple structure, based on the newly introduced concept of risk-weighted assets (RWAs), along with the general rule that the minimum amount of regulatory capital had to be at least eight per cent of the risk-weighted assets.[25] The main purpose of these provisions was to make banks increase the amount of capital held.

The structure of the risk-weighted assets framework is based on the assumption that different assets arguably carry different levels of risk. Since capital is meant to protect the institution (and its counterparties) from the risks which are embedded in its business activity, the amount of capital to hold needs to be determined relative to the riskiness of the bank's assets.

This is reflected in different risk weightings being assigned to different asset classes. In other words, assets have been grouped in different categories, each of them considered to carry different risks. Every category has been given a percentage resulting from its perceived riskiness. The higher the percentage, the higher the riskiness of the assets, and vice versa.[26] In turn, the higher such a percentage is, the more capital a bank is required to set aside. Accordingly, if an asset is given a risk weight of 20 per cent, this means that the bank owning that asset in its balance sheet has to hold an amount of capital at least equal to 20 per cent of eight per cent of the value of such asset.[27] A loan to the British Government, for example, is considered to be risk-free (ie zero per cent) because the British Government is

[23] n 1, 86.

[24] See n 10, 28, underlining that typically capital is considered more expensive than debt.

[25] See Bank for International Settlements: History of the Basel Committee, available at www.bis.org/bcbs/history.htm; see also P Shakdwippe and M Mehta, 'From Basel I to Basel II to Basel III' (2017) 3 *International Journal of New Technologies and Research* 66; L Balthazar, *From Basel 1 to Basel 3: The Integration of State of Art Risk Modelling in Banking Regulation* (New York, Palgrave Macmillan, 2006).

[26] See n 2, 91, emphasising that loans to Organisation for Economic Co-operation and Development (OECD) countries would have a zero risk-weighting, while loans to countries outside the OECD were subject to the full 100% risk-weighting. All loans to business and individuals were subject to the same risk-weightings, whereas mortgage loans were subject to a 50% risk-weighting.

[27] See n 1, 86.

deemed to be able to repay its own debt. As a result, such a loan, on the grounds of being considered risk-free, does not impact the amount of capital the bank is required to hold.[28]

Regulatory capital could be sourced from different tiers: Tier 1 (core capital); and Tier 2 (supplementary capital). Tier 2 could not exceed 100 per cent of Tier 1. While Tier 1 capital includes common equity shares, equivalent instruments and retained earnings (going concern capital), Tier 2 capital is mainly represented by subordinated debt and other bonds and debt-like instruments, such as preference shares and convertible instruments (gone concern capital).

Even though Basel I significantly increased the amount of capital held by banks, it also had a number of shortcomings. In particular, it lacked risk-sensitivity as well as risk-mitigation techniques. Although banks are typically exposed to a number of different risks, Basel I mainly focused on credit risk. Market risk and operational risk were not taken into due account and, as a consequence, banks were not requested to hold capital in relation to the growing amount of assets they were trading in the capital markets. Also, these regulatory requirements only applied to loans recorded in the bank's balance sheet. Banks, therefore, developed techniques (such as securitisation and purchase of credit derivatives) to move assets and/or related risks off their balance sheet with a view to reducing the amount of capital to hold.[29]

The Market Risk Amendment to Basel I was adopted in 1996 by the BCBS with a view to tackling some of those weaknesses in response to the collapse of Barings. Accordingly, capital requirements were extended to enable banks to absorb losses resulting from market risk exposures. In so doing, banks were allowed to use their own data and value-at-risk (VaR) models to calculate the regulatory capital concerning their trading book.[30]

V. The Adoption of Basel II

With a view to addressing the remaining shortcomings affecting Basel I, in 2005 the BCBS adopted Basel II, which significantly amended the previous framework.[31] Basel II introduced the so-called three pillars, namely: the first pillar based on a revised minimum capital framework; the second pillar with the supervisory review process; and the third pillar regarding market discipline based on mandatory and voluntary disclosure.[32]

[28] On the risk weight attributed to government debt in the Basel framework and on its consequences see S Gleeson, 'Bank Capital Regulation and Sovereign Debt Restructuring' (2018) 13 *Capital Markets Law Journal* 467, 482.

[29] n 2, 92.

[30] JC Hull, *Risk management and financial institutions* (New York, Wiley, 2012) 183–201.

[31] Basel Committee on Banking Supervision, 'Basel II: International Convergence of Capital Measurement and Capital Standards: A Revised Framework' (2006), available at www.bis.org.

[32] See G Walker, 'Basel III Market and Regulatory Compromise' (2011) 12 *Journal of Banking Regulation* 95.

The main purpose of Basel II was to give banks the possibility to internally weight their own assets in the face of their riskiness as perceived by the banks themselves.[33] Banks were already counting and calculating internally their economic capital, so they were deemed to know better than supervisors their own situation and to be better suited to determine the amount of capital they needed. On these grounds, banks were permitted to use their internal models also to calculate their risk-weighted assets.[34]

As foreseeable, however, the practical effect of Basel II was mainly that banks using internal models to calculate risk-weighted assets managed to considerably decrease the amount of capital held. This was also due to supervisors often lacking internally the sophisticated skills needed to challenge the banks' internal models.[35]

The global financial crisis of 2007–09 occurred with the Basel II standards in place. In this regard, Alan Greenspan argued that:

> The Basel Committee on Banking Supervision, representing regulatory authorities from the world's major financial systems, promulgated a set of capital rules that failed to foresee the need that arose at the height of the crisis for much larger capital and liquidity buffers.[36]

Clearly, the Basel II framework proved to be inadequate for achieving its stated goals. In particular, its rules were unable to limit the excessive building-up of leverage and did not take into account the importance of liquidity, two of the main causes for the crisis.[37] Also, the amount of capital held by banks was considered to be largely insufficient.[38]

VI. The Adoption of Basel III

In response to the global financial crisis, the BCBS adopted Basel III in 2011 in order to 'strengthen global capital and liquidity rules with the goal of promoting a more resilient banking sector'.[39] In other words, the main goal of Basel III was to make the banks' regulatory capital increase both in terms of quantity and quality.[40]

[33] A Cornford, 'Basel II: The Revised Framework of 2004', United Nations Conference on Trade and Development (UNCTD), Discussion Paper No 178, 2005; A Belratti and G Paladino, 'Basel and Regulatory Arbitrage. Evidence from Financial Crises' (2016) 39 *Journal of Empirical Finance* 180.

[34] n 2, 94.

[35] n 1, 87.

[36] A Greenspan, 'Speech Given at the Federal Reserve of Chicago Bank Structure Conferences', 7 May 2010, available at www.chicagofed.org.

[37] E Avgouleas, *Governance of Global Financial Markets: The Law, the Economics, the Politics* (Cambridge, Cambridge University Press, 2012).

[38] See P Yeoh, 'Basel IV: International Bank Capital Regulation Solution or the Beginning of a Solution?' (2018) 39 *Business Law Review* 176.

[39] Basel Committee on Banking Supervision, 'Basel III: A Global Regulatory Framework for More Resilient Banks and Banking Systems' (2011), available at www.bis.org.

[40] M Barr, H Jackson and M Tahyar, *Financial Regulation: Law and Policy. Foundation Press* (New York, Eagan, 2016); F Cannata and M Quagliariello, *Basel III and Beyond: A Guide to Banking Regulation After the Crisis* (London, Risk Books, 2011).

This goal has been pursued in several ways.[41]

Quality, consistency and transparency of regulatory capital have been significantly increased. Quality of capital has been enhanced through the provision that Tier 1 has to be mostly made up of equity and reserves and CET1 has to be much higher than in the past. Quantity has been increased through the provision that more capital is now required. Accordingly, CET1 (ie equity and retained earnings) is more than doubled, increasing from two to 4.5 per cent against risk-weighted assets.[42] This is supplemented by a capital conservation buffer of 2.5 per cent which, along with the other provisions, brings the CET1 to seven per cent.[43]

Additionally, banks have been required to build a counter-cyclical capital buffer and global systemically important banks (G-SIBs) have been requested to hold a capital surcharge. A leverage ratio has also been introduced as a supplementary measure to the existing framework. Such a ratio, which performs a very important function considering the excessive level of debt characterising many institutions during the crisis, is calculated by dividing the book value of the assets by the value of equity. The ratio cannot exceed 30 per cent. Even though this is a very important innovation, many argue that the ratio is still too high, with the consequence that banks can continue to be excessively leveraged.[44]

A number of measures for the reduction of procyclicality and stronger provisioning practices with a forward-looking approach have also been introduced. Prominent among them are the above-mentioned counter-cyclical capital requirements. These measures represent a macro-prudential tool, since they link the regulatory capital to the economic cycle. By contrast, under Basel II, banks were required to increase their capital during periods of crisis, which was a mechanism that clearly proved ineffective during the global financial crisis of 2007–09 when banks were not able to raise capital from the markets.

Also, liquidity has been recognised as being of paramount importance in reducing externalities. Based on these premises, specific requirements have been introduced. In particular, a liquidity coverage ratio has been adopted, and to comply with it, banks are required to hold a stock of high-quality liquid assets that can be easily sold to match withdrawals.[45] Additionally, a stable funding ratio has been introduced requiring illiquid assets to be backed by stable funding.

Equally significant are the new measures concerning the so-called Pillar 2. Corporate governance and risk management oversight have accordingly been enhanced. From a practical perspective, supervisors are now requested to more carefully examine the bank's corporate governance arrangements and the

[41] See n 32, 95, underlining that 'The final arrangements are more remarkable in terms of their balance and moderation rather than for the time that they took to agree'.

[42] n 1, 88.

[43] n 32, 95, underlining that 'Banks operating between 4.5 and 7 per cent will be subject to restrictions on dividend and bonus payments to protect capital from short-term dilution'.

[44] See D Miles, J Yang and G Marcheggiano, 'Optimal Bank Capital. Bank of England, External MPC Unit' (2011) 31, arguing that the amount of capital to hold should be 20% of unweighted assets.

[45] See n 28, 467.

way in which they actually work, namely the way in which the bank's decisions are made. The main concern relates to the board's awareness of the internal situation within the institution, given that in the past boards often demonstrated that they did not fully understand the risks and complexities of their bank's business model.[46]

VII. The Adoption of Basel IV

In December 2017, the BCBS adopted the so-called Basel III reforms with a view to complementing the improvements introduced with the issuance of the Basel III package in 2011.[47] The 'revisions seek to restore credibility in the calculation of risk-weighted assets and improve the comparability of banks' capital ratios'.[48]

Despite qualifying the new measures as simply a revision of the principles already in place, their intrusive impact on banking institutions is the reason why they have been immediately labelled by the industry as 'Basel IV'.[49]

The new measures have been introduced on the grounds that Basel III was considered insufficient, as banks were still over-relying on their internal models for calculating risk-weighted assets.[50] In particular, the BCBS was of the idea that higher levels of capital and higher buffers were needed to help preserve financial stability.[51] Based on this assumption, Basel IV has introduced a number of new provisions that, either directly or indirectly, will affect the calculation of risk-weighted assets and thereby increase the amount of regulatory capital to hold.

The main innovations introduced relate to:

(a) 'enhancing the robustness and risk sensitivity of the standardised approaches for credit risk and operational risk';
(b) 'constraining the use of the internal model approaches, by placing limits on certain inputs used to calculate capital requirements under the internal ratings-based (IRB) approach for credit risk and by removing the use of the internal model approaches for operational risk';
(c) 'introducing a leverage ratio buffer to further limit the leverage of global systemically important banks (G-SIBs)'; and
(d) 'replacing the existing Basel II output floor with a more robust risk-sensitive floor based on the BCBS's revised Basel III standardised approaches'.[52]

[46] About this specific issue see M Bodellini, 'Corporate Governance of Banks and Financial Stability: Critical Issues and Challenges Ahead' (2018) 39 *Business Law Review* 160.

[47] Basel Committee on Banking Supervision, 'Finalising Post-Crisis Reforms' (2017), available at www.bis.org.

[48] ibid.

[49] See n 38.

[50] See n 1, 90.

[51] M Magnus, A Margerit, B Mesnard and A Korpas, 'Upgrading the Basel Standards: From Basel III to Basel IV?' (2017) Economic Governance Support Unit, European Parliament Briefing Paper.

[52] Basel Committee on Banking Supervision, 'High Level Summary of Basel III Reforms' (2017), available at www.bis.org.

A. The New Standardised Approach

As credit risk is often the most significant risk taken on by banks, the BCBS has deemed it necessary to redesign the standardised approach applied for its determination. Such decision was also grounded in the consideration that the standardised approach is used by the majority of banking institutions around the globe. The revision is expected to improve the granularity of the standardised approach and hence its risk-sensitivity. Accordingly, while Basel II used to assign a flat risk weight to every residential mortgage, in the current framework the risk weight assigned to mortgage loans will depend on their loan-to-value (LTV) ratio.[53]

Moreover, Basel IV aims to reduce the excessive reliance on credit ratings. Thus, banks are requested to conduct their own due diligence in order to price the risk(s) more efficiently.[54] The most relevant measures in this context are as follows:

(1) '[A] more granular approach has been developed for unrated exposures to banks and corporates, and for rated exposures in jurisdictions where the use of credit ratings is permitted'.
(2) '[F]or exposures to banks, some of the risk weights for rated exposures have been recalibrated. A standalone treatment for covered bonds has also been introduced'.
(3) '[F]or exposures to corporates, a more granular look-up table has been developed. A specific risk weight applies to exposures to small and medium-sized enterprises (SMEs). In addition, the revised standardised approach includes a standalone treatment for exposures to project finance, object finance and commodities finance'.
(4) '[F]or residential real estate exposures, more risk-sensitive approaches have been developed, whereby risk weights vary based on the Loan-To-Value ratio of the mortgage (instead of the existing single risk weight) and in ways that better reflect differences in market structures'.
(5) 'For retail exposures, a more granular treatment applies, which distinguishes between different types of retail exposures'.
(6) 'For commercial real estate exposures, approaches have been developed that are more risk-sensitive than the flat risk weight which generally applies'.
(7) '[F]or subordinated debt and equity exposures, a more granular risk weight treatment applies'.
(8) '[F]or off-balance sheet items, the credit conversion factors which are used to determine the amount of an exposure to be risk-weighted, have been made more risk-sensitive'.[55]

With regard to operational risks, in contrast, the global financial crisis showed two main shortcomings within the framework then in force. On one hand, capital

[53] n 47.
[54] ibid.
[55] n 52.

requirements for operational risk proved insufficient to cover losses incurred by some banks, and on the other, the nature of these losses – covering events such as misconduct and inadequate systems and controls – highlighted the difficulty resulting from using internal models to estimate capital requirements for operational risk.[56]

On these grounds, the operational risk framework has been streamlined and, accordingly, the advanced measurement approaches (which were based on banks' internal models) and the existing three standardised approaches have been replaced with a single risk-sensitive standardised approach to be used by every bank.[57]

The new standardised approach for operational risk will determine a bank's operational risk capital requirements based on the bank's incomes and its historical losses:[58]

> Conceptually, it assumes: (i) that operational risk increases at an increasing rate with a bank's income; and (ii) banks which have experienced greater operational risk losses historically are assumed to be more likely to experience operational risk losses in the future.[59]

B. Internal Rating-Based Approaches for Credit Risk and the Leverage Ratio Framework

The financial crisis of 2007–09 also highlighted a number of shortcomings related to the use of internally modelled approaches for regulatory capital calculation, including the IRB approaches for the calculation of credit risk.[60] These shortcomings include the excessive complexity of the IRB approaches, the lack of comparability in banks' internally modelled IRB capital requirements and the lack of robustness in modelling certain asset classes.[61]

To address these shortcomings, the BCBS has made the following revisions to the IRB approaches:

> '(i) removed the option to use the advanced IRB (A-IRB) approach for certain asset classes;
> (ii) adopted "input" floors (for metrics such as probabilities of default (PD) and loss-given-default (LGD)) to ensure a minimum level of conservativism in model parameters for asset classes where the IRB approaches remain available; and
> (iii) provided greater specification of parameter estimation practices to reduce RWA variability.'[62]

[56] See P Sands, G Liao and Y Ma, 'Rethinking Operational Risk Capital Requirements' (2018) 4 *Journal of Financial Regulation* 1.
[57] n 47.
[58] n 1, 91.
[59] n 52.
[60] n 1, 92.
[61] See n 38.
[62] n 52.

In this regard, Stefan Ingves, then Chair of the Basel Committee on Banking Supervision, claimed that Basel IV will help reduce excessive variability in RWAs simultaneously improving the comparability and transparency of banks' risk-based capital ratios.[63]

A new leverage ratio buffer has also been introduced, the function of which is to complement 'the risk-weighted capital requirements by providing a safeguard against unsustainable levels of leverage and by mitigating gaming and model risk across both internal models and standardised risk measurement approaches'.[64] Such a buffer applies to G-SIBs and has to be met with Tier 1 capital. It is set at 50 per cent of a G-SIB's risk-weighted higher-loss absorbency requirements.[65]

The leverage ratio buffer has the same structure as capital buffers in the risk-weighted framework. The BCBS noted that 'as is the case with the risk-weighted framework, capital distribution constraints will be imposed on a G-SIB that does not meet its leverage ratio buffer requirement'.[66]

C. The Output Floor

The most relevant measure introduced by Basel IV as to its impact on the amount of capital to hold is the 'output floor'. The concept of the output floor is not novel, since with Basel II, the BCBS had already introduced this mechanism, based on the Basel I capital requirements. However, the floor under Basel II, which amounted to 80 per cent of the relevant Basel I capital requirements, never functioned effectively since its implementation proved to be inconsistent across countries, mainly because of differing interpretations of the underlying requirements.[67]

With Basel IV, the BCBS has replaced the previous floor with a new one based on the revised Basel III standardised approaches.[68] As with the original floor, the new one 'places a limit on the regulatory capital benefits that a bank using internal models can derive relative to the standardised approaches'.[69] In effect, such instrument represents a risk-based backstop that limits the extent to which banks can decrease their capital requirements relative to those resulting from the application of standardised approaches.[70] This is meant to help keep a level playing field between banks using internal models and those using the standardised approaches.[71] It also

[63] Bank for International Settlements, 'Governors and Heads of Supervision Finalise Basel III Reforms' (2017), available at www.bis.org/press/p171207.htm.

[64] n 52.

[65] ibid, stating that 'a G-SIB subject to a 2% risk-weighted higher-loss absorbency requirement would be subject to a 1% leverage ratio buffer requirement'.

[66] ibid.

[67] See accordingly n 38.

[68] See n 1, 93.

[69] n 52.

[70] n 47.

[71] ibid.

supports the credibility of banks' risk-weighted calculations and is expected to improve comparability through the related disclosure obligations.[72]

On these grounds,

> banks' risk-weighted assets must be calculated as the higher of: (i) total risk-weighted assets calculated using the approaches that the bank has supervisory approval to use in accordance with the Basel capital framework (including both standardised and internal model-based approaches); and (ii) 72.5 per cent of the total risk-weighted assets calculated using only the standardised approaches.[73]

In other words, the floor is a limit to the outcomes in terms of the value of RWAs as calculated by applying the internal model-based approaches. And such a limit is linked to the value of RWAs as resulting from the application of the default standard model. As a consequence, banks have to, either directly or indirectly, take into account the standardised model that acts like a proxy to a lower limit below which RWAs cannot fall. This is expected to cause banks to have to hold much more capital than they used to.[74] Importantly, such new output floor will ensure that the value of banks' RWAs calculated according to internal models is not lower than 72.5 per cent of the RWAs as calculated by applying the Basel III framework's standardised approaches. Banks will also be required to disclose their RWAs based on these standardised approaches.[75]

The output floor will be introduced only gradually on the grounds that these new measures will require banks to raise additional capital. As a consequence, banks need to be given a reasonable amount of time to plan and carry out the requested capital increase. Thus, the 72.5 per cent limit will be progressively reached over a number of years. The mechanism has entered into force in January 2022 with a limit of 50 per cent that will, year upon year, increase up to 72.5 per cent in January 2027.[76]

VIII. Early Intervention Measures

Early intervention measures are procedures and tools of a different nature and with a different level of intrusiveness, commonly activated and applied by authorities with a view to ensuring that banks address their weaknesses promptly before the triggers for their submission to a crisis management procedure are met.

[72] See n 38.
[73] n 47.
[74] See n 1, 93.
[75] n 47.
[76] With regard to the output floor, a phase-in period has been agreed as follows: 1 January 2022: 50%; 1 January 2023: 55%; 1 January 2024: 60%; 1 January 2025: 65%; 1 January 2026: 70%; 1 January 2027: 72.5%; see n 47.

The objective of such measures is either to put banks back on a sound footing or, when this is not possible, to mitigate the consequences of a failure to be then handled in the context of a crisis management procedure.[77] But to try to restore the bank's viability, the measure needs to be implemented when the institution concerned has still a minimum amount of capital left, despite (some of) the regulatory requirements having probably been already breached. Also, for the intervention to be successful, a number of measures might have to be adopted simulataneously, ranging from the appointment of a new management team and/or a new board of directors, to implementation of a new business plan and restructuring of the business activities.

In this regard, the BCBS has emphasised that

> adopting a forward-looking approach to supervision through early intervention can prevent an identified weakness from developing into a threat to safety and soundness. This is particularly true for highly complex and bank-specific issues (eg. liquidity risk) where effective supervisory actions must be tailored to a bank's individual circumstances.[78]

The importance of early intervention arises from the fact that depositors, customers and investors are sensitive to any sign of vulnerability, and this in turn might prompt them to quickly terminate their contractual relationships with their bank. Such sensitivity is further boosted by the perception that banks have incentives to delay loss recognition in their financial statements.[79]

Early intervention measures and their triggers differ from jurisdiction to jurisdiction with both the EU and the US providing their authorities with a number of options to rely upon depending on the seriousness of the issues affecting the bank concerned.

A relevant distinction has been drawn between the so-called regular supervisory frameworks and the formal intervention regimes, where the former are the ones in which supervisors use their powers to take action based on their own judgment and following high-level principles as stated in their mandates, while in the latter, actions by supervisors are grounded in specific legal or regulatory provisions specifying both triggers for intervention and available options.[80]

The triggers for the implementation of such measures can have different nature, ranging from capital-based triggers, to asset quality and liquidity indicators, to supervisory ratings. Yet, capital-based indicators are backword-looking indicators that can end up reinforcing weak banks' incentives to inflate reported solvency ratios.[81] Also, once the bank has become under-capitalised, it is usually too late

[77] See on this JP Svoronos (2018) 'FSI Insights on policy implementation No 6. Early intervention regimes for weak banks' 2.

[78] Basel Committee on Banking Supervision, 'Core Principles for Effective Banking Supervision' (2012) 4.

[79] See n 77, 2.

[80] ibid, 2.

[81] ibid, 2.

for it to recover; an effective way to tackle the drawbacks of capital-based triggers could be to set them at levels that are significantly higher than the respective minimum capital requirements.[82] By contrast, the use of forward-looking indicators as triggers is expected to make the early intervention regime more effective and really proactive. Such indicators should be able to promptly detect vulnerabilities that would likely lead to a significant deterioration of the bank's financial conditions. In this way, they could enable for a more timely supervisory intervention.[83]

A. Early Intervention Measures in the EU

Early intervention measures and their triggers are regulated in the EU by the BRRD, which has established a formal early intervention regime. Accordingly, the competent authorities (ie the bank supervisors) are meant to assess whether the bank's conditions for early intervention are met and when that is the case, then they will decide if such early intervention measures are appropriate. The conditions for early intervention measures in turn require a breach or a likely breach of prudential requirements in the near future.[84]

The early intervention measures allow the competent authorities to:

(a) require the management body of the institution to implement one or more of the arrangements or measures set out in the recovery plan, or, update such a recovery plan when the circumstances that led to the early intervention are different from the assumptions set out in the initial recovery plan and implement one or more of the arrangements or measures set out in the updated plan within a specific timeframe and in order to ensure that the conditions referred to in the introductory phrase no longer apply;
(b) require the management body of the institution to examine the situation, identify measures to overcome any problems identified and draw up an action programme to overcome those problems and a timetable for its implementation;

[82] ibid, 2.

[83] ibid, 14, arguing that 'triggers could also include the quality of a bank's risk control function, underwriting practices, corporate governance framework and other indicators relating to credit, market, liquidity or operational risk. The main drawback of this type of indicator is that they are typically more subject to interpretation, and thus harder to enforce and potentially more subject to litigation'.

[84] According to Art 27 of the BRRD, early intervention measures can be implemented 'where an institution infringes or, due, inter alia, to a rapidly deteriorating financial condition, including deteriorating liquidity situation, increasing level of leverage, non-performing loans or concentration of exposures, as assessed on the basis of a set of triggers, which may include the institution's own funds requirement plus 1,5 percentage points, is likely in the near future to infringe the requirements of Regulation (EU) No 575/2013, Directive 2013/36/EU, Title II of Directive 2014/65/EU or any of Articles 3 to 7, 14 to 17, and 24, 25 and 26 of Regulation (EU) No 600/2014, Member States shall ensure that competent authorities have at their disposal, without prejudice to the measures referred to in Article 104 of Directive 2013/36/EU where applicable'.

(c) require the management body of the institution to convene, or if the management body fails to comply with that requirement, convene directly a meeting of shareholders of the institution, and in both cases set the agenda and require certain decisions to be considered for adoption by the shareholders;
(d) require one or more members of the management body or senior management to be removed or replaced if those persons are found unfit to perform their duties;
(e) require the management body of the institution to draw up a plan for negotiation on restructuring of debt with some or all of its creditors according to the recovery plan, where applicable;
(f) require changes to the institution's business strategy;
(g) require changes to the legal or operational structures of the institution; and
(h) acquire, including through on-site inspections, and provide to the resolution authority, all the information necessary in order to update the resolution plan and prepare for the possible resolution of the institution and for valuation of the assets and liabilities of the institution.[85]

Such measures are complemented by the removal of senior management and management body[86] and the appointment of a temporary administrator.[87] However, the removal of senior management and management body can be ordered only when the other, less intrusive, measures are not sufficient to reverse the deterioration and, similarly, the appointment of a temporary administrator can take place only when the removal of the senior management and the management body is not sufficient to reverse the deterioration.

[85] Article 27 of the BRRD.

[86] According to Art 28 of the BRRD, 'where there is a significant deterioration in the financial situation of an institution or where there are serious infringements of law, of regulations or of the statutes of the institution, or serious administrative irregularities, and other measures taken in accordance with Article 27 are not sufficient to reverse that deterioration, Member States shall ensure that competent authorities may require the removal of the senior management or management body of the institution, in its entirety or with regard to individuals. The appointment of the new senior management or management body shall be done in accordance with national and Union law and be subject to the approval or consent of the competent authority'.

[87] According to Art 29 of the BRRD, '1. Where replacement of the senior management or management body as referred to in Article 28 is deemed to be insufficient by the competent authority to remedy the situation, Member States shall ensure that competent authorities may appoint one or more temporary administrators to the institution … 2. The competent authority shall specify the powers of the temporary administrator at the time of the appointment of the temporary administrator based on what is proportionate in the circumstances. Such powers may include some or all of the powers of the management body of the institution under the statutes of the institution and under national law, including the power to exercise some or all of the administrative functions of the management body of the institution … 3. The role and functions of the temporary administrator shall be specified by competent authority at the time of appointment and may include ascertaining the financial position of the institution, managing the business or part of the business of the institution with a view to preserving or restoring the financial position of the institution and taking measures to restore the sound and prudent management of the business of the institution … 7. The appointment of a temporary administrator shall not last more than one year. That period may be exceptionally renewed if the conditions for appointing the temporary administrator continue to be met'.

With regard to early intervention measures, Italy is an interesting case study as it has had in place special rules on the so-called special administration (*amministrazione straordinaria*) for decades, and such administrative procedure has been used often to handle early-stage crises. Special administration under Italian law represents now the transposed version of temporary administration, regulated by the BRRD, and is, therefore, conceived as an early intervention measure.[88]

Pursuant to the Italian Consolidated Banking Act,[89] when there are serious violations of laws and regulations or of the articles of association as well as when there are serious irregularities in the management or when the situation of the bank is significantly deteriorating or there are relevant losses or there is a specific request from the bank itself and the other early intervention measures are not sufficient, the Bank of Italy can place such bank under special administration, thereby removing the members of the governing and oversight bodies and appointing new administrators and auditors.[90]

The appointed administrators are requested to perform all the tasks and functions of the dissolved governing body.[91] Yet, the banking licence is not withdrawn, since the bank is meant to continue operating and performing its business activity. Additionally, the administrators are required to analyse the economic and financial situation, remove the irregularities and find out the solutions needed in the interests of depositors as well as of the bank itself.[92]

In exceptional circumstances, in order to safeguard the bank's creditors, the administrators may decide to interrupt the repayment of the bank's liabilities as well. Such a decision needs to be authorised by the Bank of Italy and the interruption cannot last more than one month. This one-month period can, however, be extended for a further two months. In such a period no enforcement action can be brought by creditors against the bank.

The special administration has a limited duration of no longer than one year but can be extended for additional one-year periods, if needed. Its primary objective is to resolve all the problems affecting the bank with a view to enabling it to restart doing business as usual.

Although after the adoption and transposition of the BRRD, and the subsquent introduction of the resolution procedure, one could have thought that there was no longer need for the special administration, this has not been the case. Indeed, in recent years, two Italian banks (ie *Cassa di Risparmio di Genova – Carige* and *Banca Popolare di Bari*), one of which significant (ie *Carige*), were submitted

[88] See M Bodellini, 'The Quest for European Harmonised Deposit Guarantee Scheme-Centred Special Administrative Regimes to Handle Troubled Banks' (2020) 25 *The Uniform Law Review* 222.

[89] Legislative Decree No 385 of 1993.

[90] Article 70(1) of Legislative Decree no 385 of 1993.

[91] Article 72 of Legislative Decree no 385 of 1993.

[92] See n 88.

to such procedure.[93] This shows that there are still situations where the special administration in the view of the authorities can be useful.

In the past, such a procedure was often used to try to resolve mild bank crises. But even when the crisis concerned turned out to be severe, the previous submission of the bank to special administration often proved useful to gain time and properly prepare the following crisis management procedure. The administrators, appointed by the Bank of Italy, indeed had the chance to analyse the economic and financial situation and find out its causes. Typically, as a result of this preliminary assessment, the administrators had to write down the loans' book value, thereby recording a loss.[94] When the loss could be somehow absorbed and the bank was seen as capable of recovery, the special administration ended. This often took place through a merger with another bank or through the acquisition by another larger and more solid bank, typically supported by the DGS. By contrast, when the loss was too great and the bank was not deemed able to recover, it was placed into compulsory administrative liquidation. Still, the previous submission to special administration was useful to plan a strategy for managing the crisis,[95] for example by finding another bank willing to purchase assets and liabilities so that the transfer could take place simultaneously or immediately after the submission of the FOLF bank to compulsory administrative liquidation.[96]

B. Prompt Corrective Action in the US

In 1991, the US Congress passed the Federal Deposit Insurance Corporation Improvement Act (FDICIA), which contains the provisions governing the prompt corrective action (PCA) framework for bank supervision. The objective of the framework is to resolve issues affecting insured depository institutions (IDIs) with the least possible long-term impact for the Deposit Insurance Fund (DIF). To try to reach this goal, timely (or prompt) and forceful (or corrective) supervisory intervention is needed with a view to preventing banks' problems from affecting the deposit insurer and/or taxpayers. This means that the intervention should take place when the institutions concerned still have some capital left to absorb their losses. To limit supervisory forbearance, many PCA provisions are mandatory and the room for discretion is limited. Specifically, pursuant to

[93] See C Dias, J Deslandes and M Magnus, 'Recent measures for Banca Carige from a BRRD and State Aid perspective' (2019) European Parliament Briefing, 1; see also F Capriglione, 'Banking crises and systemic crises. The Italian case' (2019) 8 *Law and Economics Yearly Review*, 222.

[94] See n 88.

[95] See U Belviso, 'Il trasferimento dell'azienda bancaria nella liquidazione coatta amministrativa' (1972) I *Banca Borsa Titoli di Credito* 356; U Belviso, 'La liquidazione coatta nel quadro di una riforma delle procedure concorsuali' (1979) I *Giurisprudenza Commerciale* 274.

[96] See G Fauceglia, 'La cessione di attività e passività nella liquidazione coatta amministrativa delle banche e la successione nei rapporti contrattuali' (1997) I *Banca Borsa Titoli di Credito* 452, emphasising that it has been common practice over time to transfer assets and liabilities at the same time when the Bank of Italy submitted the FOLF bank to compulsory administrative liquidation.

Section 38 of the FDICIA, regulators are required to classify supervised banks into one of five capital categories according to capital-based triggers and to take specific action when these are breached.[97] The five capital categories are: well capitalised; adequately capitalised; undercapitalised; significantly undercapitalised; and critically undercapitalised.

Restrictions start applying once an institution is categorised as adequately capitalised. When that is the case, the institution concerned can only accept brokered deposits with an FDIC waiver. It cannot pay interest significantly exceeding market rates and its risk-based deposit premium may be increased. Further restrictions apply to banks which are classified as undercapitalised. The restrictions become increasingly stringent as the bank's conditions deteriorate. They are also cumulative.[98]

Importantly, undercapitalised banks have to adopt a capital restoration plan (CRP) that is subject to supervisory approval and contains specific provisions. The CRP must be submitted within 45 days from the categorisation of the bank as undercapitalised. The CRP will be analysed to determine whether it is based on realistic assumptions and is likely to succeed in restoring the institution's capital. If the bank fails to submit a CRP within the prescribed deadline or to comply with an approved plan, it will then be reclassified as significantly undercapitalised.

Banks that have been categorised as critically undercapitalised are to be placed in conservatorship (or receivership) within 90 days of such a determination, unless the FDIC and the appropriate regulator grant a 90-day extension, which can be renewed once.[99] In this regard, the Federal Deposit Insurance Act (FDIA) provides that, subject to these time limits, the appropriate federal regulator must appoint a conservator. A conservator is appointed with the task to preserve the going-concern value of the institution. The goal is for the institution to return viable, but when this is not possible it will be wound up in a receivership. The conservator plays a role which is similar to the one performed by the temporary administrator(s) under EU law. Both have the power to operate the troubled bank in order to restore it and with a view to avoiding crisis management procedures. The decision to appoint a conservator requires the concurrence of the FDIC.[100]

IX. The Effectiveness of Capital and Early Intervention Measures as First Lines of Defence

Although there is no doubt as to the effectiveness of capital as a tool to make institutions more robust and thereby more equipped to face a crisis, it has been

[97] See n 77, 19.
[98] ibid.
[99] ibid, 19.
[100] ibid, 19.

sometimes regarded as a controversial regulatory instrument. Showing sympathy to the banking industry, politicians have been in some cases highly critical of the BCBS rules on capital. In a letter sent to the Chair of the Board of Governors of the Federal Reserve System, the Vice Chairman of the Financial Services Committee of the Congress of the Unites States – House of Representatives pointed out that

> agreements like the Basel III Accords were negotiated and agreed to by the Federal Reserve with little notice to the American public, and were the result of an opaque, decision-making process. The international standards were then turned into domestic regulations that forced American firms of various sizes to substantially raise their capital requirements, leading to slower economic growth here in America.[101]

The banking industry itself already raised its serious concerns about the effects resulting from the implementation of the new Basel IV measures. In a paper published in May 2018 by the Association of German Public Banks, it was claimed that the new 'Basel IV' package would determine a 23 per cent increase in RWAs for the 16 largest German banks.[102] As a consequence, their CET1 capital ratio would fall by 2.8 per cent.[103] The output floor itself is meant to cause a RWAs increase of more than 11 per cent.[104] On these grounds, the Association of German Public Banks argued that the original purpose of the new package to avoid a significant increase of RWAs for banking institutions has not been achieved.[105]

Similarly, in a survey published by PWC in December 2017, it was pointed that the increase of RWAs for the largest banks in Europe would be €1–2.5 trillion and an increase of capital between 13 per cent and 22 per cent would be needed.[106]

Yet, despite such criticisms, there are not many legal tools as effective as capital to enhance banks' solidity and resilience.[107] This is why many have recommended a further significant increase of capital to be held by banking institutions.[108] If the main goal of a balanced system is to avoid systemic crises – since these can generate financial instability that can in turn provoke long periods of recession – it is fair and reasonable to have serious and demanding capital requirements in force

[101] See P McHenry, Letter sent to the Chair of the Board of Governors of the Federal Reserve System, 2017, available at www.ftalphaville-cdn.ft.com.

[102] VÖB, DekaBank, DZ BANK, BayernLB, Helaba, LBB, LBBW, NORD/LB, 'ApoBank: The Consequence of 'Basel IV' – A Quantitative Impact Study' (2018).

[103] ibid.

[104] ibid.

[105] ibid.

[106] PricewaterhouseCoopers, '"Basel IV": Big Bang – or the Endgame of Basel III? BCBS finalises on Risk Weighted Assets (RWA)' (2017); see also n 38, underlining that 'research findings suggest, if banks do nothing to mitigate their impact, the reform measures would require about EUR 120 billion in additional capital, while reducing the banking sector' s return on equity by 0.6% points'; see S Schneider, G Schiock, S Koch and R Schneider, 'Basel "IV": What's Next for Banks?: Implications of Intermediate Results of New Regulatory Rules for European Banks' (2017) McKinsey Global Risk Practice Paper.

[107] See n 1, 95.

[108] See D Miles, J Yang and G Marcheggiano, 'Optimal Bank Capital' (2011) External MPC Unit Discussion Paper, 31, arguing for unweighted capital ratios of up to 20%. This is mainly based on the assumption that the higher the capital, the lower the risk of needing a public bail-out to rescue the bank in question.

for banks.[109] As such, in the BCBS's view, Basel IV represents the answer for the prevention of future global financial crises.[110]

However, the approach of the new rules on the grounds that banks are different from each other requires further analysis. Some banks have business models that support high-risk decisions, whereas others prefer low-risk operations. Importantly, there are also banks whose legal structure does not allow them to effectively raise capital on the market. This is, for instance, the case of the Italian cooperative mutual banks (so-called *banche di credito cooperativo*) that can only distribute a very low amount of dividends, with the consequence that investors are not willing to buy large shareholdings. Hence, they can comply with capital rules only through retained earnings.[111] Capital requirements rules need to take into consideration these differences. In the same vein, from a more general perspective, further analysis on the optimal amount of capital to hold is important. This arises from the consideration that a balanced mixture of equity and debt needs to be found in order for banks to be safe and sound yet profitable. Safety, soundness and profitability are equally important elements for an efficient bank and for a well-functioning banking system. This rests on the grounds that profitability is of paramount importance for a bank to be able to increase its equity capital by attracting investors on the market, which, in turn, is the prerequisite for its safety and soundness.[112] In other words, a bank which is not profitable cannot distribute dividends. This in turn affects its ability to raise capital on the market.

It now seems possible to argue that the banking system, thanks in part to the recently adopted Basel III and Basel IV rules, is more sound and resilient than it used to be.[113] Nevertheless, there is still a need for the legal framework to be more conscious of the subjective differences among banks, and thereby more efficient.[114]

Relatedly, early intervention measures are also an effective first line of defence, as their use can prevent a bank crisis from further escalating, thereby becoming irreversible. Several measures have been developed in different jurisdictions, but their common characteristic is that to be effective they are to be initiated at the early stages of a crisis. This rests on the grounds that the later the intervention, the higher the risk that the amount of capital left is no longer sufficient to effectively tackle the crisis. The legal frameworks in place in Italy and US provide some early intervention options that have, over time, shown to be rather effective.

[109] See n 1, 95.

[110] See n 38.

[111] See M Bodellini, *Attività Bancaria e Impresa Cooperativa* (Bari, Cacucci Editore, 2017), *passim*.

[112] n 1, 95.

[113] Accordingly see M Carney, 'Reports to G20 Leaders' (2017) Financial Stability Board (FSB) Chairman's Memo to G20 Leaders, available at www.fsb.org/wp-content/uploads/P030717-1.pdf, underlining that the largest banks are now required to have 10 times more of the highest quality capital than before the crisis and are subject to greater market discipline as a result of globally agreed standards to resolve TBTF entities.

[114] See n 1, 95.

4

The Crisis of Non-Systemic Institutions

Bank Insolvency Regimes

I. Introduction

The global financial crisis of 2007–09 made it clear that many jurisdictions around the globe were unprepared to face the shocks which affected many banking and financial institutions, since they lacked specific legal regimes to deal with their crises.[1] Due to the absence of special tools and procedures, while systemic institutions in crisis were typically rescued with public money, the non-systemic ones were often submitted to normal corporate insolvency proceedings.[2] Nevertheless, it was, and still is, widely recognised that such insolvency proceedings, which typically apply to non-financial institutions, are not suitable for the crisis of peculiar entities such as banks, even more so if the latter are systemic.[3] This mainly results from their slowness and the fact that they often do not ensure the continuation of the bank's core business lines[4] and critical functions[5] (particularly payment

[1] This concept is clearly underlined also by Recital 1 of the BRRD, which states that 'The financial crisis has shown that there is a significant lack of adequate tools at Union level to deal effectively with unsound or failing credit institutions and investment firms ("institutions"). Such tools are needed, in particular, to prevent insolvency or, when insolvency occurs, to minimise negative repercussions by preserving the systemically important functions of the institution concerned'.

[2] This has, to a certain extent, changed in recent times, since according to data collected by the World Bank, approximately 69% of jurisdictions have some form of separate bank insolvency regime, see World Bank, 'Bank Regulation and Supervision Survey, 2019 Database – 2021 Update', available at www.datacatalog.worldbank.org/dataset/bank-regulation-and-supervision-survey#tab2.

[3] See WG Ringe, 'Bail-in between Liquidity and Solvency' University of Oxford Legal Research Paper Series no 33 (2016) 5; see also A Shleifer and R Vishny, 'Fire Sales in Finance and Macroeconomics' (2011) 25 *Journal of Economic Perspectives* 29.

[4] Core business lines are defined by Art 2(1)(36) of the BRRD as 'business lines and associated services which represent material sources of revenue, profit or franchise value for an institution or for a group of which an institution forms part'.

[5] Critical functions are defined by Art 2(1)(35) of the BRRD as 'activities, services or operations the discontinuance of which is likely in one or more Member States, to lead to the disruption of services that are essential to the real economy or to disrupt financial stability due to the size, market share, external and internal interconnectedness, complexity or cross-border activities of an institution or group, with particular regard to the substitutability of those activities, services or operations'.

services, lending activities and prompt availability of deposits).[6] As a consequence, the submission of banks to these proceedings can endanger financial stability,[7] and, in extremely serious situations, can even create systemic risk.[8] Also, normal corporate insolvency proceedings usually aim at liquidating the entity[9] without a view to maintaining the so-called franchise value (or going concern value) resulting from the business ability to generate profits, which is in fact a value that should be preserved in the interest of the involved stakeholders.[10] Consequently, they often end up destroying value, thereby harming the bank's creditors.

Thus, because of the absence of effective legal frameworks to handle troubled banks, those countries whose governments and authorities did not want to place failing institutions under normal corporate insolvency proceedings for the reasons discussed above had to rescue them with taxpayers' money, through public bailouts. Yet, such an approach had a number of negative consequences, ranging from the deterioration of public finance, to the increase of public debt and the creation of moral hazard.[11]

Against this background, the EU legislator intervened in 2014 with the adoption of the Bank Recovery and Resolution Directive (BRRD). The BRRD gives

[6] Recital 4 of the BRRD also adds that they are inappropriate because they do not ensure 'the preservation of financial stability', whilst, according to Recital 45, 'A failing institution should in principle be liquidated under normal insolvency proceedings. However, liquidation under normal insolvency proceedings might jeopardise financial stability, interrupt the provision of critical functions, and affect the protection of depositors. In such a case it is highly likely that there would be a public interest in placing the institution under resolution and applying resolution tools rather than resorting to normal insolvency proceedings. The objectives of resolution should therefore be to ensure the continuity of critical functions, to avoid adverse effects on financial stability, to protect public funds by minimising reliance on extraordinary public financial support to failing institutions and to protect covered depositors, investors, client funds and client assets'.

[7] See D Arner, *Financial Stability, Economic Growth, and the Role of Law* (Cambridge, Cambridge University Press, 2007) 72, who defines financial stability as 'the primary target in preventing financial crises and reducing the severe risks of financial problems which do occur from time to time'; see M Andenas and I Chiu, 'Financial Stability and Legal Integration in Financial Regulation' (2013) 38 *European Law Review* 342, defining financial stability as a general policy objective that should guide regulators and policymakers; see also R Lastra, *Legal Foundations of International Monetary Stability* (Oxford, Oxford University Press, 2006) 92 and 302, outlining that financial stability is an evolving concept that 'encompasses a variety of elements'.

[8] See Ringe (n 3) 6, who argues that 'bankruptcy entails a court-supervised process that is designed to protect the substantive and procedural rights of all creditors without particular regard for broader public interests'; see P Calello and W Erwin, 'From Bail-Out to Bail-In' *The Economist* (30 January 2010) *passim*, arguing that a 15% haircut of Lehman Brothers' senior debt would have avoided its collapse by recapitalising the bank; see KP Wojcik, 'Bail-in in the Banking Union' (2016) 53 *Common Market Law Review* 92, arguing that the decision to let Lehman Brothers fail 'made visible the risks such failures entail for the financial system'.

[9] See T Huertas, 'The case for bail-ins' in A Dombret and S Kenadjian (eds), *The Bank Recovery and Resolution Directive*, (Philadelphia, Institute for Law and Finance Series, 2013) 167–68.

[10] See RD Guynn, 'Are Bailouts Inevitable?' (2012) 29 *Yale Journal on Regulation* 29, 121, 137–40, arguing that bankruptcy intervention destroys the financial institution's value exacerbating the losses for creditors.

[11] See European Central Bank, 'The Fiscal Impact of Financial Sector Support During the Crisis' (2015) 6 ECB Economic Bulletin, 80, available at www.ecb.europa.eu/pub/pdf/other/eb201506_article02.en.pdf?fadae43a45a35a30cd17d3213277042d.

resolution authorities the power to decide how to handle banks in crisis, by allowing them to choose between resolution and winding up under insolvency proceedings. Yet, while resolution is regulated by the BRRD and is therefore harmonised at EU level, insolvency proceedings continue being regulated and administered at national level, thereby diverging from Member State to Member State.

Obviously, the introduction of a new bank resolution regime harmonised at EU level and based on the application of resolution tools has represented a significant step forward if compared to the framework in force during the global financial crisis of 2007–09.[12] Nevertheless, although the new system might have been expected to make resolution the main way to handle 'failing or likely to fail' (FOLF) banks, it soon became clear that this is not the case.[13] In 2017, the Single Resolution Board (SRB) decided that there was no public interest at stake in the crises of two significant banks, Veneto Banca and Banca Popolare di Vicenza,[14] thereby clarifying that in its view the resolution procedure should only be activated in the event of crises involving the largest banks operating within the Banking Union and the ones the failure of which (irrespective of the size) could negatively affect the system, as

[12] Pursuant to the BRRD, the four resolution tools are: the bail-in tool; the sale of business tool; the asset separation tool; and the bridge institution tool.

[13] See M Bodellini, 'Alternative forms of deposit insurance and the quest for European harmonised deposit guarantee scheme-centred special administrative regimes to handle troubled banks' (2020) 25 *The Uniform Law Review* 213.

[14] On 23 June 2017, the ECB decided that both Banca Popolare di Vicenza and Veneto Banca were 'failing or likely to fail as they repeatedly breached supervisory capital requirements'; see European Central Bank, 'ECB deemed Veneto Banca and Banca Popolare di Vicenza failing or likely to fail' (Frankfurt, 2017), available at www.bankingsupervision.europa.eu/press/pr/date/2017/html/ssm.pr170623.en.html. The ECB's decision was somewhat surprising also in that both banks were already issuing bonds with Italian state guarantees under Art 32.4(d)(ii) of the BRRD on the grounds of being considered as solvent and not FOLF. As a consequence of the ECB's decision, the two banks were submitted to liquidation under the Italian insolvency law on the basis of the lack of a public interest for resolution, as decided by the SRB. The SRB's decision was grounded on the consideration that the functions performed by the two banks (deposit-taking, lending activities and payment services) were not deemed to be critical since they were provided to a limited number of third parties and could be replaced in an acceptable manner and within a reasonable timeframe. Therefore, their failure was not considered likely to result in significant adverse effects on financial stability, particularly due to their limited financial and operational interconnections with other financial institutions; see Single Resolution Board, 'The SRB will not take resolution action in relation to Banca Popolare di Vicenza and Veneto Banca' (Brussels, 2017), available at www.srb.europa.eu/en/node/341. Interestingly, two days after the SRB's decision, the Commission approved state aid measures in order to facilitate the liquidation of the two institutions and to avoid a 'serious impact on the real economy'; see European Commission, 'State aid: Commission approves aid for market exit of Banca Popolare di Vicenza and Veneto Banca under Italian insolvency law, involving sale of some parts to Intesa Sanpaolo' (Brussels, 2017), available at www.europa.eu/rapid/press-release_IP-17-1791_en.htm. In its decision, the Commission seems to have relied considerably upon the assessment made by the Bank of Italy on the negative consequences of the credit crunch. According to the Bank of Italy, (point 49 of the Commission's decision), the atomistic liquidation without public support can cause relevant losses 'to non-professional and non-protected customers, as well as the sudden termination of credit relationships for both households and SMEs. This would lead to the disorderly wind down of the institutions, causing disturbance in the economy, especially at local level … The credit crunch could hit around 55,000 firms for an aggregated shortfall of ca. 22bn, without taking into consideration the second round effects'.

shown in the recent cases of Sberbank d.d. and Sberbank banka d.d.[15] Yet, if this is the new paradigm, then the effectiveness of insolvency proceedings applying to banks that cannot be submitted to resolution becomes even more important in that such proceedings will be initiated in the event of the majority of institutions becoming FOLF.[16]

On these grounds, the new policy and legislative objective at European level should be to develop a harmonised bank insolvency regime dedicated to FOLF

[15] Banca Popolare di Vicenza and Veneto Banca were requested by the ECB to be consistently recapitalised (€3.3 billion and €3.1 billion respectively) after failing the stress tests. However, in that situation, it was very difficult to find a market solution where other private financial players could be involved in the recapitalisation. Additionally, the simultaneous submission to resolution of the two banks and the bail-in of a significant amount of their liabilities were perceived as potentially able to generate financial instability, probably not only at national level. That was the reason why the authorities involved were rather concerned. And that was also why one of the main options under their consideration was precautionary recapitalisation. Such a tool would have allowed to avoid resolution (with the application of the bail-in tool) and the two institutions would have been recapitalised with public money provided by the Italian Government, after the absorption of previous losses by shareholders and subordinated creditors, unless the Commission had decided not to apply the burden-sharing mechanism to avoid financial instability. But in order to undertake a precautionary recapitalisation, banks have to be assessed as solvent and not FOLF by the authorities, and the intervention of the state has to be assessed as compatible with the state aid framework by the Commission. After a long negotiation between the ECB, the Commission and the SRB, on one side, and the Bank of Italy, the Italian Ministry of Finance and the two banks on the other, it was eventually decided that Veneto Banca and Banca Popolare di Vicenza, having been assessed as FOLF and being considered as not able to affect the market with their failure, had to be wound down. Nevertheless, in a controversial decision, the Commission authorised the provision of state aid measures to use in order to orderly manage the liquidation of the two banks. On the other hand, with regard to Sberbank d.d., on 1 March 2022, the SRB decided that resolution action was needed for the achievement of, and proportionate to, avoiding significant adverse effects on financial stability as the winding up of the bank under normal insolvency proceedings would have not met the resolution objectives to the same extent. As a consequence, the SRB adopted a resolution scheme providing for the application of the sale of business tool. Thus, following a marketing procedure, the SRB decided to transfer all the shares issued by the Croatian bank to the Hrvatska Poštanska Banka. As to Sberbank banka d.d. (€1.8 billion in assets at the end of 2020, representing approximately 4% of the banking assets in Slovenia), the SRB decided that resolution action was necessary for the achievement of, and proportionate to: ensuring the continuity of the critical function of lending to small and medium sized enterprises (SMEs); and avoiding significant adverse effects on financial stability, also in that winding up of the bank under normal insolvency proceedings would have not met the resolution objectives to the same extent. As a consequence, the SRB adopted a resolution scheme providing for the application of the sale of business tool. Accordingly, following a marketing procedure, the SRB decided to transfer all the shares issued by the Slovenian bank to Nova Ljubljanska Banka d.d; see Single Resolution Board, 'Notice summarising the decision taken in respect of Sberbank Europe AG', 1 March 2022, available at www.srb.europa.eu/system/files/media/document/20220103%20SRB%20Notice%20summarising%20the%20decision%20taken%20in%20respect%20of%20Sberbank%20Europe%20AG%20parent%20company.pdf.

[16] Elsewhere I argued that the differences featuring Member States' national insolvency proceedings can ultimately determine that an institution might be deemed as resolvable in that it can be effectively liquidated thanks to the rules of its Member State, whilst another in similar conditions might be considered as not resolvable due to the insolvency proceeding rules of its Member State. This can therefore impact upon the resolvability assessment, thereby influencing the authorities' action as well as threatening the level playing field between institutions established in different Member States; see on this M Bodellini, 'Impediments to resolvability: critical issues and challenges ahead' (2019) 5 *Open Review of Management, Banking and Finance* 50.

banks that do not meet the public interest test for resolution.[17] In order to develop such regime, the Italian experience and legal framework in place (particularly before the transposition of the BRRD) as well as the US experience and framework, might prove particularly helpful, since in both systems a resolution-like procedure is typically activated to effectively manage small and medium-sized non-systemic bank crises.[18] The analysis of the UK framework and experience is also relevant for these purposes.

This chapter focuses on the main characteristics of successful bank insolvency proceedings in light of both the BRRD rules and the Italian, UK and US bank crisis management frameworks and experience, thereby contributing also to the policy debate taking place at EU level on the adoption of a harmonised non-systemic bank insolvency regime.[19]

II. The New EU Regime and its Weaknesses

The new bank crisis management regime introduced in the EU by the BRRD, which implements the FSB Key Attributes, is based on the distinction between two alternative procedures to initiate in the event of banks being determined as FOLF. Accordingly, resolution authorities have been given the power to decide on whether to submit FOLF banks[20] either to resolution[21] or to winding up[22] (also referred to as liquidation)[23] under normal insolvency proceedings.[24] A partially similar structure applies in the UK, which had already transposed the BRRD before leaving the EU.

[17] On the importance of the harmonisation of bank insolvency regimes within the EU see also JH Binder, M Krimminger, M Nieto and D Singh, 'The choice between judicial and administrative sanctioned procedures to manage liquidation of banks: a transatlantic perspective' (2019) 14 *Capital Markets Law Journal* 178.

[18] See n 13, 215.

[19] See European Commission, 'Targeted Consultation Review of the Crisis Management and Deposit Insurance Framework, 2021', available at www.ec.europa.eu/info/consultations/finance-2021-crisis-management-deposit-insurance-review-targeted_en.

[20] The EU framework defines banks, namely institutions taking deposits from the public and making loans, as credit institutions. The terms 'bank' and 'credit institution' will be used interchangeably across the book with reference to EU entities.

[21] 'Resolution' means, under Art 2(1)(1) of the BRRD, the application of a resolution tool in order to achieve one or more of the resolution objectives referred.

[22] 'Winding up' means, according to Art 2(1)(54) of the BRRD, the realisation of assets of an institution.

[23] The terms 'winding up' and 'liquidation' will be used interchangeably across the book with reference to the EU framework.

[24] 'Normal insolvency proceedings' are defined, according to Art 2(1)(47) of the BRRD, as 'collective insolvency proceedings which entail the partial or total divestment of a debtor and the appointment of a liquidator or an administrator normally applicable to institutions under national law and either specific to those institutions or generally applicable to any natural or legal person'.

In this vein, elsewhere we argued that the new EU framework is based on the dichotomy between resolution and liquidation.[25] In other words, resolution authorities have the discretion to decide how to handle a bank crisis by selecting the most appropriate procedure on a case-by-case basis.[26] The discretion in the choice given to the resolution authorities is, however, limited by a number of elements, included in the broad concept of public interest, which are to guide their decision-making process. Thus, in the face of a bank's crisis, firstly, resolution authorities have to assess whether the submission of the FOLF bank to winding up under national insolvency proceedings can reach the resolution objectives to the same extent as resolution and, if that is the case, then the FOLF bank is to be placed under such insolvency proceedings.[27] The resolution objectives to take into account when choosing the procedure to initiate are: to ensure the continuity of critical functions; to avoid a significant adverse effect on the financial system, in particular by preventing contagion, including to market infrastructures, and by maintaining market discipline; to protect public funds by minimising reliance on extraordinary public financial support; to protect depositors and investors; and to protect client funds and client assets.[28]

The resolution authorities' decision is hence grounded in the forecast ability of the winding up under national insolvency proceedings to allow for the achievement of the resolution objectives to the same extent as resolution. This should be the case, particularly, in the event of bank crises that are not expected to create financial instability, for instance because such banks are small (or at least not too large) relative to the system where they operate, they do not provide functions the interruption of which could threat financial stability and/or they are not closely interconnected with many other financial institutions. In these cases, it is said that there is no public interest in resolving them, as their failure is not expected to result in significant adverse effects on the stability of the system.

Nevertheless, when the resolution authority comes to the opposite conclusion that the submission of the FOLF bank to normal insolvency proceedings does not allow it to reach the resolution objectives to the same extent as resolution, then the bank concerned should be resolved,[29] provided that it is

[25] See R Lastra, C Russo and M Bodellini, 'Stock Take of the SRB's activities over the past years: What to Improve and Focus On?' (2019) Study Requested by the ECON Committee of the European Parliament, 11.

[26] These regimes where two different bank crisis management procedures are available, such as in the EU, are also referred to as 'dual-track regimes'. This is in opposition to single-track regimes, such as in the US, where only one procedure is to be activated when the triggers are met.

[27] See n 16, 50.

[28] Art 31(2) of the BRRD.

[29] This general principle is clearly explained by Recital 49 of the BRRD, under which 'the resolution tools should therefore be applied only to those institutions that are failing or likely to fail,

effectively resolvable.[30] In other words, if there is a public interest in avoiding the submission of the bank in crisis to insolvency proceedings, for example because this can create financial instability, then such an institution is to be resolved.

The introduction in the EU framework of the concept of public interest, whose safeguard would justify the start of a resolution procedure, has broadened the scope of application of resolution envisaged in the FSB Key Attributes. While the latter mostly target institutions which are systemically significant or critical in failure, the resolution procedure in the EU is to be started every time that this is in the public interest. And resolution is in the public interest when winding up according to national insolvency proceedings would not ensure to achieve the resolution objectives to the same extent as resolution. This means that even smaller institutions could have to be resolved if their winding up would not ensure primarily the continuity of critical functions and the avoidance of significant adverse effects on the financial system. But this, irrespective of the institutions concerned, could also depend on the features of the domestic banking system and the characteristics of the national legal frameworks for their winding up as shown by the recent cases of Sberbank d.d. in Croatia and Sberbank banka d.d. in Slovenia. Despite their limited size in absolute terms both banks were resolved by the SRB, while their holding bank company, significantly larger as to the amount of assets, was liquidated pursuant to Austrian law.

Against this background, for the sake of simplicity, in the context of the EU framework this work will refer to systemic institutions as to the ones which will be resolved (as opposed to be liquidated) should they be FOLF.

Yet, while the BRRD has harmonised at EU level the resolution procedure rules, insolvency proceedings applying to FOLF banks remain regulated and administered at national level. Hence, they differ between Member States, thereby affecting the effectiveness of bank crisis management and possibly impacting on the stability of the European banking system as well.

and only when it is necessary to pursue the objective of financial stability in the general interest. In particular, resolution tools should be applied where the institution cannot be wound up under normal insolvency proceedings without destabilising the financial system and the measures are necessary in order to ensure the rapid transfer and continuation of systemically important functions and where there is no reasonable prospect for any alternative private solution, including any increase of capital by the existing shareholders or by any third party sufficient to restore the full viability of the institution'.

[30] Under Art 15(1) of the BRRD, 'An institution shall be deemed to be resolvable if it is feasible and credible for the resolution authority to either liquidate it under normal insolvency proceedings or to resolve it by applying the different resolution tools and powers to the institution while avoiding to the maximum extent possible any significant adverse effect on the financial system, including in circumstances of broader financial instability or system-wide events, of the Member State in which the institution is established, or other Member States or the Union and with a view to ensuring the continuity of critical functions carried out by the institution'.

III. Towards the Establishment of a New EU Harmonised Bank Insolvency Regime Inspired by the Italian, UK and US Frameworks and Experiences

Despite the recent cases of Sberbank d.d. and Sberbank banka d.d., within the Banking Union, resolution action seems to be still regarded by the authorities as the solution for large, complex and interconnected institutions, whereas winding up under normal insolvency proceedings is the default option for the majority of them.[31] Yet, the two cases in Croatia and Slovenia reminded that in making the choice between resolution and liquidation, authorities should pay special attention to both the conditions of the national banking system and the domestic legal framework for bank winding up as they might actually cause the need for resolution. These two cases are further discussed in chapter five.

Against this backdrop, there is widespread consensus in considering normal corporate insolvency proceedings run by law courts and purely aimed at liquidating the FOLF entity as generally ill-suited for peculiar institutions like banks.[32] If not properly managed, in fact, even the winding up of banks that do not satisfy the public interest test for their submission to resolution could negatively affect the banking and financial system – or a part of it – thereby creating instability and possibly harming the economy too.[33] This is obviously not the case for ordinary non-financial companies, with regard to which these proceedings are typically designed.

EU Member States have different regimes in force to handle the crisis of non-systemic banks. While some of them rely entirely upon normal corporate insolvency proceedings, others have in place modified insolvency proceedings which differ slightly from the previous ones to take into account some of the bank's peculiarities. A number of Member States, including Italy, on the other hand, already have special regimes for banks in force.[34]

[31] See J Dias, C Deslandes and M Magnus, 'Recent measures for Banca Carige from a BRRD and State Aid perspective' European Parliament Briefing (2019) 7, quoting Andrea Enria (then Chair of the European Banking Authority) who, referring to Veneto Banca and Banca Popolare di Vicenza, said that 'The decision that there was no EU public interest at stake in the crises of two ECB-supervised banks that were hoping to merge and operate in the same region with combined activities of around EUR 60 billion sets the bar for resolution very high'.

[32] See n 10, 137–40, arguing that bankruptcy intervention produces erosion of the financial institution's value exacerbating the losses for creditors; see Ringe (n 3) 5, who argues that there is consensus on regarding traditional bankruptcy procedures as not appropriate to deal with failing global banks since they are usually long and complicated and therefore can undermine market confidence and destabilise the financial system; see n 9, 167–68; see also Shleifer and Vishny (n 3) 29.

[33] Accordingly, see European Forum of Deposit Insurers, 'EFDI State of Play and Non-Binding Guidance Paper, Guarantee Schemes' Alternative Measures to Pay-out for Effective Banking Crisis Solution' (7 November 2019) 27, arguing that 'it cannot be excluded that liquidation through pay-out of non-systemic banks (particularly if multiple) may be a threat to public confidence and financial stability in a specific situation of a single Member State and a particular credit institution'.

[34] See P Baudino, A Gagliano, E Rulli and R Walters, 'FSI insights on policy implementation no 10 Why do we need bank-specific insolvency regimes? A review of country practices' (2018) *passim*,

On these grounds, one of the most relevant issues at stake relates to how insolvency proceedings take place pursuant to the jurisdiction-specific[35] rules of the Member State in which the FOLF bank is established.[36] The key aspects in this regard concern the objectives pursued through these proceedings, their institutional set-up, their triggers for initiation, the tools which the authorities can employ in order for the winding up to be orderly, and funding.[37]

While the objectives typically pursued by normal corporate insolvency proceedings refer to value maximisation of the insolvency estate to enhance payments to creditors, the proceedings applying to banks cannot only focus on value maximisation and thus should also ensure that depositors are protected thereby maintaining financial stability.

With regard to their set-up, while normal corporate insolvency proceedings have typically a judicial nature, modified insolvency proceedings and bank specific proceedings can be categorised into two main models:

- predominantly administrative models, where the proceeding is administered by an administrative authority with limited or no involvement of judicial authorities; and
- predominantly court-based models, where the proceeding is run by a court-appointed liquidator, with limited or no involvement for administrative authorities.

Views vary as to which model is more effective, but there seems to be a preference for models where administrative authorities (mainly the bank supervisor or the resolution authority) are involved in administering the proceeding on the grounds that their expertise and access to information are crucial. Also, administrative models are often deemed to be faster and administrative authorities are typically considered more capable of taking into account public interest objectives, applying non-conventional insolvency tools, such as those aiming at the transfer of deposits to another bank, and making decisions on the use of external funding.

With regard to the grounds for opening these proceedings, while normal corporate insolvency proceedings usually rely on balance-sheet insolvency (liabilities exceeding the assets) or illiquidity (inability to pay debts as they fall due), such

arguing that the insolvency regimes for troubled banks can be grouped as follows: corporate insolvency law (adopted by France, Spain and Germany); modified corporate insolvency law (adopted by the UK and Ireland); free-standing bank insolvency regime (adopted by Italy, Greece, Luxembourg, Switzerland, the US and Canada and many others outside Europe).

[35] Elsewhere we argued that the introduction of an administrative bank liquidation tool to be assigned to the SRB 'could reduce fragmentations along national lines arising from different domestic insolvency regimes and thereby increase the effectiveness of the EU legal framework through legislative harmonisation'; see on this n 25, 18; accordingly see also International Monetary Fund, 'Euro Area Policies, Financial System Stability Assessment' IMF Country Report No 18/226 (2018) 7.

[36] All this will, therefore, depend on the domestic rules of the jurisdiction where the FOLF bank is established. As a consequence, the fact that the insolvency proceedings rules of Member States are not harmonised represents a further issue undermining the effectiveness of the Banking Union.

[37] See International Monetary Fund and the World Bank, 'An Overview of the Legal, Institutional, and Regulatory Framework for Bank Insolvency' (2009) 4.

triggers might be inappropriate for banks, so proceedings applying to them should be started on the basis of different conditions. In this vein, waiting for the bank to be balance-sheet insolvent to initiate the proceeding may cause a considerable and detrimental destruction of value, thereby possibly leading to contagion. On the other hand, the concept of illiquidity, as applied in corporate insolvency proceedings, may be inadequate on the grounds that banks perform a key function in maturity transformation, which makes liquidity tensions rather common, despite often being only temporary. Accordingly, the triggers for opening bank insolvency proceedings should be forward-looking triggers and/or regulatory triggers. Relatedly, in dual-track regimes, like the EU, the triggers for initiating them should be aligned with the triggers for resolution so as to avoid the risk of banks ending up in a limbo where no proceeding can be started due to misalignments between the two regimes. Also, such proceedings should be regarded as a last resort measure to be utilised if there are no other supervisory or market-based alternatives.

Crucially, insolvency proceedings applying to FOLF banks should provide the involved authorities with tools enabling to handle them in such a way that every negative impact on both the banking system and the real economy can be avoided or, at least, minimised. To reach this goal it is often necessary to find a way for the FOLF bank's core business lines and most important functions (such as depositors' access to their deposits, payment services and borrowers' financing) to continue.[38] In this way, the so-called atomistic liquidation, which is often deemed inappropriate as the activities are immediately interrupted and the assets are sold piece by piece, can to a large extent be avoided.[39] Atomistic liquidation is ill-suited for banks as it could cause value destruction as a result of assets being sold at fire-sale prices; borrowers might be exposed to liquidity constraints and creditors (other than insured depositors) would likely need to wait for a long time to receive a reimbursement, which typically is only partial. Should depositors be unable to access their deposits, confidence in the system might also be harmed. These negative externalities can be avoided through the creation of an ad hoc toolkit. Thus, the legal tools that can be applied in order to avoid atomistic liquidation with a view to keeping the FOLF bank's core business lines and main functions working are, to a significant extent, similar to some of the resolution tools regulated by the BRRD. These tools are: a sale of business-like tool; a bridge institution-like tool; and an asset separation-like tool.[40] Accordingly, insolvency proceedings applying to FOLF banks should provide the authorities involved with the power to use such tools that in fact will be chosen on a case-by-case basis. In this way, the risk of

[38] See M Schillig, 'Bank Resolution Regimes in Europe: Recovery and Resolution Planning, Early Intervention, Resolution Tools and Powers' (2014) 24 *European Business Law Review* 754, arguing that 'traditional banks perform quasi-utility function' as they are the primary source of liquidity for many financial and non-financial institutions.

[39] The terms 'atomistic liquidation' and 'piecemeal liquidation' are used interchangeably across the book to refer to situations in which, in the context of a liquidation procedure, the bank's assets are sold piece by piece according to the liquidation timeframe and at liquidation prices.

[40] See n 13, 215.

affecting the stability of the system (or a part of it) can be reduced and the destruction of value can be minimised.

The last key point relates to funding. In this regard, while the use of public funds should be avoided in order to reduce moral hazard, protect the public budget and preserve a level playing field as far as possible, other sources of financing become thus key. Financial support can then be provided by deposit guarantee schemes on the grounds that even in the event of a depositors' pay-out they would be called to disburse resources. Accordingly, their support can also take forms other than depositors' reimbursement; for example, they can finance the application of the transfer tool.

Interestingly, the Italian experience and the Italian legal framework are an important case study in this regard. Italian failing banks have always been handled in the context of special administrative procedures, other than corporate judicial insolvency proceedings. Also, the solutions implemented over time by Italian authorities to handle FOLF banks show that piecemeal liquidations (also referred to as 'atomistic liquidations') with deposit guarantee schemes (DGSs) reimbursing covered depositors were conducted only a few times in relation to very small institutions, on the grounds that the application of resolution-like tools allows for a more efficient crisis management. Likewise, looking at the Italian framework before the transposition of the BRRD, it can be said that a resolution-like procedure was typically activated to handle bank crises, ie that every FOLF bank was to be resolved. The main difference with the resolution regime under the BRRD currently in place is that typically creditors were not affected by burden-sharing mechanisms. As a consequence, only shareholders suffered losses along with the DGS (in compliance with the least cost principle), the Bank of Italy extending loans with interest rates below market rates and, in cases involving systemic banks, the taxpayers, due to the public intervention.[41]

On the other hand, the UK bank crisis management regime is rooted in the centrality of the Bank of England, which through its different units and directorates acts both as supervisor and resolution authority. FOLF banks that do not meet the public interest test for resolution are handled in the context of so-called modified insolvency proceedings. Irrespective of their judicial nature, the main feature of modified insolvency proceedings is that the resolution authority has the power to transfer either only deposits or a larger bulk of assets and liabilities to other banks.

Similarly, the US regime for failing banks is based on the key role of the FDIC, which acts as both deposit insurer and receiver. The centrality of the FDIC is often regarded as one of the most important reasons for the effectiveness of the US system. The FDIC has developed a number of methods to successfully deal with failing banks, thereby using several transaction structures to transfer assets and liabilities from failing banks to other private players with a view to reducing as

[41] See n 13, 215.

much as possible the costs of crisis management to taxpayers. These transactions can also be successfully implemented because the FDIC can dispose of the deposit insurance resources.[42]

The next sections discuss the Italian, UK and US regimes, identifying their main strengths with a view to exploring whether some of them could be imported into a harmonised EU bank insolvency regime to be developed.

IV. The Italian Legal Framework

Italy has had a special regime for bank crisis management since the beginning of the twentieth century.[43] Since then, small and mid-sized troubled banks have been handled through the application of special tools, in the context of special administrative procedures pursuant to special rules, rather than through their submission to normal corporate insolvency proceedings run by law courts and applicable to non-financial firms.[44] However, when the bank in crisis was considered systemic it was typically rescued through a public intervention – sometimes in the context of a crisis management procedure, sometimes outside, simply with the injection of public money to recapitalise it.[45]

Before the adoption and transposition of the BRRD in 2014–15,[46] the Italian system already relied upon two different administrative procedures to handle troubled banks: special administration (*amministrazione straordinaria*); and compulsory administrative liquidation (*liquidazione coatta amministrativa*).

The main reasons for having these two administrative procedures dedicated to troubled banks are:

- an ability to allow administrative authorities, namely the Bank of Italy, and to a certain extent the Ministry of Finance, to quickly react and intervene when the first symptoms of a bank's problems arise;

[42] See M Bodellini, 'Old Ways and New Ways to Handle Failing Banks across the Atlantic' (2021) 2 *Journal of Comparative Law* 584.

[43] See S Fortunato, 'Sulla liquidazione coatta delle imprese bancarie' (1991) I *Banca Borsa Titoli di Credito* 715, arguing that even before the adoption of the first Banking Act (*Legge Bancaria*) in 1936, which introduced special administrative procedures to handle troubled banks, the system had in place rules dealing with the crisis of some special credit institutions, such as *casse di risparmio* and *casse rurali e artigiane*.

[44] From a more general perspective see n 34 *passim*, arguing that the insolvency regimes for troubled banks can be grouped as follows: corporate insolvency law (adopted by France, Spain and Germany); modified corporate insolvency law (adopted by the UK and Ireland); free-standing bank insolvency regime (adopted by Italy, Greece, Luxembourg, Switzerland, US, Canada, and many others outside Europe).

[45] See C Brescia Morra, 'Crisi bancarie e disciplina degli aiuti di Stato: un chiarimento importante dalla Corte di Giustizia' (2019) II *Banca Borsa Titoli di Credito*, *passim*.

[46] The BRRD has been transposed in Italy mainly through the adoption of two legislative decrees: Legislative Decree no 180 of 2015 and Legislative Decree no 181 of 2015.

- involvement of external and independent experts who take over the entity's decision-making and identify the causes for such problems;
- the banking supervisor's oversight on the whole procedure; and
- a capability to implement solutions which are considered more effective for depositors, other bank's counterparties, the banking and financial system as well as the real economy.[47]

This argument is, in turn, reinforced by the consideration that normal law-court-run insolvency proceedings, applying to non-financial institutions, do not have the same abilities.[48] But it also means that, in the view of the Italian legislator, in bank crises (regardless of the institution's size, complexity and business model) there is always a special twofold public interest to protect, which can be identified in the safeguard of depositors and in the stability of the system. Such a special twofold public interest is considered more effectively protected through special administrative procedures run by administrative authorities, as opposed to law-court-run procedures.

In light of the satisfactory results achieved over time, after the adoption and transposition of the BRRD with the introduction of the resolution procedure, the Italian legislator decided to keep these two procedures in place. Thus, there are now three different administrative procedures that could be initiated to handle a troubled bank depending on the actual circumstances: special administration; compulsory administrative liquidation; resolution. The conditions for a bank to be placed under these procedures are different, however, since the reason for having them all in force is to allow the authorities to choose the most suitable procedure on a case-by-case basis.[49]

[47] See n 13, 221.

[48] Accordingly, see Ringe (n 3) 6, who argues that 'bankruptcy entails a court-supervised process that is designed to protect the substantive and procedural rights of all creditors without particular regard for broader public interests'; see also F Restoy, 'How to improve crisis management in the banking union: a European FDIC?' CIRSF Annual International Conference 2019 on 'Financial supervision and financial stability 10 years after the crisis: achievements and next steps' (Lisbon, 4 July 2019), available at www.bis.org, arguing that these regimes are particularly inefficient in 'those jurisdictions that do not have bank-specific rules and have to rely on regular court-based corporate insolvency procedures. The application of those procedures tends to be lengthy and less able to preserve the residual value of a bank's franchise and of its net assets, thereby contributing to the generation of stress that could eventually spread to other institutions'.

[49] This was not the case prior to the transposition of the BRRD, when special administration and compulsory administrative liquidation used to have very similar activation triggers. The two procedures could be initiated in the event of unsafe and unsound conducts, fraud and illegal behaviours, violations of laws, or non-compliance with prudential regulations. The difference between the elements triggering the two procedures was grounded in the seriousness of the situation, ie serious in the case of special administration and particularly serious in the case of compulsory administrative liquidation; see on this G Boccuzzi, 'Towards a new framework for banking crisis management: The international debate and the Italian model' (2011) *Quaderni di Ricerca Giuridica della Consulenza Legale della Banca d'Italia* 193.

V. Compulsory Administrative Liquidation under Italian Law

The Italian proceeding to activate in the event of non-systemic banks being FOLF is the so-called compulsory administrative liquidation. This procedure is initiated when the bank crisis is thought to be irreversible and the bank is not deemed able to continue operating. This is based on the grounds that FOLF Italian banks cannot be placed under normal insolvency proceedings applicable to non-financial firms, as expressly stated in law.[50] Nevertheless, the rules of the Insolvency Act[51] concerning the insolvency proceedings of non-financial firms apply also to FOLF banks as far as they are compatible with the compulsory administrative liquidation rules.[52]

The Minister of Finance, upon Bank of Italy proposal, places a bank into compulsory administrative liquidation when: the bank is FOLF; there is no reasonable prospect that any alternative private sector measures, including measures by an Institutional Protection Scheme (IPS), or supervisory action, including early intervention measures taken in respect of the institution, would prevent the failure of the institution within a reasonable timeframe; and there is no public interest in resolving the bank.[53] In other words, a FOLF Italian bank that does not meet the public interest test for its submission to resolution will be placed under compulsory administrative liquidation.[54] In this regard, aligning the triggers for the initiation of the two procedures, except for the public interest, means that the risk of so-called limbo situations can be avoided. These situations occur when the conditions for resolution are met, apart from resolution being in the public interest, but the triggers for initiating insolvency proceedings, being different, are not met. When that is the case, the bank concerned is stuck in a limbo situation, which turns out to be very difficult for the authorities to handle, as happened to ABLV Luxembourg in 2018.[55] In this regard, the ECB and the SRB took a strong stance in favour of the regimes of those Member States, such as Italy, that have aligned the triggers for resolution and insolvency proceedings.[56]

[50] Article 80(6) of Legislative Decree no 385 of 1993.

[51] Royal Decree no 267 of 1942.

[52] See A Nigro, 'La disciplina delle crisi bancarie: la liquidazione coatta amministrativa' (1996) I *Giurisprudenza Commerciale* 144.

[53] These conditions are set out by Art 80(1) of Legislative Decree no 385 of 1993, Art 17(1), Art 20(1)-(2) and Art 21(1)-(2) of Legislative Decree no 180 of 2015.

[54] See n 13, 223.

[55] See European Central Bank, 'Notice "Failing or Likely to Fail" Assessment of ABLV Bank, AS', available at www.bankingsupervision.europa.eu/press/pr/date/2018/html/ssm.pr180224.en.html; see Single Resolution Board, 'Notice summarising the decision taken in respect of ABLV Bank, AS' (2018), available at www.srb.europa.eu/sites/srbsite/files/20180223-summary_decision_-latvia.pdf.

[56] See European Central Bank, 'ECB contribution to the European Commission's targeted consultation on the review of the crisis management and deposit insurance framework', available at www.ecb.europa.eu/pub/pdf/other/ecb.consultation_on_crisis_management_deposit_insurance_

After submitting the FOLF bank into compulsory administrative liquidation, the Bank of Italy appoints the liquidator(s) as well as the members of the oversight committee and exercises the power to instruct them.

The main legal effects arising from the submission of a bank to compulsory administrative liquidation are: withdrawal of the banking licence; interruption of all liabilities' payment as well as of the return of assets to clients and counterparties; termination of contractual relationships, such as loans, overdrafts and current accounts, with the effect that loans and credit lines are immediately called back; and stay of individual enforcement actions, which cannot be brought against the bank in that assets' liquidation and creditors' repayment must take place pursuant to the special rules set out by the Consolidated Banking Act and, to a certain extent, the Insolvency Act.[57]

Special rules apply in the case of banking groups. When the bank parent company is submitted to compulsory administrative liquidation and the other banks of the group are also FOLF, the latter are placed into compulsory administrative liquidation as well, with the aim of coordinating the various procedures.[58] A clear example of this coordination effort is the possibility of appointing the same liquidators for each FOLF bank of the group.

The final objective of the procedure is the liquidation of the assets and the payment of the creditors, which are to be carried out by the liquidators. The creditors' interest to be repaid should then drive the action of both authorities and liquidators. Yet, other extremely relevant interests are always taken into due consideration by the Italian authorities in running the procedure, the stability of the system, the confidence of depositors and investors and the safeguard of the franchise value of the FOLF bank being the most important.

Relatedly, the rationale for having such a procedure in place is similar – in some respects – to that which prompted the introduction of the resolution procedure through the BRRD based on the FSB's Key Attributes of Effective Resolution Regimes for Financial Institutions. To this end, normal insolvency proceedings (typically run by law courts), which apply to non-financial firms, are not suitable for banks, often irrespective of their size.[59] They are usually lengthy, slow and primarily aimed at simply liquidating the assets, thereby using the arising proceeds to pay (typically only some of) the creditors.[60] As a consequence, they often do not allow for the continuation of the FOLF bank's core business lines and main functions with a potential destabilising impact on its counterparties, the banking and

202105~98c4301b09.en.pdf; see Single Resolution Board, 'SRB replies to consultation on Review of the Crisis Management and Deposit Insurance Framework', available at www.srb.europa.eu/sites/default/files/2021-04-20_srb_replies_consultation_cmdi_review.pdf.

[57] See n 13, 224.

[58] See S Fortunato, 'La liquidazione coatta amministrativa delle società del gruppo bancario' (1997) I *Banca Borsa Titoli di Credito* 317.

[59] See n 9, 167–68; n 10, 137–40; n 3, 6.

[60] See M Bodellini, 'Greek and Italian "Lessons" on Bank Restructuring: Is Precautionary Recapitalisation the Way Forward?' (2017) 19 *Cambridge Yearbook of European Legal Studies* 145.

financial system and possibly its geographical area of operation.[61] On the other hand, compulsory administrative liquidation is a flexible procedure that has often allowed for the achievement of a number of key objectives, namely value maximization and depositors' protection thereby keeping financial stability.

For the same reasons, in the context of compulsory administrative liquidation, Italian authorities have seldom carried out an atomistic liquidation. Aimed at selling the assets one by one, this process does not ensure the continuation of the main functions and core business lines thereby potentially harming the bank's counterparties. In particular, irrespective of the size of the bank concerned, the interruption of key functions and core business lines might end up affecting financial stability and destroying the franchise value (of the good parts) and therefore can be detrimental for both the bank's creditors and potentially for the system.[62]

The wish to avoid negative effects on financial stability and to safeguard the franchise value is also the reason why the submission of a bank to compulsory administrative liquidation does not need to wait for it to be balance-sheet insolvent. Even before the adoption of the BRRD with the introduction of the forward-looking FOLF concept,[63] Italian banks were placed into compulsory administrative liquidation when there were serious elements leading the authorities to think that the bank concerned was no longer able to properly perform the banking activity in a sound manner. Such inability is not necessarily equivalent to insolvency. Despite including insolvency, this broad condition encompasses a number of different situations and can be met much earlier than when the bank is balance-sheet insolvent. Obviously, the determination of when the bank was considered no longer able to perform the banking activity in a sound manner was based on a relevant amount of discretion granted to the Bank of Italy. But this anticipatory, yet discretionary, approach was regarded as the most effective way to protect depositors and, in turn, the whole system.

On these grounds, the management of bank crises in Italy has most of the time taken forms resembling – to a large extent – the ones of the resolution procedure under the BRRD.[64] This result has been achieved mostly through the use of a legal tool called *cessione di attività e passività*, meaning transfer of assets and liabilities, which looks substantially similar to the so-called sale of business tool regulated by Articles 38 and 39 of the BRRD.[65] Both tools aim at transferring assets and

[61] See n 13, 224.

[62] See M Bodellini, 'To Bail-In, or to Bail-Out, that is the Question' (2018) 19 *European Business Organization Law Review* 369.

[63] Article 32(4) of BRRD.

[64] See n 13, 225.

[65] According to Art 2(1)(58) of BRRD, the sale of business tool is 'the mechanism for effecting a transfer by a resolution authority of shares or other instruments of ownership issued by an institution under resolution, or assets, rights or liabilities, of an institution under resolution to a purchaser that is not a bridge institution'. According to Art 38(1) of BRRD, 'Member States shall ensure that resolution authorities have the power to transfer to a purchaser that is not a bridge institution … (b) all or any assets, rights or liabilities of an institution under resolution'.

liabilities of the FOLF bank to another bank, without the former's consent and at market prices, which are expected to be higher than liquidation prices, thereby allowing for the continuation of at least some activities of the FOLF bank through the purchasing institution, and safeguarding in this way the franchise value of the FOLF entity.[66]

Thus, compulsory administrative liquidation under Italian law has rarely been applied as a procedure intended purely to dissolve the bank in crisis after the sale piece by piece of the assets and the repayment of the creditors. In other words, it has not often been conducted as a piecemeal liquidation; rather, it has been primarily run with a view to allowing for the continuation of the failing bank's activity through a different bank, thereby merging the dissolving function of the liquidation procedure with the business continuity character of the transfer of assets and liabilities tool.[67] Only after the transfer of assets and liabilities was the residual, almost empty, entity liquidated and then dissolved. In so doing, a number of key outcomes have been achieved:

- deposits have been transferred to the purchasing bank and thus depositors have been fully protected, thereby avoiding runs on other banks and possibly systemic risk;
- borrowers have been allowed to keep on accessing financial means provided by the purchasing bank, thereby avoiding to negatively affect the real economy; and
- at least some assets and liabilities have been sold to the purchasing bank, thereby allowing for the continuation of the business activity and partially preserving the franchise value.[68]

A. The Application of the Transfer of Assets and Liabilities Tool

The Italian Consolidated Banking Act grants to the bank's liquidators every power that is necessary to efficiently liquidate the assets.[69] Among other measures, thus liquidators can: sell assets and liabilities; sell the business or just some parts of the business; and sell a bulk of assets and contractual relationships.[70]

[66] See n 13, 225.

[67] See S Fortunato, 'La liquidazione coatta delle Banche dopo il Testo Unico: lineamenti generali e finalità' (1995) I *Banca Borsa Titoli di Credito* 777.

[68] See G Fauceglia, 'La cessione di attività e passività nella liquidazione coatta amministrativa delle banche e la successione nei rapporti contrattuali' (1997) I *Banca Borsa Titoli di Credito* 452, emphasising that the public interest of safeguarding depositors has been protected through keeping the business function and continuing the previous contractual relationships of the failing bank.

[69] Article 90(1) of the Legislative Decree no 385 of 1993.

[70] Article 90(2) of the Legislative Decree no 385 of 1993.

The wording of this provision of the Italian Consolidated Banking Act is not entirely clear, and might appear somewhat misleading in that a bank's assets and liabilities are principally the banking-related contractual relationships, and those are also the main components of the business. Thus, it seems that the three options given to the liquidators are, in fact, just one whose extent will vary depending on the amount and type of assets and liabilities included in the perimeter of the transfer. Indeed, the transfer can also be just partial. Still, the FOLF bank's creditors have the right to be treated according to the *pari passu* principle on the basis of the creditor ranking as set forth by the law.

In several previous cases, liquidators tried to find another bank willing to purchase all (or a relevant part) of the assets and liabilities of the FOLF bank.[71] Yet, the main issue was that the value of the liabilities to transfer obviously exceeded the value of the assets. This could of course dissuade other banks from getting involved by acquiring such assets and liabilities with a net negative value. Hence, in order to compensate the purchasing bank willing to take on such a negative mismatch, two main instruments were typically deployed: the involvement of the DGS, when the amount of resources to provide was estimated to be lower than the amount that the DGS should have paid to covered depositors in the context of an atomistic liquidation without the transfer of deposits to another bank; and/or a collateralised loan with capped interest rates of one per cent extended by the Bank of Italy to the purchasing bank.[72] When interest rates were rather high, obtaining a loan with very low rates transferred to the Bank of Italy the cost of the crisis management.[73]

A key aspect of the transfer of assets and liabilities relates to the timing. Since assets and liabilities are mostly contractual relationships that would automatically terminate upon the submission of the bank to compulsory administrative liquidation, either their transfer takes place at the start of the procedure or a special tool interrupting the effects of the contracts' termination needs to be employed. In this regard, with a view to allowing liquidators to gain more time to find the best way to liquidate the assets, they also have the power to continue some or all of the FOLF bank's activities.[74] The exercise of this power must be authorised by the Bank of Italy[75] and prevents the contractual relationships from being terminated,

[71] See n 68, arguing that the role played by Bank of Italy in this phase is particularly relevant since the choice of the purchasing bank needs to be authorised by the authority, which, in practical terms, in the past often ended up making the choice itself.

[72] This tool was provided for by the Decree of Minister of Finance 27 September 1974 (the so-called *Sindona* Decree that was adopted to deal with the crisis of Banca Privata Italiana).

[73] See G Minervini, 'Il "ristoro" ex d.m. 27 settembre 1974 e il fondo interbancario di tutela dei depositi' (1996) I *Giurisprudenza Commerciale* 6, who argued that the generalised approach to rescue every failing bank through such a tool would end up increasing moral hazard and affecting the free market competition with the final outcome of having an inefficient banking system.

[74] Article 90(3) of Legislative Decree no 385 of 1993. Also, the Bank of Italy itself can decide that the bank's activity is to continue when the liquidators take office.

[75] The Bank of Italy will decide whether to authorise the continuation of the activity or not after consulting with the oversight committee. According to G Fauceglia, 'L'esercizio provvisorio nella

as would otherwise be the case. This power can be particularly useful in that it does not cause the contractual relationships to automatically terminate upon submission of the bank to compulsory administrative liquidation, thereby keeping intact the business organisation and maintaining its going-concern value.[76] This, in turn, allows liquidators to continue looking for another bank willing to buy the FOLF bank's assets and liabilities at market prices rather than just some assets at liquidation prices. The conditions to meet in order for this power to be exercised are: urgency; and that such a strategy would be more effective to liquidate the assets.[77] This power, however, raised a lively debate among legal scholars, as it permits a bank that no longer has a banking licence to continue performing reserved activities.[78] In other words, the authorisation to continue the bank's activity freezes the effects of the banking licence withdrawal. Nevertheless, the debts arising from acts performed in this phase acquire a super priority in the liquidation ranking. This could negatively affect previous unsecured creditors should the bank's assets become insufficient to pay their credits as a result of the continuation of the activity.[79]

Also, the crisis management strategy was typically prepared well in advance, and banks facing a crisis were not immediately submitted to compulsory administrative liquidation, unless it was clear since the start that they were unequivocally insolvent and/or that their crisis was irreversible. Before the submission to compulsory administrative liquidation, the bank in crisis was often placed into special administration during which the administrators, appointed by the Bank of Italy, were requested to analyse the economic and financial situation and determine its causes as well as possible solutions for recovery. As a result of this assessment, often the administrators had to write down the loans' book value, thereby recording a loss. When the loss could be absorbed and the bank was seen as able to recover, the special administration ended. This often occurred through a merger with another bank or through the acquisition by another larger and more solid bank. However, when the loss was too high and the bank was not seen as able to recover, it was submitted to compulsory administrative liquidation. Still, the previous special administration, as discussed in chapter three, was useful to plan a strategy for

liquidazione coatta amministrativa delle banche' (1996) I *Giurisprudenza Commerciale* 711, the oversight committee is also meant to point out how the continuation of the bank's activity should take place.

[76] See n 13, 231.

[77] See L Desiderio, *La liquidazione coatta amministrativa delle aziende di credito* (Milano, Giuffrè, 1981) 270.

[78] See n 75; A Colavolpe, 'Decreto EUROSIM: le modifiche al T.U. bancario' (1996) I *Società* 1072; B Libonati, *Contratto bancario e attività bancaria* (Milano, Giuffrè, 1965) 34; CM Pratis, *La disciplina giuridica delle aziende di credito* (Milano, Giuffrè, 1972) 463; Desiderio (ibid).

[79] This power was exercised, inter alia, to handle the crisis of Banca Network Investimenti. Banca Network Investimenti was placed into compulsory administrative liquidation on 16 July 2012, and, on 18 July 2012, the Bank of Italy authorised the continuation of the provision of investment services; see Banca d'Italia, 'Provvedimenti rilevanti di carattere particolare delle autorità creditizie. Sezione XI Provvedimenti straordinari. Banca Network Investimenti S.p.A.' (2012) *Bollettino di Vigilanza* no 7 (July 2012), available at www.bancaditalia.it.

managing the crisis,[80] for example by finding a bank willing to purchase assets and liabilities so that the transfer could take place at the start of the compulsory administrative liquidation.[81]

B. The Liquidation Strategy: Transfer of Assets and Liabilities vis-à-vis Atomistic Liquidation

In the context of a compulsory administrative liquidation, liquidators have the discretion to decide how to liquidate the FOLF bank's assets and, to this end, they are granted every power they need for the liquidation to be effective and orderly. Among the tools they can utilise is also the power of transferring the whole bulk (or a part) of assets and liabilities to another bank. This tool has been typically treated as an alternative to the bank's atomistic liquidation and has been applied as the main instrument to manage bank crises.[82]

The choice between these two alternatives (ie atomistic liquidation, and transfer of assets and liabilities) has to be based on a comparative assessment and on the prospective valuation of which of them is supposed to be the most efficient solution in the crisis concerned. The cases of Banca Popolare di Vicenza and Veneto Banca provide a clear example of how this comparative assessment is performed.[83] Banca Popolare di Vicenza and Veneto Banca were placed into compulsory administrative liquidation in 2017, through a special law,[84] and the Bank of Italy developed a counterfactual scenario to compare both options in view of which the liquidation strategy was eventually informed.[85]

Based on this counterfactual scenario, the Bank of Italy came to the conclusion that the wind-down of the two banks under normal insolvency proceedings without state aid would have increased the liquidation costs: 'The wind-down scenario was developed based on the assumption of the sale of all the assets, rights and liabilities in part'.[86] The main assumptions applied were grounded on the sale of

[80] See U Belviso, 'Il trasferimento dell'azienda bancaria nella liquidazione coatta amministrativa' (1972) I *Banca Borsa Titoli di Credito* 356; U Belviso, 'La liquidazione coatta nel quadro di una riforma delle procedure concorsuali' (1979) I *Giurisprudenza Commerciale* 274.

[81] See n 68, emphasising that it had been common practice to transfer assets and liabilities simultaneously when the Bank of Italy placed the FOLF bank into compulsory administrative liquidation.

[82] See n 13, 232.

[83] See Banca d'Italia, 'La Crisi di Veneto Banca S.p.A. e Banca Popolare di Vicenza S.p.A.: Domande e risposte' (2017) *passim*, available at www.bancaditalia.it/media/notizie/2017/crisi-banche-venete/20170811_QA_venete.pdf.

[84] Law no 121 of 2017.

[85] See European Commission, Decision of 25 June 2017 on State aid measures in the context of *Veneto Banca* and *Banca Popolare di Vicenza* liquidation (State Aid SA. 45664, 2017/N – Italy – Orderly Liquidation of *Banca Popolare di Vicenza* and *Veneto Banca* – Liquidation Aid) *passim*, where it is said that in order to choose between the liquidation strategy eventually adopted and the alternative atomistic liquidation, the Bank of Italy run a counterfactual scenario focusing on the consequences potentially resulting from the adoption of the latter strategy.

[86] ibid, para 52.

the 'loans portfolio to private investors, using a table of discounted values for each asset class with a 3 to 5 year time horizon'.[87] The counterfactual scenario consisted of the liquidation of both banks

> under normal insolvency proceedings without any State support. Under that scenario, the liquidator would have overseen the termination of the activities, the seizure of the pledged performing assets by the secured creditors, the administration of the unencumbered assets and the activation of the DGS to protect depositors.[88]

In other words, the counterfactual scenario looked at what the outcomes would have been should an atomistic liquidation have taken place without any public support. Such outcomes would have been: assets' liquidation taking place at liquidation prices and according to the long liquidation timeframe; contractual relationships simultaneously terminated with liquidators immediately calling back all of the loans and credit lines previously granted; DGS fully paying covered depositors; and activities performed by the two banks automatically interrupted.[89]

According to the Bank of Italy, the inherent consequences would have been extremely severe, as approximately 100,000 SMEs and 200,000 households would have been obliged to pay back overnight their loans for about €26 billion. This, in turn, could have created a domino effect triggering a huge number of failures affecting many more operators.[90] Uninsured depositors and senior creditors would have had to wait for many years to try to get their money back, amounting to approximately €20 billion.[91] The DGS should have had to immediately reimburse covered depositors for an amount of approximately €10 billion, and after that it could have exercised the subrogation right to the depositors' rights in the liquidation procedure. Nevertheless, due to the limited amount of immediately available resources, the DGS should have asked its members for extra contributions.[92] The guarantees released by the state with regard to bonds issued by the two banks in the first months of 2017 would have been immediately enforced. As a consequence, the state would have had to pay immediately €8.6 billion and then it could have exercised the subrogation right in the liquidation procedure.[93]

In the view of the Italian authorities, these negative consequences could be avoided only with the measures eventually adopted, namely the transfer of some assets and liabilities to Intesa San Paolo with the provision of public support.[94]

Regardless of the provision of public financial support, these two cases (along with others) show that it has been common practice over time to prefer the transfer

[87] ibid, para 52.
[88] ibid, para 105.
[89] See n 83.
[90] See Banca d'Italia, 'Informazioni sulla Soluzione della Crisi di Veneto Banca S.p.A. e Banca Popolare di Vicenza S.p.A.' (2017) Memoria per la VI Commissione Finanze della Camera dei Deputati, available at www.bancaditalia.it/media/notizie/2017/Nota-Venetobanca-e-BPV.pdf.
[91] ibid.
[92] ibid.
[93] ibid.
[94] See n 13, 233.

of assets and liabilities to another bank over atomistic liquidation of the assets, since the former has been regarded as able to allow for the continuation of core business lines and main functions as well as for the protection of the franchise value. Consequently, the atomistic liquidation with the DGS reimbursing covered depositors took place only in some residual cases involving very small banks, as further discussed in chapter six.[95]

C. The Position of Banks' Creditors and the Law Courts' Judicial Review of Decisions taken in the Context of Compulsory Administrative Liquidation

When the transfer of assets and liabilities tool is applied, the FOLF bank's creditors have the right to be treated according to the *pari passu* principle on the basis of the creditor ranking.[96] This rule should allow creditors negatively and unfairly affected by the transfer to bring a legal claim against the bank, the liquidators and the authorities. Despite this being the case, there are two key aspects to consider in this regard.

Firstly, usually all of the bank's liabilities were transferred to the purchasing bank with the effect that only shareholders had to bear the losses;[97] hence each bank's creditor was fully safeguarded. When this did not happen, as in the case of Veneto Banca and Banca Popolare di Vicenza, another way to compensate retail investors, who purchased the subordinated bonds which were left within the failing banks, was found, namely through the so-called Solidarity Fund.[98]

Secondly, there is case law concerning claims brought forward by the failing bank's shareholders and former directors complaining about: the lack of conditions

[95] See Fondo Interbancario di Tutela dei Depositi, 'FIDT's Interventions, Interventions Report' 1, available at www.fitd.it/Cosa_Facciamo/Interventi, according to which between 1988 and 2018, the main Italian DGS intervened twice to reimburse depositors. In the case of Banca di Tricesimo the Italian DGS paid €3.4 million to covered depositors, whereas in the case of Banca Network Investimenti it paid €73.9 million to covered depositors. With regard to the mutual banks' DGS, see F Baldi, M Bredice and R Di Salvo, 'Bank-Crisis Management Practises in Italy (1978–2015). Perspectives on the Italian Cooperative Credit Network' (2015) 2 *The Journal of European Economic History* 144, 145, underlining that in the period between 1997 and 2015, the mutual banks' DGS intervened 80 times and only once did it reimburse covered depositors.

[96] Article 90(2) of Legislative Decree no 385 of 1993.

[97] See n 45; see also S Maccarone, 'Il ruolo e l'ambito di intervento dei fondi di risoluzione e dei DGS nelle crisi bancarie' (2015) 2 *Diritto della Banca e del Mercato Finanziario* 177.

[98] The so-called Solidarity Fund was established in 2015 by Law no 208 of 2015; pursuant to Law no 119 of 2016, the Italian DGS was tasked to manage and finance the Solidarity Fund. At the outset, the Solidarity Fund has been established in order to compensate the retail investors who bought subordinated bonds of four small-sized banks (Banca delle Marche, Banca Popolare dell'Etruria, Cassa di Risparmio di Ferrara and Cassa di Risparmio di Chieti) which were resolved in 2015. Subsequently, Law no 121 of 2017, through which Banca Popolare di Vicenza and Veneto Banca were liquidated, has given also the retail investors who bought subordinated bonds issued by such banks the possibility to obtain a compensation to be paid by the Solidarity Fund.

for the submission of their bank to compulsory administrative liquidation; and the way in which liquidation was conducted. In these cases, typically law courts ruled that the Bank of Italy had to be given substantial discretion in making its own choices.[99] And such discretionary choices could not be questioned by law courts unless they were manifestly wrong or adopted by violating procedural rules. This reading of the rules has so far enabled the Bank of Italy, and thereby the bank's liquidators, to avoid any overruling of their decisions.[100]

As to the potential impact of the transfer of assets and liabilities tool on fundamental rights, a BRRD-oriented reading would lead to an argument that negatively affecting fundamental rights is only justified for public interest purposes in resolution. The main issue in this regard is that resolution tools, potentially affecting property rights and creditor claims, can be employed also when the bank is just FOLF and not necessarily balance-sheet insolvent. Against this backdrop, public interest acts as the legal basis permitting to negatively affect fundamental rights before the main condition for submission to an insolvency proceeding (namely balance-sheet insolvency) is met.

Yet, when there is no public interest to safeguard and the bank is just FOLF, but not (yet) balance sheet insolvent, the legal basis to justify the negative impact on fundamental rights might be missing.[101] This could be the case when resolution-like tools, such as the transfer of assets and liabilities tool, are adopted in the context of a bank's liquidation. Still, it is worth recalling that tools similar to the resolution tools affecting fundamental rights were used even before the adoption of the BRRD and therefore outside a resolution procedure justified by public interest concerns. This occurred in the case of the application of burden-sharing measures adopted, according to the 2013 European Commission Banking Communication, in order for a bank to be entitled to receive state aid provision.[102] To justify the application of burden-sharing measures to shareholders and subordinated creditors, the Court of Justice of the European Union ruled that

> The scale of losses suffered by shareholders of distressed banks will, in any event, be the same, regardless of whether those losses are caused by a court insolvency order because no State aid is granted or by a procedure for the granting of State aid which is subject to the prerequisite of burden-sharing.[103]

[99] See *Tribunale Amministrativo Regionale del Lazio*, 7 January 2017 no 166; *Tribunale di Arezzo*, 11 February 2016; *Tribunale di Roma*, 27 April 1977, (concerning the compulsory administrative liquidation of Banca Privata Italiana and the shareholders' and creditors' legal claims brought against the Bank of Italy); see also n 52; F Capriglione, 'Discrezionalità del provvedimento amministrativo di messa in liquidazione coatta di un'azienda di credito e pretesa risarcitoria del socio (1978) II *Banca Borsa Titoli di Credito* 90.

[100] See n 13, 235.

[101] ibid, 235.

[102] Communication from the Commission of 30 July 2013 on the application, from 1 August 2013, of state aid rules to support measures in favour of banks in the context of the financial crisis ('2013 Banking Communication') [2013] OJ C216/1.

[103] Court of Justice of the European Union, Case C-526/14 *Kotnik and Others v Drzavni zbor Republike Slovenije*, judgment of 19 July 2016.

This means that, when powers affecting fundamental rights are exercised outside an insolvency proceeding (eg to prevent it), it is relevant for the authorities to demonstrate that the outcomes for shareholders and creditors would have been equally negative in the event of a liquidation. If that is the case, then a similar argument could be advanced when equivalent powers are exercised in the context of an insolvency proceeding where tools other than an atomistic liquidation are deployed. Here the point of reference to consider in evaluating advantages and disadvantages for shareholders and creditors would be the outcomes arising from an atomistic liquidation, where typically the assets are sold at discounted prices. Accordingly, in order to justify the transfer of assets and liabilities in an insolvency proceeding, should it negatively affect fundamental rights, the authorities could have to show that such a strategy is not more detrimental for shareholders' and creditors' fundamental rights than an atomistic liquidation. A further safeguard to avoid litigation arising from the application of this tool could be a specific provision requiring the authorities to run a counterfactual scenario. The latter might be a preventive assessment of whether the transfer of assets and liabilities would have more negative effects on shareholders' and creditors' fundamental rights than a piecemeal liquidation. The decision on the strategy to adopt then should be based on the outcomes of such an assessment.[104]

D. The Application of Other Resolution-Like Tools in the Context of Compulsory Administrative Liquidation

Liquidators can exercise every power needed to efficiently liquidate the bank's assets, and accordingly some of such powers are listed in legislation.[105] In this list, however, a bridge-bank-like tool and an asset-separation-like tool (similar to the resolution tools regulated by the BRRD) are not mentioned.[106] This does not necessarily mean, however, that similar tools cannot be employed in a compulsory administrative liquidation. Some past cases provide interesting insights in this regard.

In the Banco Ambrosiano crisis in the 1980s, a pool of market participants, holding a considerable amount of debt instruments issued by the bank in crisis, set up a new entity with a view to buying some assets and liabilities from the latter. Such a tool looks similar – at least from the substantial perspective and irrespective

[104] See n 13, 236.

[105] Article 90(2) of the Consolidated Banking Act.

[106] According to Art 2(1)(60) of BRRD, the bridge institution tool is 'the mechanism for transferring shares or other instruments of ownership issued by an institution under resolution or assets, rights or liabilities of an institution under resolution to a bridge institution'; according to Art 2(1)(55) of BRRD, the asset separation tool is 'the mechanism for effecting a transfer by a resolution authority of assets, rights or liabilities of an institution under resolution to an asset management vehicle'.

of the private nature of the vehicle and its promoters – to the bridge bank tool currently regulated by the BRRD.[107]

Also, a tool similar to the asset separation tool, which is not explicitly regulated by Italian law in the context of compulsory administrative liquidation, was employed in the cases of Veneto Banca and Banca Popolare di Vicenza. The legal basis for the application of such a tool was a law decree then converted into law.[108] The liquidation strategy provided for the transfer of non-performing loans to a state-owned company named SGA. The latter was expected to manage these assets with a long-term view, supposedly more efficient for the recovery of the transferred credits. Interestingly, SGA was established in 1997 to deal with the Banco di Napoli crisis.[109] Banco di Napoli was not submitted to compulsory administrative liquidation but rescued with public money,[110] through a special law,[111] and its bad loans were transferred to SGA.[112] SGA is, therefore, a clear example of an asset separation tool *ante litteram*.[113]

These cases can be called upon to argue that, if needed, even a bridge-bank-like tool could, in principle, be adopted in the context of a compulsory administrative liquidation. A key aspect to consider in this regard pertains to the high operating costs relating to the establishment and running of a bridge bank. Therefore, a bridge bank tool could be efficiently employed only in those cases in which the franchise value of the FOLF bank is assessed as considerably higher than such operating costs. Also, it might be necessary to ground the use of such a tool in some solid legal foundations, such as a specific law.

VI. Bank Liquidation and the EU State Aid Framework: The So-called Liquidation Aid

The EU framework on state aid limits the possibility for a Member State to intervene in rescuing banks (and more in general private firms) with public money.[114]

[107] See E Rulli, *Contributo allo studio della risoluzione bancaria* (Torino, Giappichelli, 2017) 108.

[108] Law no 121 of 2017, converting Law Decree no 99 of 2017, *recante disposizioni urgenti per la liquidazione coatta amministrativa di Banca Popolare di Vicenza S.p.A. e di Veneto Banca S.p.A.*

[109] See V Giglio and R Setola, 'La disciplina degli aiuti di Stato e le crisi bancarie italiane' (2002) 1 *Mercato Concorrenza Regole* 230.

[110] See U Belviso, 'La liquidazione coatta amministrativa e il caso Banco di Napoli' (1998) I *Banca Borsa Titoli di Credito* 1.

[111] Law no 588 of 19 November 1996. Interestingly, the European Commission did not find any breach of the state aid prohibition rules; see n 109; M Sepe, 'La vecchia e la nuova socializzazione delle perdite: elementi di continuità e di discontinuità' (2017) 4 *Rivista Trimestrale di Diritto dell'Economia* 22.

[112] See N Salanitro, 'La cessione dei crediti anomali ad una società di gestione (c.d. bad bank)' (1997) I *Banca, Borsa Titoli di Credito* 409; n 109.

[113] See n 13, 237.

[114] See M Dewatripont, 'European Banking: Bailout, Bail-in and State Aid Control' (2014) 34 *International Journal of Industrial Organization* 40, pointing out that the EU is 'the only jurisdiction in the world with State Aid Control policies'.

The rationale behind this limitation is grounded in the need to ensure that firms established in different Member States can compete fairly amongst themselves without benefiting from public resources granted by their governments. The absence of such a rule would favour those firms established in the most financially solid Member States, while penalising those firms which are established in Member States that are less financially sound. However, this general rule is subject to some exceptions. Article 107 TFEU states that any state aid is incompatible with the internal market,[115] unless it qualifies as one of the exceptions laid down in Article 107(2) TFEU,[116] or unless it has been approved by the Commission for one of the reasons set out in Article 107(3) TFEU.[117] In relation to the banking sector, the most suitable justification to allow for public intervention, according to Article 107(3)(b) TFEU, has so far been 'to remedy a serious disturbance in the economy of a Member State'. The argument advanced in this regard is that in order to remedy a serious disturbance in the economy of a Member State the use of public resources might be necessary.

Between 2008 and 2011, the Commission adopted six communications to clarify the criteria to apply in assessing the compatibility of state aid with the provisions of the TFEU.[118] Then, in 2013, in light of the adoption of the new regulatory

[115] Article 107(1) TFEU provides for a general prohibition of any aid granted by a Member State: 'save as otherwise provided in the Treaties, any aid granted by a Member State or through State resources in any form whatsoever which distorts or threatens to distort competition by favouring certain undertakings or the production of certain goods shall, in so far as it affects trade between Member States, be incompatible with the internal market'.

[116] Article 107(2) provides that 'the following shall be compatible with the internal market: (a) aid having a social character, granted to individual consumers, provided that such aid is granted without discrimination related to the origin of the products concerned; (b) aid to make good the damage caused by natural disasters or exceptional occurrences; and, (c) aid granted to the economy of certain areas of the Federal Republic of Germany affected by the division of Germany, in so far as such aid is required in order to compensate for the economic disadvantages caused by that division. Five years after the entry into force of the Treaty of Lisbon, the Council, acting on a proposal from the Commission, may adopt a decision repealing this point'.

[117] Article 107(3) of the TFEU establishes that 'the following may be considered to be compatible with the internal market: (a) aid to promote the economic development of areas where the standard of living is abnormally low or where there is serious underemployment, and of the regions referred to in Article 349, in view of their structural, economic and social situation; (b) aid to promote the execution of an important project of common European interest or to remedy a serious disturbance in the economy of a Member State; (c) aid to facilitate the development of certain economic activities or of certain economic areas, where such aid does not adversely affect trading conditions to an extent contrary to the common interest; (d) aid to promote culture and heritage conservation where such aid does not affect trading conditions and competition in the Union to an extent that is contrary to the common interest; and, (e) such other categories of aid as may be specified by decision of the Council on a proposal from the Commission'.

[118] These are the so-called 'Crisis Communications': 'Communication from the Commission of 25 October 2008 on the application of state aid rules to measures taken in relation to financial institutions in the context of the current global financial crisis' ('2008 Banking Communication') [2008] OJ C270/8; 'Communication from the Commission of 15 January 2009 on the recapitalisation of financial institutions in the current financial crisis: limitation of aid to the minimum necessary and safeguards against undue distortions of competition ('Recapitalisation Communication') [2009] OJ C10/2; 'Communication from the Commission of 26 March 2009 on the treatment of impaired assets in the Community financial sector' ('Impaired Assets Communication') [2009] OJ C72/1; 'Communication

architecture, namely the Banking Union and the new bank resolution regime, the Commission published the 2013 Banking Communication,[119] also providing for the application of the 'burden sharing' mechanism to (shareholders and) subordinated creditors, and requesting the adoption of a restructuring plan to be approved before obtaining the aid.[120] Accordingly, state aid can be given only if equity and subordinated debt-holders will absorb the losses through the conversion and/or the write-down of their instruments. However, the Commission has always emphasised that in the state aid authorisation process in the banking sector, maintaining financial stability is key.[121] For this reason, it has the power to exclude the application of the burden-sharing mechanism when this 'would endanger financial stability or lead to disproportionate results'.[122]

In the context of a liquidation procedure, the Commission Banking Communication allows for the granting of a so-called liquidation aid. Particularly,

> the Commission recognises that, due to the specificities of credit institutions and in the absence of mechanisms allowing for the resolution of credit institutions without threatening financial stability, it might not be feasible to liquidate a credit institution under ordinary insolvency proceedings. For that reason, State measures to support the liquidation of failing credit institutions may be considered as compatible aid, subject to compliance with the burden sharing mechanism.[123]

However, this possibility has raised severe criticism, also on the grounds that it appears that the use of public money in the context of liquidation can paradoxically take place more easily than in resolution. Under the resolution regime, the use of public money can occur only after a strict application of the bail-in tool has taken place (at least to eight per cent of the bank's liabilities). This is not the case in the context of liquidation, where such conditions are not requested. These misalignments can create incentives to prefer liquidation – with the provision of

of the Commission of 19 August 2009 on the return to viability and the assessment of restructuring measures in the financial sector in the current crisis under the state aid rules' ('Restructuring Communication') [2009] OJ C195/9; Communication from the Commission of 7 December 2010 on the application, from 1 January 2011, of state aid rules to support measures in favour of financial institutions in the context of the financial crisis' ('2010 Prolongation Communication') [2010] OJ C329/7; Communication from the Commission of 6 December 2011 on the application, from 1 January 2012, of state aid rules to support measures in favour of financial institutions in the context of the financial crisis' ('2011 Prolongation Communication') [2011] OJ C356/7.

[119] n 102.

[120] See G Lo Schiavo, 'State Aids and Credit Institutions in Europe: What Way Forward?' (2014) 25 *European Business Law Review* 442, arguing that 'burden sharing entails that the aid shall be limited to the minimum necessary and that the beneficiary undertakes the required level of "own contribution" in order to receive the State aid'.

[121] See S Micossi, G Bruzzone and M Casella, 'Bail-in Provisions in State Aid and Resolution Procedures: Are They Consistent with Systemic Stability?' (2014) 318 *CEPS Policy Brief* 4, available at www.ceps.eu/publications/bail-provisions-state-aid-and-resolution-procedures-are-they-consistent-systemic.

[122] 2013 Banking Communication (n 102) (point 45); C Hadjiemmanuil, 'Limits on State-Funded Bailouts in the EU Bank Resolution Regime' (2016) 2 *European Economy* 100, argues that the 2013 Banking Communication 'is framed in terms sufficiently flexible for enabling the approval of almost every conceivable solution by way of exception'.

[123] 2013 Commission Banking Communication (n 102) point 66.

taxpayers' money – over resolution.[124] The wish to avoid the politically and socially burdensome application of the bail-in tool, which can negatively affect many retail investors as well as depositors (with deposits over €100,000), is indeed an incentive for national authorities to prefer a publicly funded liquidation over resolution. This can however be seen as a deviation from the Financial Stability Board's Key Attributes of Effective Resolution Regimes, which express disapproval for the use of public funds.[125]

Also, as national insolvency laws vary across Member States, a differential treatment of creditors, depending on where the procedure is initiated, might take place.[126] The unacceptable outcome is that some creditors might be better off in liquidation than in resolution, even if the aggregate cost for the state is higher as a result of the provision of public support.[127] This can also end up creating an uneven playing field for banks' funding costs.[128]

The risk of a more relaxed approach to the provision of public funds in liquidation than in resolution is the reason why elsewhere we advocated in favour of the alignment of the two regimes as to the conditions for public intervention.[129] Highlighting the same shortcomings, the IMF emphasised that solutions based on a less stringent application of the burden-sharing requirements, namely the ones which can be adopted in a liquidation procedure, should be restricted.[130]

The provision of a liquidation aid was authorised by the European Commission in 2017 with regard to Veneto Banca and Banca Popolare di Vicenza. Both banks, after having been assessed as FOLF by the ECB[131] were submitted to winding up

[124] In a similar vein see Single Resolution Board, 'SRB Multi-Annual Planning and Work Programme 2018' (2017) 5, where it is underlined that 'other crisis cases in 2017 also revealed the need to take a broader look at the overall regulatory framework, in particular the interplay between the Bank Recovery and Resolution Directive (BRRD), the national insolvency regimes and the rules regarding State Aid and whether incentives are set correctly'.

[125] See Financial Stability Board, 'Key Attributes of Effective Resolution Regimes for Financial Institutions' (2014), where the Board has recommended the implementation of these principles into the domestic laws in order to 'resolve financial institutions in an orderly manner without taxpayer exposure to loss from solvency support, while maintaining continuity of their vital economic functions'. The Financial Stability Board's main objective is therefore to allow the orderly resolution of banks without impacting the public finances as was the case in the past with bail-outs. But in so doing, the resolution authorities should also pursue the aim to avoid the creation of 'severe systemic disruption'.

[126] See n 35, 7.

[127] See n 25, 18.

[128] See n 35, 27.

[129] See n 25, 18.

[130] See n 35, 7–27, also arguing that 'this approach should be balanced with the introduction of a financial stability exemption allowing for the disapplication of the rule providing that at least 8% of the bank's liabilities have to be bailed in before the use of public resources is permitted. This exemption should be granted in cases of either Eurozone-wide or country-wide crisis subject to some conditions. After all, the SRM has been designed to deal with idiosyncratic events. Such a financial stability exemption is necessary since under the current BRRD/SRMR regime the only flexible option is 'precautionary recapitalisation'. However, precautionary recapitalisation can take place only when the institution in question is solvent and not when flexibility is really needed, namely during a system-wide crisis when banks are typically undercapitalised.

[131] See European Central Bank (n 14) *passim*.

under Italian law on the grounds of being considered by the SRB as unable to negatively affect the system with their failure.[132] Against this backdrop, the European Commission authorised the use of state aid measures to manage the liquidation of the two institutions.[133] This decision was criticised as it was considered somehow at odds with the rationale behind the rules of the BRRD.[134] The underlying argument was that if the two institutions were submitted to liquidation, this was due to the fact that the SRB did not envisage any public interest to safeguard through their resolution. But if that was the case, then it would be difficult to understand the justification for the use of public resources in the winding-down phase, although the Banking Communication 2013, with a provision which is not in line with the rationale behind the BRRD, allows for the provision of liquidation aid with a view to orderly managing bank liquidation.

VII. The UK Regime

In the UK, according to the Banking Act,[135] the statutory modified insolvency regimes for banks, building societies and credit unions are applied either alongside the stabilisation options (resolution tools) or when using a stabilisation option is not appropriate.[136] Against this backdrop, there are two available judicial procedures, namely the bank insolvency procedure (BIP) and the bank administration procedure (BAP). Despite both being initiated upon court order, the Bank of England, in its capacity as resolution authority, plays a key role. Indeed, it is the Bank of England which typically submits the application to the court to initiate the appropriate procedure when it deems the requested conditions to be met. In other words, the Bank of England decides which procedure should be initiated on a case-by-case basis and accordingly submits an application to the competent court.

The bank insolvency procedure is designed to ensure either rapid reimbursement of covered depositors by the FSCS or the transfer of covered deposits to a viable firm. Either the Bank of England can apply for the initiation of this procedure, or an application can be made by the Secretary of State or the PRA. The conditions requested for activating this procedure are that: the firm is unable or likely to become unable to pay its debts; winding-up would be fair; or in the case of an application made by the Secretary of State, winding-up would be in the public interest.

If a bank is placed into bank insolvency procedure, a liquidator is to be appointed, along with a liquidation committee to supervise and advise on how the

[132] See Single Resolution Board (n 14) *passim*.

[133] See European Commission (n 14).

[134] See E Avgouleas and C Goodhart, 'Bank resolution 10 years from the global financial crisis: a systematic reappraisal' (2019) 7 LUISS University School of European Political Economy, Working Paper 11.

[135] Banking Act 2009, ss 91, 130 and 131, respectively.

[136] See H Malek, J Potts and S Dzwig, *Bank Resolution – Key Issues and Local Perspectives* (London, Insol International, 2019) 172.

liquidator should deal with deposits.[137] The liquidator's priority, according to the Banking Act, is to work with the FSCS to pay out protected deposits within seven days. The secondary statutory aim is to wind up the bank.

In contrast, the bank administration procedure is used where part of a bank has been sold to a private purchaser.[138] The procedure typically starts upon application of the Bank of England. The court then appoints an administrator. The conditions to initiate the bank administration procedure are that the Bank of England intends to use the private-sector purchaser tool and that the bank is unable to pay its debts or is likely to become unable to pay its debts as a result of the use of that tool.[139] The administrator appointed by the court has two statutory objectives: supporting the commercial purchaser, and normal administration, that is, to rescue the firm as a going concern or achieve a better result than winding up the firm without prior administration.[140]

The bank insolvency procedure was activated in 2009 with regard to the Scottish Dunfermline Building Society (DBS), which had 350,000 customers, 550 staff and 34 branches.[141] In March 2009, the bank's supervisor (FSA) deemed that an injection of £60 million was needed to stabilise the institution. Due to the lack of alternatives, the Bank of England decided then to apply the private-sector purchaser tool, and accordingly, Nationwide Building Society acquired retail and wholesale deposits, branches and residential mortgages, while social-housing loans and related deposits were transferred to a bridge bank.[142] The remainder of DBS was eventually put into bank insolvency procedure by a court order on 30 March 2009.[143]

The bank insolvency procedure was used also to handle the crisis of Southsea Mortgage and Investment Company Limited in 2011.[144] However, due to the very small size of the institution, which was a building society and had approximately 250 depositors and retail deposits of £7.4 million, it was decided to simply liquidate it with the FCSC reimbursing covered depositors up to £85,000. Its liquidation did not create any disruption to the customers. This case shows that the conditions for initiating resolution were found to be met but the institution was deemed too small for the application of both the bail-in tool and the private-sector purchaser tool.[145]

[137] ibid, 173.
[138] ibid, 173.
[139] The private sector purchaser tool involves the transfer of all or part (in a partial transfer) of a firm's shares or property to an authorised private purchaser. It does not require the consent of the firm, nor of its shareholders, customers or counterparties. The transfer process usually follows an auction. The marketing process must be transparent, without conflicts of interest, must take account of the need to act quickly and must maximise the sale price as far as possible.
[140] See n 136, 174.
[141] ibid, 175.
[142] ibid, 176.
[143] ibid, 176.
[144] ibid, 177.
[145] ibid, 177.

The bank administration procedure was initiated with regard to Strand Capital Limited, which collapsed in May 2017. Strand Capital had approximately 3,000 customers and investments, and cash deposits of approximately £12.5 million.[146] The FSCS started paying client money balances up to £50,000 per customer. By November 2018, the FSCS had paid £5.8 million in compensation.[147]

VIII. The US Regime

The US bank crisis management framework has been introduced in 1933 as one of the policy initiatives adopted in response to the great financial crisis of the late 1920s. Since then, it has been revised many times with a view to fixing the weaknesses shown while handling bank crises. It has been applied in a significant number of cases and, due to this, US agencies have acquired relevant experience and developed very sophisticated skills in managing banks' crises. For all these reasons its analysis can be rather useful in the context of the debate on the adoption of a harmonised bank insolvency regime at EU level.

Taking into account the typical American banking group structure, the US crisis management framework provides specific rules for IDIs, which are different to those applying to BHCs. In the event of a crisis, while the former are always subject to a special regime (so-called receivership), the latter, by default, are to reorganise or liquidate pursuant to the Bankruptcy Code, like any non-financial firm, unless they are considered systemically important. When that is the case, the Orderly Liquidation Authority (OLA) applies to them according to the Dodd-Frank Act.[148] OLA in the US is discussed vis-à-vis resolution in the EU and UK in chapter five.

Over its almost 90-year existence, the FDIC has developed a broad range of methods to successfully deal with failing banks, thereby relying upon a significant host of transaction structures to transfer assets and liabilities of failing banks to other private players with a view to reducing the costs of crisis management for the public finance. Interestingly, between 2008 and 2013, the FDIC managed to close down nearly 500 insured depository institutions (IDIs), including some large banks, without destabilising the market.[149]

IX. Receivership

The procedure to activate in the event of an IDI failing is the so-called receivership (also referred to as resolution). Typically, the receivership starts with the

[146] ibid, 180.
[147] ibid, 180.
[148] Dodd-Frank Act, Sec 203(b)(2).
[149] See Federal Deposit Insurance Corporation, 'Crisis and Response: An FDIC History, 2008–2013' (2017) *passim*, available at www.fdic.gov/bank/historical/crisis.

chartering authority (ie the supervisory authority) withdrawing the bank's charter and appointing the FDIC as receiver.[150] The FDIC is mandatorily appointed as receiver for every failing federally chartered IDI and can also be appointed with regard to failing state-chartered insured banks. Thus, the FDIC acts as receiver for almost every failing state and federally chartered bank in the US.[151]

The triggers for initiating the receivership refer to several types of unsafe and unsound conditions, activities and violations of the law as well as statutes, regulations, regulatory settlements and enforcement orders.[152] Any of the following situations can in fact lead to the initiation of a receivership: regulatory insolvency (bank is under-capitalised under the prompt corrective action framework); balance sheet insolvency (liabilities exceed assets); inability to pay obligations or meet depositors' demands in ordinary course (illiquidity); unsafe or unsound condition; wilful violation of a cease-and-desist order; concealment of books, papers, records, or assets; and violation of anti-money laundering laws and regulations.[153]

With the start of the procedure, typically the failing bank's assets and liabilities are transferred to a dedicated legal entity, called receivership, which is established for every failed bank. The crisis management process, however, usually begins up to 90 days before the establishment of the receivership, once the IDI's primary regulator, coordinating with the FDIC, notifies the failing bank that it is critically undercapitalised or insolvent.[154] At that point, the FDIC officials meet with the bank's management to start the due diligence process as well as the marketing of both assets and liabilities.[155] After the bank closure, the winding up of the receivership may take years, but the FDIC usually manages to sell the most marketable assets within the first three to four months. This means that approximately half of the FDIC's most relevant activities are concluded on a confidential basis before the bank is closed down, while the remaining part is performed publicly after the so-called resolution weekend.[156]

Moreover, the FDIC has also the power to terminate or suspend insurance coverage, as far as it warns at least 30 days in advance both the bank's primary regulator and the bank itself. As a consequence of insurance termination, the IDI is placed into receivership. The conditions requested for insurance termination

[150] See n 42.

[151] See J Deslandes, C Dias and M Magnus, 'Liquidation of Banks: Towards an "FDIC" for the Banking Union? In-depth analysis' (2019), available at www.europarl.europa.eu/RegData/etudes/IDAN/2019/634385/IPOL_IDA(2019)634385_EN.pdf

[152] See A Gelpern and N Véron, 'An Effective Regime for Non-viable Banks: US Experience and Considerations for EU Reform' (2019) Study Requested by the ECON committee of the European Parliament, Economic Governance Support Unit (EGOV) – Directorate-General for Internal Policies of the Union, 20–21, also highlighting that the FDIC as receiver does not report to the chartering authorities that appointed it.

[153] This list is not exhaustive.

[154] See n 152, 18.

[155] See n 42.

[156] See Federal Deposit Insurance Corporation, 'Resolutions Handbook' (2019) 14, available at www.fdic.gov/bank/historical/reshandbook/resolutions-handbook.pdf, where the resolution weekend is described as the beginning of the last step of the process.

are rather similar to the ones required for receivership.[157] Although rarely used because of its inflexibility,[158] insurance termination plays an important function, since it gives the FDIC some leverage in its interaction with the other chartering authorities and regulators that may be more inclined to engage in supervisory forbearance.[159]

As to banking groups, the FDIC is given the power to make other banks within the group bear the failing bank's losses, that otherwise would negatively affect the DIF.[160] This power is expected to tackle the risk of assets' occultation and balance sheet manipulation which sometimes are put in place by insolvent banks' owners.[161] The legal effect resulting from the exercise of such power is that within the group, banks have to cross-guarantee the FDIC's exposure to their affiliates. This means that all IDIs within the same group are treated as if they were a single entity for the purposes of compensating the DIF.[162] If the receivership manages to recover enough proceeds to repay the guarantors, they are entitled to sixth-priority distribution, but in practice the enforcement of the cross-guarantee typically causes the failure of the latter as well.[163]

Between 1951 and 1991, the FDIC used to have a broader discretion in implementing the crisis management strategy and in selecting the resolution method(s) to adopt.[164] The criteria driving these choices only requested the strategy to be less costly than liquidation with depositors' pay-out.[165] Nevertheless, the FDIC Improvement Act (FDICIA) of 1991 has significantly restricted this discretion by mandating the FDIC to use the resolution method which is least costly for the DIF.[166] Also, according to the FDICIA, the FDIC is now requested to: develop a more rigorous cost assessment methodology, projecting losses to the DIF 'on a present-value basis, using a realistic discount rate'; document its reasoning and assumptions; and undergo annual reviews of its resolution practice by the Government Accountability Office (GAO). The introduction of this reinforced least-cost criterion has led to a substantial decrease of the number of whole-bank

[157] See n 42, 585.

[158] See TJ Curry, JP O'Keefe, J Coburn and L Montgomery, 'Financially Distressed Banks: How Effective Are Enforcement Actions in the Supervision Process?' (1999) FDIC Banking Review, *passim*, available at www.fdic.gov/bank/analytical/banking/9910.pdf.

[159] See n 152, 22, also noting that the FDIC's authority to terminate deposit insurance and to appoint itself as receiver, on one hand, incentivises other regulators to collaborate and, on the other, 'puts the objective of minimising losses to the DIF at the heart of the resolution process'.

[160] Federal Deposit Insurance Corporation, 'Cross Guaranty Program' (2009) FDIC Press release (30 October 2009), available at www.fdic.gov/news/news/press/2009/pr09195b.html.

[161] See n 152, 24.

[162] See n 42, 585.

[163] See RS Carnell, JR Macey and GP Miller, *The Law of Financial Institutions* (New York, Wolters Kluwer, 2017) 417–18.

[164] See n 152, 2.

[165] Federal Deposit Insurance Corporation, 'The First Fifty Years: A History of the FDIC 1933–1983' (1984) 87, available at www.fdic.gov/bank/historical/firstfifty.

[166] See n 152, 6.

purchase and assumption (P&A) transactions and, as a result, to a relevant increase of the losses suffered by uninsured depositors.[167]

In its capacity as receiver, the FDIC is entitled to exercise intrusive powers aimed at disposing of assets, assuming or repudiating contracts, and paying or rejecting claims.[168] Accordingly, the FDIC has the power to decide on whether to enforce or walk away from the failed IDI's contracts. Such authority is extremely broad as the FDIC can decide to terminate contracts that are not completely performed when the receivership is established. Nonetheless, this power needs to be exercised within a reasonable timeframe and must meet the conditions that the performance of the contract's obligations is considered 'burdensome' and its termination is deemed able to promote orderly administration.[169] As a consequence of the contract's termination, the FDIC will become liable for the damages caused to the counterparty, but the scope of such liability is more limited than in the case of a breach of contract outside the receivership. Indeed, the receiver will not be liable for consequential damages and for certain penalty provisions.[170]

The FDIC is also given the authority to administer the claims against the receivership. Accordingly, the FDIC is mostly meant to review proof of claims; this process is subject to judicial review.[171] Every claim recognised as valid by the FDIC gives title to a proportional share of the liquidation proceeds, according to the creditor ranking. Claims are paid in the following order: secured debt (up to the collateral value with the remaining portion to be paid along with general unsecured and unsubordinated claims); administrative expenses of the receivership; insured and uninsured depositors (including FDIC subrogating to insured depositors' rights); general unsecured and unsubordinated claims; subordinated debt; cross-guarantee claims; and equity.[172]

Nonetheless, mainly in order to prevent uninsured depositors' runs, the FDIC can also pay claims before liquidating the assets by using its own funds.[173] The FDIC's maximum liability as receiver is capped to the amount that the claim would have received in liquidation.[174] Hence, creditors have no claim against the FDIC's own funds in excess of the amount that they would have received in liquidation, even when similarly situated creditors have received more than them as a consequence of P&A.[175]

[167] See n 42, 586.
[168] See n 152, 20.
[169] ibid, 27.
[170] ibid, 27, also arguing that 'critics of the receivership approach to bank insolvency have highlighted the receiver's ability to cherry-pick contracts as unfair and potentially distortive'.
[171] ibid, 27.
[172] Obviously, lower-priority claims are not paid until claims which are senior to them are paid in full.
[173] See n 152, 27.
[174] ibid, 28.
[175] ibid, 28.

Being able to rely on the DIF allows the FDIC to quickly and successfully access huge financing sources.[176] Nevertheless, this possibility is regarded as potentially capable of creating moral hazard.[177]

X. The FDIC Strategies

The FDIC primarily relies upon two tools, ie liquidation (sometimes also referred to as payoff) and P&A.[178] These tools can be used either singularly or together, depending on the estimated result arising from the application of the least cost principle. In addition, the FDIC can also set up a bridge bank with a view to facilitating resolution while preparing a P&A transaction or as an intermediate step preceding liquidation.[179]

Liquidation takes place when the FDIC pays creditors using the proceeds arising from the sale of assets. The payments can also occur in advance based on the FDIC's asset recovery estimates.[180]

This resolution method can be implemented in different ways.[181] Through the 'straight deposit payoff', the FDIC just pays insured depositors.[182] In such scenarios, it first gathers and then sells the bank's assets, remaining responsible for its liabilities as well as for the administrative costs of resolution. The FDIC can also transfer insured deposits to another bank to effect payoff ('insured deposit transfer').[183] The acquiring bank in this way acts as the FDIC's agent. When it is not possible to transfer deposits quickly, the FDIC can establish a deposit insurance national bank (DINB) to allow insured depositors to keep on accessing their deposits.[184]

Still, P&A is the most common resolution method adopted in the US and refers to a number of diverse transactions between the FDIC and acquiring institutions, which are usually other banks.[185] Its goal is to find another institution willing to take over some or all of the assets and liabilities of the failed bank, with or without financial support provided by the FDIC.[186]

In a basic P&A transaction, the acquiring institution acquires all the failed bank's insured deposits (and possibly uninsured deposits as well) along with its

[176] See n 163, 410.
[177] See n 152, 20.
[178] Qualifying liquidation as a resolution method differs from the EU setting where liquidation is often understood as the procedure to be initiated as an alternative to resolution when there are no public interest concerns at stake.
[179] See n 42, 587.
[180] See n 152, 21.
[181] See n 151, 6.
[182] See n 152, 10, underscoring that the terms 'liquidation' and 'pay off' are often used interchangeably.
[183] See n 42, 587.
[184] See n 152, 21, underscoring that the DINB is a temporary special-purpose bank with no capital, specifically established to pay off insured deposits.
[185] See n 151, 6.
[186] See n 152, 21.

most liquid assets. The acquiring bank is also given the option to buy a portfolio of loans or individual loans at book value within 30 days. Acquiring banks normally purchase deposits at a premium since they are considered a cheap and stable source of funding. This is particularly important as it lowers the cost of resolution for the FDIC compared to a straight payoff.[187] After the transfer, the FDIC is meant to liquidate the remaining assets and then pay the claims against the receivership.[188] Since the acquiring bank usually does not assume all of the bank's assets and liabilities, basic P&As might end up being more expensive than whole bank P&As due to greater upfront cash outlays and administrative burdens.[189]

On the other hand, whole bank P&As were the FDIC's preferred resolution method in the late 1980s, because the conditions of the banking sector had deteriorated and the FDIC ended up holding a significant amount of non-performing assets.[190] Such a strategy sometimes enabled the failing bank to bypass receivership altogether.[191] Although whole bank P&As require less cash and have lower administrative expenses upfront for the FDIC, sometimes they can turn out being more costly for the DIF.[192] This results from acquiring banks typically submitting negative bids aimed at covering the (negative) mismatch between assets and liabilities to transfer.[193]

In the context of a P&A, the FDIC can also accept sharing prospective losses on transferred assets with the acquiring bank using a negotiated formula.[194] In a loss-sharing agreement, the FDIC is usually expected to absorb 80 per cent of the losses, up to a cap. Acquiring banks may, on the other hand, offer to split the gains on transferred assets by issuing value recovery instruments to the FDIC.[195] The goal of a loss-sharing agreement is to transfer as many non-performing assets as possible to private sector acquirers 'in a manner that aligns the interests and incentives of the acquiring bank and the FDIC'.[196] The development of loss-sharing agreements was mainly motivated by the problems the FDIC faced in resolving large banks with complex commercial and real estate loan portfolios, due to the limited amount of time that potential acquirers were given to perform the due diligence.[197]

[187] See n 42, 588.
[188] See n 151, 6.
[189] See n 152, 22.
[190] ibid 22.
[191] Government Accountability Office, '1992 Bank Resolutions: FDIC Chose Methods Determined Least Costly, but Needs to Improve Process' GGD-94-107 (May 1994) 10.
[192] See n 42, 588.
[193] Federal Deposit Insurance Corporation, *Managing the Crisis: The FDIC and RTC Experience 1980–1994* (1998) 88, available at www.fdic.gov/bank/historical/managing/index.html.
[194] See n 151, 11, underscoring that during the global financial crisis, the FDIC used to offer a loss-sharing agreement whereby the acquiring institution was to accept a certain percentage of the losses, depending on the bid. They also note that 'shared loss assets' were usually distressed assets that without some incentive or protection from losses would not have raised the interest of potential acquirers.
[195] See n 152, 22.
[196] n 193, 96.
[197] n 152, 23.

Yet, the extent to which P&A transactions can be used to handle large institutions as well as in future financial crises is still uncertain, and indeed Washington Mutual has been so far the only significant recent precedent.[198]

The FDIC has also the authority to charter a bridge bank to facilitate P&A transactions and/or liquidation. Although bridge banks are rarely used, a notable example is the case of IndyMac during the global financial crisis.[199] The benefit that the creation of a bridge bank is expected to bring is mostly to provide the receiver with more time for conducting the due diligence as well as marketing activities.[200] If after the establishment of a bridge bank a P&A is put in place, the receiver transfers assets and liabilities three times. The first transfer is from the failed institution to the receivership, the second one is from the receivership to the bridge bank, and the final one is from the bridge bank to the acquiring bank. The conditions for the use of a bridge bank are typically met when the FDIC can show 'that the franchise value of the bank is greater than the marginal costs of operating the bridge bank'.[201]

XI. Concluding Remarks

The analysis of the Italian, UK and US frameworks and experiences provide valid arguments supporting the usefulness of the adoption of a special Union-wide harmonised regime dedicated to FOLF banks which do not meet the public interest test for resolution. The importance of the adoption of such a regime is also supported by the fact that several EU Member States still apply normal corporate insolvency proceedings, designed for non-financial firms, to FOLF banks.[202]

The objectives of this regime should not excessively diverge from the resolution objectives listed by the BRRD on the grounds that, despite the systemic nature of banks to place into resolution, most of their critical issues also feature small and medium-sized (non-systemic) banks that are not to be resolved. This results from the consideration that banks, regardless of their size, complexity and interconnectedness within the banking system, are special creatures. They are the depository of people's savings, payment intermediaries and the principal source of credit to the

[198] See Reuters, 'JPMorgan ends WaMu disputes with FDIC, to receive $645 million' (19 August 2016), available at www.reuters.com/article/us-jpmorgan-settlement-washing-mut-bk/jpmorgan-ends-wamu-disputes-with-fdic-to-receive-645-million-idUSKCN10U28M; Washington Mutual had assets amounting to US $307 billion when it failed in September of 2008. Its resolution caused substantial losses for its creditors and for the DIF, and also generated significant legal liability for its acquirer JP Morgan Chase.

[199] See n 152, 23.

[200] See n 42, 589.

[201] Federal Deposit Insurance Corporation, 'Resolutions Handbook, 2019', available at www.fdic.gov/bank/historical/reshandbook/resolutions-handbook.pdf.

[202] See n 34, 6, arguing that about one-third of the countries globally do not have bank-specific provisions in their insolvency legal framework. These countries include also mature economies such as France, Germany, Japan and Spain. Other developed countries, such as the UK and Ireland, have modified corporate insolvency regimes which apply to banks.

economy, especially in bank-dominated financial systems. Thus, the objectives of a special regime dedicated to FOLF banks which do not meet the public interest test for resolution should take into account such a special nature. Accordingly, while the primary objective of any corporate insolvency proceeding is to maximise the value of the insolvency estate to repay as many creditors as possible, a bank insolvency regime, because of the special characteristics of banks, should not only focus on this objective.[203] In this vein, depositor protection and financial stability, which are closely interconnected among each other, should be added to value maximisation among the objectives to pursue. The depositor protection objective, in turn, should not be limited to insured depositors but rather include the whole category of depositors. This position is justified in that in the context of liquidation, while insured depositors would only suffer a freeze of their funds until the DGS payout, non-insured depositors would be subject to uncertainties as to the timing and amount of the deposits they will recover. Yet, their inability to promptly access their funds may create destabilising effects and trigger a contagion.

Moreover, maintaining financial stability should also be one of the objectives to achieve. This argument rests on the assumption that financial stability issues might arise even in the event of small and medium-sized bank crises and are often difficult to foresee in advance as well as at the moment in which the crisis management procedure has to be started. Such issues are linked to the special nature of banks previously discussed. In other words, the crisis of a non-systemic bank can also harm the confidence in the system, even more so in peculiar situations, such as a negative phase of the business cycle, when the number of banks facing difficulties might be relatively high. In these situations, financial stability, at least at a regional level, could be at risk. Financial stability considerations, the protection of depositors as well as the monetary nature of bank liabilities (particularly deposits) are the main elements supporting the case for banking regulation, regardless of their size, complexity, systemic importance and interconnectedness within the system. The same considerations should then support the case for qualifying them as objectives of bank insolvency proceedings. In particular, including financial stability among the objectives of bank insolvency regimes is grounded in the important function that banks play in supporting the real economy, ie as transmission channels for monetary policy. An explicit reference to maintaining financial stability should then be included among the objectives of this regime, or, at least, financial stability should be treated as a minimum safeguard for the authorities involved to take into account when dealing with small and medium-sized bank crises. Disregarding entirely financial stability considerations might indeed lead

[203] Interestingly, while value preservation is not listed among the resolution objectives in the SRMR nor in the BRRD, Art 14(2) of the SRMR recognises that 'destruction of value' may be necessary to achieve the 'resolution objectives'; accordingly, it is stated that 'When pursuing the objectives referred to in the first subparagraph, the Board, the Council, the Commission and, where relevant, the national resolution authorities, shall seek to minimise the cost of resolution and avoid destruction of value unless necessary to achieve the resolution objectives'.

to suboptimal solutions and could also create a number of practical issues to those authorities which are mandated to contribute to keeping financial stability. The practical difficulty of including financial stability among the institutional objectives of bank insolvency regimes seems to be mostly an EU issue. The EU has in place a dual-track regime whereby the right procedure (resolution vis-à-vis liquidation) is chosen by resolution authorities on the basis of what is in the public interest. The latter in turn is mostly associated with financial stability, with the result being that resolution is understood as the procedure to initiate if financial stability is regarded as potentially threatened, while liquidation is commenced when authorities do not envisage financial stability concerns. However, as previously discussed, financial stability might be always affected by a bank crisis and often it is very difficult (if not impossible at all) to forecast in advance if a bank failure can impact on the stability of the system since counterparties' reactions cannot be precisely foreseen. That is one of the reasons why an argument against dual-track regimes is often advanced. In this regard, single-track regimes might be considered more effective in that they would pursue the same objectives irrespective of the institutions in crisis and the main difference would then relate to the crisis management strategies and tools designed and applied by the competent authorities.

From the institutional perspective, such regime should have an administrative nature and, accordingly, empower the resolution authorities to run the proceedings. The involvement of administrative authorities ensures expertise, sophisticated skills and access to bank-related information. As a result, administrative regimes are typically faster and allow authorities to take into due consideration public interest objectives, such as depositor protection and financial stability.

The triggers applied to initiate these proceedings should be designed based on the special nature of banks. As a consequence, they should have a forward-looking approach, as the ones which apply in resolution (particularly FOLF), and unlike the backward-looking ones which are typically used for initiating normal corporate insolvency proceedings. In this regard, triggers such as balance-sheet insolvency and illiquidity might be inadequate. As to the first of these, such a condition is met when liabilities already exceed the assets, and thus when the crisis has already reached a point of no-return. On the other hand, illiquidity can even be just a temporary issue that can be tackled with other tools, for instance emergency liquidity assistance provided by the central bank, without necessarily causing the bank to be liquidated and dissolved. In this vein, also triggers linked to serious regulatory breaches might prove particularly suitable. Such regulatory breaches would concern capital requirements, on one hand, and other violations of laws and regulations prompting the authorisation's withdrawal, on the other hand.[204]

[204] On this see International Association of Deposit Insurers, 'General Guidance for the Resolution of Bank Failures' (2005) 46, holding that a rule-based or statutory trigger mechanism for early intervention into the affairs of a troubled bank and for determining whether a bank has failed would be ideal. 'The trigger criteria should involve either quantitative or qualitative measures. The quantitative ratios

Relatedly, the use of the same triggers applied for resolution, apart from the public interest, would have a number of advantages. Firstly, they are forward-looking. Secondly, in dual-track regimes, such as the EU model, where two different crisis management procedures are available and the authorities are given the power to choose resolution according to EU law or liquidation according to national law (depending on what is in the public interest), a risk always exists for banks to end up in so-called limbo situations. The latter are those situations in which the conditions for resolution are met except for resolution being in the public interest; however, the conditions for initiating the insolvency proceedings are different pursuant to national law and the bank concerned ends up in a limbo where, despite being FOLF, it can be neither resolved nor liquidated. That is what happened in 2018 to ABLV Bank Luxembourg, which was placed into liquidation under Luxembourgish law more than one year after being declared FOLF by the ECB.[205] Such issue can be effectively tackled by aligning the triggers for resolution with the ones for insolvency proceedings, with the exception of the public interest that will be the element on the basis of which the authorities will decide on whether to resolve or liquidate the FOLF bank. A good point of reference to align the triggers is the Italian legislation, where the conditions for placing a bank either into resolution or into compulsory administrative liquidation are exactly the same, in that they are the result of the transposition of the BRRD. The only difference relates to the public interest, the lack of which determines that the procedure to activate is the compulsory administrative liquidation, on the grounds that such a procedure is considered by the authorities as able to reach the resolution objectives to the same extent as resolution.

Still, the initiation of the procedure should rest on a comprehensive assessment to be discretionarily conducted by the competent authorities. Discretion and

should include measures such as regulatory capital and asset quality. Qualitative indexes should include measures of management quality and any material breaches of standards of sound business and financial practices, violations of regulatory requirements, or the inability of a bank to fulfil its obligations resulting from the claims of depositors'.

[205] In 2018, ABLV Bank AS was declared FOLF by the European Central Bank; see European Central Bank, 'ECB determined ABLV Bank was failing or likely to fail' (24 February 2018), available at www.bankingsupervision.europa.eu/press/pr/date/2018/html/ssm.pr180224.en.html. Following the ECB's ruling, the SRB decided that the bank did not pose public interest concerns to justify resolution and thus it could be dealt with by the Latvian authorities according to national law; see Single Resolution Board, 'Notice summarising the decision taken in respect of ABLV Bank, AS' (2018), available at www.srb.europa.eu/en/system/files?file=media/document/20180223-summary_decision_-_latvia.pdf. The subsidiary established in Luxembourg, ABLV Bank Luxembourg SA, was also considered FOLF by the ECB and the SRB deemed resolution not to be needed. The Luxembourg resolution authority, CSSF, then requested to the local court both an order for the liquidation of ABLV Luxembourg SA and stay of proceedings procedure. The bank requested the court to order a stay of proceedings to give it enough time to orchestrate a takeover. The court found the application for the procedure of suspension of payment admissible and decided that the suspension should last for six months. The temporary administrators applied to the court on 5 October 2018 for an extension and an additional four months were granted for the sale of the bank to proceed. Due to the lack of interested purchasers, however, the bank was placed into judicial liquidation by judgment rendered on 2 July 2019 by the District Court of Luxembourg; on the ABLV case; see D Singh, *European Cross-Border Banking and Banking Supervision* (Oxford, Oxford University Press, 2020) 178.

flexibility are in fact particularly important when forward-looking and qualitative triggers have to be assessed.

Furthermore, on the grounds that this regime is to be regarded as a last resort measure, its initiation should also be based on the ascertained absence of alternatives. The alternatives to consider before placing a bank into these proceedings would relate to supervisory measures, including early intervention measures, and market alternatives, whereby other players are willing (*rectius* not willing) to acquire the bank concerned. The absence of such alternatives is to be determined by the authority empowered to start the procedure, or the burden of proof as to the presence of such alternatives could be placed on the bank concerned. This would simplify the role of the authorities also reducing the risk of their decisions being challenged before a law court.

Among the effects arising from the submission of a bank to this procedure should also be the authorisation withdrawal on the basis that the bank concerned should, as a result, be dissolved and exit the market. Yet, the continuation of the banking activity for a short period of time (typically some days/weeks) after the authorisation's withdrawal might be needed to achieve value maximisation, depositors' protection and thereby maintaining financial stability. This would be the case particularly when resolution-like tools are to be employed.

Building on the Italian, UK and US experiences, this new regime should ensure that the authorities have the power to transfer assets and liabilities from the FOLF bank to another institution at market prices. In addition, a bridge-bank-like tool and an asset-separation-like tool should be available as well. The availability of these tools is particularly important to maintain the stability of the system, protect depositors and reduce the destruction of value, as shown by the Italian, UK and US experiences.

All these tools might be very effective, despite also having some weaknesses. The transfer tool, to be financed by the DGS, will be useful when its costs are expected to be lower than the estimated loss for the DGS arising from a pay-out, but also when it is considered to be less disruptive compared to a pay-out and is deemed to be in the best interests of the bank's depositors.[206] On the other hand, a bridge-bank-like tool is expected to be useful when the bank concerned still has an attractive franchise, the value of which should be preserved while looking for acquirers willing to pay for it. Through this tool, the daily operations of the failed bank can be maintained, and this allows to gain time in the search for purchasers while keeping the organisation intact. The asset-separation like tool should be used when there are solid expectations that some particular assets (for example non-performing loans) can be more efficiently managed by specialised

[206] See on this International Association of Deposit Insurers, 'General Guidance for the Resolution of Bank Failures' (2005) 23, arguing that the same would hold true in cases where the liquidator is reluctant to proceed with the formal liquidation because either the failed bank is too large and thus no adequate funds would be available for reimbursement, or there is not enough time to market the bank's assets to potential acquirers as well as when the number of failed financial institutions is very large and the failures have occurred during a short period of time.

institutions, other than the bank in crisis. In this way, with a view to preserving value, such assets should be transferred to entities specialised in their management on the grounds that such a strategy would enable to recover more value to repay creditors. All in all, what really matters is that these tools are available according to the legal framework and are at the authorities' disposal. The authorities should then be given discretion in deciding on a case-by-case basis which tool(s) should be employed.

As to funding, while public support should be ruled out insofar as possible, the resources provided by deposit guarantee schemes are crucial, as further discussed in chapter six.

Yet, if administrative insolvency proceedings similar to the Italian and US ones were introduced at EU level, then the distinction between liquidation and resolution[207] could be seen as merely artificial, since the former could be regarded simply as one of the tools to apply, after the deployment of the others, to the residual parts of the FOLF bank.[208] The latter will be often just a near-empty entity in which only equity instruments and (mostly subordinated) debt instruments will be left within the liabilities side of the balance sheet after the deployment of resolution-like tools.[209] Such an interpretation would be in line with the Financial Stability Board's Key Attributes of Effective Resolution Regimes for Financial Institutions, where liquidation is listed among the resolution powers.[210] As a consequence, every FOLF bank would be resolved, in one way or another, and after the application of resolution (or resolution-like) tools, the residual (nearly empty) entity would be liquidated.[211]

In relation to the Italian experience before the transposition of the BRRD, it can be argued that a resolution-like procedure was typically activated to handle bank crises, ie that every FOLF was to be resolved. The main difference with the resolution regime currently in place is that creditors typically were not affected by burden-sharing (or bail-in or write-down) mechanisms, which means that only shareholders suffered losses along with the DGS (in compliance with the least-cost principle), the Bank of Italy extending loans with very low interest rates below market rates and, in cases involving systemic banks, the taxpayers, because of the public intervention.[212]

[207] See Restoy (n 48), arguing that this is not the case in many other jurisdictions outside the EU where such a distinction does not exist.

[208] See R Leckow, A Gullo and E Emre, 'Bank Resolution Frameworks: Key Legal Design Issues' in S Brodie (ed), *Bank Resolution Key Issues and Local Perspectives* (London, INSOL International, 2019) 31.

[209] See n 13, 253.

[210] Financial Stability Board, 'Key Attributes of Effective Resolution Regimes for Financial Institutions' (2014) 8, stating that 'Resolution authorities should have at their disposal a broad range of resolution powers, which should include powers to do the following: … (xii) Effect the closure and orderly wind-down (liquidation) of the whole or part of a failing firm with timely payout or transfer of insured deposits and prompt (for example, within seven days) access to transaction accounts and to segregated client funds)'.

[211] See also n 35, 7.

[212] See n 13, 254.

Nonetheless, in order for this special administrative regime to properly work and, so for the liquidation to be orderly, as provided by the BRRD, an active and leading role should be played by the DGSs. This is clearly shown by both the Italian and US experiences, where bank liquidations typically did not negatively affect the market because of the support granted by DGSs. Still, from this perspective a review of the EU legal framework concerning state aid measures and depositor preference is needed to permit DGSs to properly and effectively carry out their function through the optional measures, as discussed in chapter six.

Also, building on these considerations, an argument could be advanced in favour of converting the EU framework into a single-track regime similar, to a certain extent, to the US one, thereby removing the artificial distinction between resolution and liquidation. While such a conversion would address the issues arising from having to choose between resolution and liquidation, depending on the public interest test, still for a single-track regime to properly work centralisation of decision-making at EU level would be required. And, despite the expected achievable efficiencies, this seems to be still far from being wanted by Member States.

5

The Crisis of Systemic Institutions

Resolution and Orderly Liquidation Authority

I. Introduction

Many jurisdictions across the world found it difficult to respond to the violent impact of the global financial crisis of 2007–09 on banking and financial institutions as they lacked special legal regimes and effective tools. As a consequence, many failing banking and financial institutions were either submitted to normal corporate insolvency proceedings or rescued with public money. Both solutions are, however, often inefficient. While normal corporate insolvency proceedings are typically not suitable for banks, as discussed in chapter four, public rescues negatively impact the country's finance and generate moral hazard.[1]

Building on the lessons learned from the global financial crisis, the regulators of the most prominent jurisdictions within the G20 conducted a policy-driven debate about the introduction of new legal instruments which could help handle banks in crisis without using taxpayers' money.[2] This policy-driven debate led to the adoption by the Financial Stability Board (FSB) of the Key Attributes of Effective Resolution Regimes for Financial Institutions, which represent the new principle-based paradigm to effectively manage systemic bank crises.[3] The rationale behind the FSB's Key Attributes is to avoid using taxpayers' money to

[1] In this sense, International Monetary Fund, 'Resolution of Cross-Border Banks – A Proposed Framework for Enhanced Coordination' (2010) Policy Papers 3, outlined in 2010 that 'The recent financial crisis has given renewed urgency to the need for resolution systems for financial institutions, which both safeguard financial stability and limit moral hazard. However, experience demonstrates that these systems will not be effective unless progress is also made in developing a framework that applies on a cross-border basis. Since many systemically important financial groups operate globally, an uncoordinated application of resolution systems by national authorities will make it much more difficult to both secure the continuity of essential functions (thereby limiting contagion), and ensure that shareholders and creditors bear the financial burden of the resolution process'.

[2] See Financial Stability Board, 'Key Attributes of Effective Resolution Regimes for Financial Institutions' (2014) 3; see also WG Ringe, 'Bail-in between Liquidity and Solvency' (2016) 33 University of Oxford Legal Research Paper Series 5, who in this regard refers to the 'political will to end taxpayer-funded bailouts'.

[3] See Financial Stability Board (n 2) *passim*; see also Financial Stability Board, 'Key Attributes Assessment Methodology for the Banking Sector – Methodology for Assessing the Implementation

rescue banking institutions in crisis, while preserving financial stability. The Key Attributes set out the 12 core elements that the FSB considers to be necessary for a resolution regime to be effective on the grounds that 'their implementation should allow authorities to resolve financial institutions in an orderly manner without taxpayer exposure to loss from solvency support, while maintaining continuity of their vital economic functions'.[4] These 12 essential features relate to: scope; resolution authority; resolution powers; set-off, netting, collateralisation and segregation of client assets; safeguards; funding of firms in resolution; legal framework conditions for cross-border cooperation; crisis management groups; institution-specific cross-border cooperation agreements; resolvability assessment; recovery and resolution planning; and access to information and information-sharing.

According to the Key Attributes,

> an effective resolution regime (interacting with applicable schemes and arrangements for the protection of depositors, insurance policy holders and retail investors) should: i) ensure continuity of systemically important financial services, and payment, clearing and settlement functions; ii) protect, where applicable and in coordination with the relevant insurance schemes and arrangements such depositors, insurance policy holders and investors as are covered by such schemes and arrangements, and ensure the rapid return of segregated client assets; iii) allocate losses to firm owners (shareholders) and unsecured and uninsured creditors in a manner that respects the hierarchy of claims; iv) not rely on public solvency support and not create an expectation that such support will be available; v) avoid unnecessary destruction of value, and therefore seek to minimise the overall costs of resolution in home and host jurisdictions and, where consistent with the other objectives, losses for creditors; vi) provide for speed and transparency and as much predictability as possible through legal and procedural clarity and advanced planning for orderly resolution; vii) provide a mandate in law for cooperation, information exchange and coordination domestically and with relevant foreign resolution authorities before and during a resolution; viii) ensure that non-viable firms can exit the market in an orderly way; and ix) be credible, and thereby enhance market discipline and provide incentives for market-based solutions.[5]

of the Key Attributes of Effective Resolution Regimes for Financial Institutions in the Banking Sector' (2016) 1, where it is stated that 'The Key Attributes constitute an 'umbrella' standard for resolution regimes for all types of financial institutions. However, not all attributes are equally relevant for all sectors. Some KAs require adaptation and sector-specific interpretation of individual KAs. This document sets out a methodology to guide the assessment of a jurisdiction's compliance with the Key Attributes with respect to the banking sector'.

[4] ibid, 1 and 3, also remarking that 'the objective of an effective resolution regime is to make feasible the resolution of financial institutions without severe systemic disruption and without exposing taxpayers to loss, while protecting vital economic functions through mechanisms which make it possible for shareholders and unsecured and uninsured creditors to absorb losses in a manner that respects the hierarchy of claims in liquidation'.

[5] ibid, 3, also emphasising that 'jurisdictions should have in place a resolution regime that provides the resolution authority with a broad range of powers and options to resolve a firm that is no longer viable and has no reasonable prospect of becoming so. The resolution regime should include: i) stabilisation options that achieve continuity of systemically important functions by way of a sale or transfer of the shares in the firm or of all or parts of the firm's business to a third party, either directly or

As to scope, the resolution regime should apply to any financial institution that could be systemically significant or critical in the event of failure. The resolution regime should designate an administrative authority (or authorities) to be responsible for exercising the resolution powers over firms to resolve. Resolution should be initiated when a firm is no longer viable or likely to be no longer viable and has no reasonable prospect of returning to viability. The resolution regime should provide for timely and early entry into resolution before a firm is balance-sheet insolvent and before equity has been fully wiped out. Resolution authorities should have the powers to apply the resolution tools, including bail-in. Resolution powers should be exercised in a way that respects the hierarchy of claims while providing flexibility to deviate from the general principle of equal treatment of creditors of the same class (the *pari passu* principle), with transparency about the reasons for these departures. The justifications for such departures should be grounded in their necessity to contain the potential systemic impact of a firm's failure or to maximise the value for the benefit of all creditors. Yet, when departures from the *pari passu* principle take place, creditors should have a right to compensation where they do not receive at a minimum what they would have received in a liquidation of the firm under the applicable insolvency regime.

The Key Attributes envisage that the way to successfully resolve financial institutions without using taxpayers' money, while keeping financial stability, is to rely upon banks' internal resources, namely the ones which have been already provided by shareholders and creditors. Shareholders and creditors should, in other words, contribute to loss-absorption and recapitalisation of the institution in crisis. Shareholders' and creditors' involvement is regarded as the means to avoid (or at least reduce) the use of public resources. This new approach is motivated by the consideration that it is conceptually wrong and, thus unacceptable, to charge taxpayers for the losses suffered by a private entity to which they are not contractually linked. It is in fact hard to find a good reason to make taxpayers pay, in terms of future higher taxes, to rescue a bank with public money. This position is further reinforced by the consideration that such a strategy can encourage moral hazard.[6] In practical terms, a compromise has to be struck between two potentially conflicting goals, ie successfully handling bank crises without creating financial instability while avoiding the use of taxpayers' money in so doing. This compromise is hard to achieve because it is difficult to balance such conflicting goals.[7]

through a bridge institution, and/or an officially mandated creditor-financed recapitalisation of the entity that continues providing the critical functions; and ii) liquidation options that provide for the orderly closure and wind-down of all or parts of the firm's business in a manner that protects insured depositors, insurance policy holders and other retail customers'.

[6] See P Krugman, *The Return of Depression Economics and the Crisis of 2008* (New York, WW Norton, 2009) 63, who defines moral hazard as 'any situation in which one person makes the decision about how much risk to take, while someone else bears the cost if things go badly'.

[7] In this regard B Biljanovska, 'Aligning Market Discipline and Financial Stability: a More Gradual Shift from Contingent Convertible Capital to Bail-in Measures' (2016) 17 *European Business Organization Law Review* 105, 106, argues that 'market discipline and financial stability cannot be achieved simultaneously'.

To this end, the FSB's Key Attributes have introduced a new approach, which consists of charging the costs of a bank's crisis firstly on its shareholders and secondly on its creditors, through the so-called resolution tools, particularly bail-in. Although, typically, even shareholders and creditors are not responsible for the crisis of their banks, unlike taxpayers, the former decided to take up a risk when they bought shares and lent money to their bank. On the grounds that shareholders and creditors have deliberately taken such a risk, it is more appropriate that they bear losses in the event of their bank's crisis.[8]

Moving from this basis, this chapter discusses the resolution procedure in the EU and in the UK and the orderly liquidation authority in the US, since these are the procedures envisaged to be applied to handle FOLF systemic institutions.

II. Resolution in the EU

At EU level, the Key Attributes of the FSB have been transposed through the adoption of the BRRD in 2014, which introduced the tools to be employed by authorities in the context of a resolution procedure. Yet, in implementing the Key Attributes with the BRRD, the EU legislator has given resolution authorities the power to decide how to handle banks in crisis, by allowing them to choose, on the basis of a number of conditions, between resolution and liquidation, thereby designing a dual-track regime. As discussed in chapter four, the crisis management regime introduced with the BRRD is thus grounded in the dichotomy between resolution and liquidation.[9] Nonetheless, it can be rather difficult to understand in advance if the failure of a bank and its winding up under insolvency proceedings can or cannot reach the resolution objectives. This is to say that the choice between resolution and liquidation in practice might be a difficult one.[10] Relatedly, it is very difficult also to determine the right moment to intervene by submitting the failing bank to either resolution or liquidation, in that an excessively early intervention

[8] It is also sometimes said that, due to bail-in, shareholders and creditors are incentivized to keep their bank under control as they will bear the losses in case of failure.

[9] See R Lastra, C Russo and M Bodellini, 'Stock Take of the SRB's activities over the past years: What to Improve and Focus On?' (2019) Study requested by the ECON Committee of the European Parliament, 11.

[10] Some criteria to make this choice have been elaborated. The Bank of England has established some thresholds which act as a guide driving the choice between modified insolvency proceedings and resolution; such thresholds are: the amount of assets exceeding £15 billion; and a number of transactional accounts exceeding £40,000; see Bank of England, 'The Bank of England's approach to setting a minimum requirement for own funds and eligible liabilities (MREL)', Responses to Consultation and Statement of Policy (2016) 14, available at www.bankofengland.co.uk/financialstability/Documents/resolution/mrelpolicy2016.pdf. However, in 2015, the Bank of Italy submitted to resolution a bank (Carichieti) with just €4.7 billion of assets on the implicit assumption that such a crisis had be handled in the context of resolution because public interests were at stake; see Banca d'Italia, 'Information on the resolution of Banca Marche, Banca Popolare dell'Etruria e del Lazio, CariChieti and Cassa di Risparmio di Ferrara crisis' (2015), *passim*, available at www.bancaditalia.it/media/approfondimenti/2015/info-soluzione-crisi/info-banche-en.pdf?language_id=1.

can wrongly harm shareholders, whereas an excessively late intervention can wrongly damage creditors and, in serious situations, even the system as a whole.[11]

Resolution is an administrative procedure which is defined by the BRRD as the application of resolution tools by a resolution authority in order to achieve one or more resolution objectives.[12] The resolution objectives that should be achieved with the resolution procedure, in turn, are: to ensure the continuity of critical functions; to avoid a significant adverse effect on the financial system, in particular by preventing contagion, including to market infrastructures, and by maintaining market discipline; to protect public funds by minimising reliance on extraordinary public financial support; to protect depositors covered by Directive 2014/49/EU and investors covered by Directive 97/9/EC; and to protect client funds and client assets.[13]

In practice, resolution can be regarded as a reorganisation procedure which differs from liquidation since its main objective is to keep the fundamental operations of a failing bank working.[14] To this end, the debts of the institution are restructured on the basis of what the resolution authorities decide in light of an evaluation to be provided by an independent expert.[15] The underlying assumption is that a reduction of liabilities can enable equalisation of the negative difference between their value and the value of the assets that has been caused by the previous losses recorded by the bank. In a similar fashion, resolution has been described as an 'administrative process in which the goal is to protect the liquidity needs of short-term creditors, especially depositors, and to manage financial assets in a way that preserves their value and the franchise value of the failing institutions'[16] and as 'an umbrella term that describes the process of handling a distress bank, based on the objective of minimizing the societal costs of a bank failure'.[17]

A bank is submitted to resolution when: the institution is considered to be FOLF; having regard to timing and other relevant circumstances, there is no reasonable prospect that any alternative private sector measures, including measures by an IPS, or supervisory action, including early intervention measures or the write-down or conversion of relevant capital instruments and eligible liabilities

[11] See C Goodhart, 'Multiple Regulators and Resolutions', Paper presented at the Federal Reserve Bank of Chicago Conference on Systemic Financial Crisis: Resolving Large Bank Insolvencies (30 September – 1 October 2004), *passim*, emphasising that 'the window of opportunity between closing a bank so early that the owners may sue and so late that the depositors may sue may have become vanishingly small'.

[12] Article 2(1)(1) of the BRRD.

[13] Article 31(2) of the BRRD.

[14] See J Armour, 'Making Bank Resolution Credible' (2015) *Oxford Handbook of Financial Regulation* 471.

[15] This means that the power that resolution authorities can exercise in relation to the application of the bail-in tool is relevant; for this reason; E Ferran, 'European Banking Union: Imperfect but It Can Work' (2014) Legal Studies Research, Paper Series, University of Cambridge, 14, defined such a power as 'near-dictatorial'.

[16] See n 14, 453.

[17] See Ringe (n 2) 7.

taken in respect of the institution, would prevent the failure of the institution within a reasonable timeframe; and a resolution action is necessary in the public interest.[18] And in this regard, a resolution action shall be treated as in the public interest if it is necessary for the achievement of and is proportionate to one or more of the resolution objectives, while the winding up of the institution under normal insolvency proceedings would not meet those resolution objectives to the same extent.[19]

Resolution and winding up under normal insolvency proceedings are thus the two alternative procedures to start in the event of a bank becoming FOLF. The *discrimen* on the basis of which the ensuing decision is to be made consists of the presence of a public interest to safeguard through resolution action or its lack thereof. In other words, public interest is the key element guiding resolution authorities in deciding whether to resolve or to liquidate a FOLF institution.[20] According to the BRRD, the default option is the submission of FOLF institutions to winding up through normal insolvency proceedings pursuant to the law of the Member States where such institutions are established. This aspect has been further reiterated by the recently introduced Article 32b of the BRRD,[21] stating that Member States shall ensure that a FOLF institution in relation to which the resolution authority considers that all the conditions for resolution are met, except for the resolution action being in the public interest, shall be wound up in an orderly manner in accordance with the applicable national law. However, if and when winding up is not considered able to achieve the resolution objectives to the same extent as resolution, then the authorities are meant to resolve the FOLF institution.[22] A clear understanding of the concept of public interest and its consistent interpretation are therefore crucial.[23] We argued elsewhere that 'public interest in this context seems to be principally connected with the need to maintain financial stability, or in negative terms, to avoid instability'.[24] Arguably, resolution authorities have been given the difficult task of ascertaining *ex ante* whether the crisis of a bank and its possible winding up could create financial instability (*rectius* whether winding up can achieve the resolution objectives to the same extent as resolution).[25] Against this backdrop, we argued in favour of the introduction of some thresholds above which the public interest is implicitly presumed and therefore resolution should be initiated. Such thresholds could indeed bring greater

[18] Article 32(1) of the BRRD.
[19] Article 32(5) of the BRRD.
[20] See n 9, 10.
[21] This Article has been introduced within the BRRD by Directive (EU) 2019/879 of the European Parliament and of the Council of 20 May 2019 (BRRD 2) [2019] OJ L150/1.
[22] See M Bodellini, 'To Bail-In, or to Bail-Out, that is the Question' (2018) 19 *European Business Organization Law Review* 373, *passim*.
[23] See M Bodellini, 'Impediments to resolvability: critical issues and challenges ahead' (2019) II *Open Review of Management Banking, and Finance* 52.
[24] See n 9, 11.
[25] See KP Wojcik, 'Bail-in in the Banking Union' (2016) 53 *Common Market Law Review* 98, emphasising that this assessment requests a significant amount of discretion.

legal certainty and proportionally reduce the risk of litigation.[26] Thus, reliance on automatic thresholds could provide some more precise indication of what 'public interest' actually means and when such a criterion is in fact met. Obviously, these thresholds would limit the discretion granted to the resolution authorities, since they would be in this way driven in their decision-making process.[27] Yet, the key advantage would be to identify well in advance the crisis management procedure to initiate in the event of an institution being determined as FOLF.[28] This in turn could reduce the grounds for litigation and from a more general perspective such thresholds could help remove potential impediments to resolvability.[29]

The importance of a clear understanding and consistent interpretation of the concept of public interest is one of the reasons why the Single Resolution Board (SRB) published a paper outlining its approach to the Public Interest Assessment (PIA).[30] The PIA is conducted to determine whether the resolution of a FOLF institution is needed in the public interest. To this end, the SRB paper provides precise procedural guidelines that should drive the decision-making process.

The paper outlines that in performing the PIA, the SRB starts by assessing

> whether liquidation under insolvency proceedings would be likely to put the resolution objectives at risk … If the resolution objectives are deemed at risk, the SRB then assesses the expected effects of the chosen resolution strategy and compares such effects with those of winding up the bank under insolvency proceedings.[31]

It also identifies the key elements to consider when assessing whether the failure of a bank could have significant adverse effects on financial stability; these elements are in fact the risk of contagion and the effects of the potential action on market discipline.[32]

The SRB paper is certainly very useful as it discloses the different phases of the process that the SRB undergoes when assessing whether the resolution of a given institution is in the public interest and thus needed should such institution be FOLF. Hence, the publication of these guidelines is particularly helpful as they will likely reduce inconsistencies among decisions adopted in managing bank

[26] See n 9, 11.

[27] ibid, 11.

[28] ibid, 11, where we underline that a similar approach has been developed by the Bank of England, that 'considers that provision of fewer than around 40,000 to 80,000 transactional bank accounts (accounts from which withdrawals have been made nine or more times within a three-month period) is generally likely to indicate that a modified insolvency would be appropriate'; see Bank of England (n 10) 5.

[29] See n 23, 53.

[30] See Single Resolution Board, 'Public Interest Assessment: SRB Approach' (2019) 6, available at www.srb.europa.eu, where it is stated that the SRB approach to the PIA for the banks under its remit has been developed by the SRB itself in close collaboration with the National Resolution Authorities and in consultation with the European Central Bank in order to ensure a level playing field in the Banking Union.

[31] ibid, 7.

[32] ibid, 8.

crises in the Banking Union, and possibly beyond.[33] Nonetheless, the concept of public interest is still poorly defined, and, as a result, potentially subject to different interpretations by different authorities as well as by the same authority in different periods.

Against this background, some years after the adoption of the BRRD and the creation of the Banking Union, with the SRB empowered to manage the crisis of banks under the supervisory remit of the ECB within the SSM as well as cross-border banking groups, it seems that the authorities would submit to resolution mainly large, complex and interconnected banks should they be determined as FOLF.[34] Hence, even several significant banks under direct supervision of the ECB within the SSM and cross-border banking groups would be liquidated according to their national laws should they become FOLF, as the cases of Veneto Banca and Banca Popolare di Vicenza showed in 2017.[35] Yet, the two recent cases of Sberbank d.d. and Sberbank banka d.d. in Croatia and Slovenia (further discussed in section VIII of this chapter) showed that in making the choice between resolution and liquidation, authorities should also pay special attention to the conditions of the national banking system and the domestic legal framework for bank winding up as they might cause themselves the need for resolution.[36] In other words, even smaller banks might need to be resolved because, due to the size of the banking system where they operate and/or the features of the winding-up legal framework in their country, their liquidation might prove unable to reach the resolution objectives. This means that banks with a similar size, level of complexity and business model could be orderly wound up in some countries, while not being able to be effectively liquidated in other countries due to exogenous factors.

On these grounds, it can also be argued that the introduction in the EU framework of the concept of public interest, the protection of which could lead to the start of a resolution procedure (as discussed in chapter four) has expanded the scope of application of resolution as envisaged in the FSB Key Attributes, which focus on institutions that are systemically significant or critical in failure. Accordingly, in the EU the resolution procedure should be activated when winding up pursuant to national insolvency proceedings would not reach the resolution objectives to the same extent. On these grounds, smaller institutions might have to be resolved if their winding up would not ensure primarily the continuity of critical functions and the avoidance of significant adverse effects on the financial system. Yet, this,

[33] See n 23, 53.

[34] See J Dias, C Deslandes and M Magnus, 'Recent measures for Banca Carige from a BRRD and State Aid perspective' European Parliament Briefing (2019) 7.

[35] See n 22, 386.

[36] On 1 March 2022, the SRB decided that resolution was not necessary for the Austrian parent of Sberbank Europe AG and accordingly the insolvency procedures would be carried out according to national law; see Single Resolution Board, 'Sberbank Europe AG: Croatian and Slovenian subsidiaries resume operations after being sold while no resolution action is required for Austrian parent company', Press release (1 March 2022), available at www.srb.europa.eu/en/content/sberbank-europe-ag-croatian-and-slovenian-subsidiaries-resume-operations-after-being-sold.

irrespective of the institution concerned, could be influenced by the features of the domestic banking system and the characteristics of the national legal frameworks for their liquidation. In this vein, as mentioned, Sberbank d.d. in Croatia and Sberbank banka d.d. in Slovenia were resolved by the SRB despite having a limited size in absolute terms, while their holding bank company, significantly larger as to the amount of assets, was liquidated pursuant to Austrian law. While the failure of the latter was regarded as unable to lead to the disruption of services essential to the real economy of Austria and to the disruption of financial stability in Austria or in other Member States, resolution action was needed with regard to the two subsidiaries to avoid significant adverse effects on financial stability. Clearly, in these three cases the SRB's decisions were significantly affected by both the size and characteristics of the Austrian, Croatian and Slovenian banking systems and the features of their domestic legal frameworks for bank liquidation.

The SRB's policy position could, nevertheless, also influence the decisions of national resolution authorities (NRAs) that might consider it inappropriate to submit less significant banks, under their direct remit, to resolution according to the domestic law transposing the BRRD, provided that significant banks under the remit of the SRB would be wound up in the event of being FOLF. In this regard, today, the four small-sized Italian banks (Banca delle Marche, Banca Popolare dell'Etruria, Cassa di Risparmio di Ferrara and Cassa di Risparmio di Chieti), which were resolved by the Bank of Italy in 2015,[37] would likely be wound up, or differently handled in the context of special administration, as a consequence of the 2017 SRB's decision not to resolve Veneto Banca and Banca Popolare di Vicenza due to the alleged lack of a public interest to do so.[38] These four cases are further discussed in section V.B of this chapter.

III. The Resolution Tools

In defining the term 'resolution', the BRRD emphasises that such administrative procedure consists of the application of resolution tools to a FOLF bank.[39] In turn, resolution tools are regulated as the legal instruments that resolution authorities are empowered to apply, individually (with the exception of the asset separation tool) or in combination, to a FOLF bank submitted to resolution in order to achieve one or more resolution objectives. The resolution tools introduced by the BRRD are: the sale of business tool; the bridge institution tool; the asset separation tool; and the bail-in tool.[40]

[37] See M Bodellini, 'Greek and Italian "lessons" on bank restructuring: is precautionary recapitalization the way forward?' (2017) 19 *Cambridge Yearbook of European Legal Studies* 151.
[38] See n 22, 387.
[39] Article 2(1)(1) of the BRRD.
[40] Article 37(3) of the BRRD.

The sale of business tool is the mechanism through which the resolution authority transfers shares or other instruments of ownership issued by an institution under resolution, or its assets, rights or liabilities to a purchaser that is not a bridge institution.[41] Such a purchaser will typically be another bank. The effectiveness of this tool rests on the fact that the transfer takes place without obtaining the consent of the shareholders of the institution under resolution or of any third party other than the purchaser and without complying with key procedural requirements under company or securities law. Importantly, such transfer shall be made on commercial terms. This means that the sale of assets and liabilities (or of the shares) shall not take place at liquidation prices which are typically discounted. By doing so, the value destruction often resulting from the sale of assets at liquidation prices can be avoided. This in turn should protect the interests of the involved stakeholders.[42] When applying the sale of business tool, authorities should make arrangements for the marketing of that institution or part of its business in an open, transparent and non-discriminatory process, while aiming to maximise, as far as possible, the sale price.[43]

The bridge institution tool is the mechanism for transferring shares or other instruments of ownership issued by an institution under resolution or its assets, rights or liabilities to a bridge institution.[44] A bridge institution, in turn, is a legal person that is: wholly or partially owned by one or more public authorities, which may include the resolution authority or the resolution financing arrangement and is controlled by the resolution authority; and is created for the purpose of receiving and holding some or all of the shares or other instruments of ownership issued by an institution under resolution or some or all of its assets, rights and liabilities, with a view to maintaining access to critical functions and selling the institution itself at a later stage.[45] Importantly, what makes the transfer of assets and liabilities to a bridge institution a powerful tool is that such transfer takes place without obtaining the consent of the shareholders of the institutions under resolution or of any third party other than the bridge institution itself, and without complying with any procedural requirements under company or securities law.[46] Yet, the total value of liabilities transferred to the bridge institution cannot exceed the total value of

[41] Article 2(1)(58) of the BRRD.

[42] In this regard, under Art 38(4) of the BRRD it is provided that 'any consideration paid by the purchaser shall benefit: a) the owners of the shares or other instruments of ownership, where the sale of business has been effected by transferring shares or instruments of ownership issued by the institution under resolution from the holders of those shares or instruments to the purchaser; b) the institution under resolution, where the sale of business has been effected by transferring some or all of the assets or liabilities of the institution under resolution to the purchaser'.

[43] Recital 61 to the BRRD also states that 'where, for reasons of urgency, such a process is impossible, authorities should take steps to redress detrimental effects on competition and on the internal market'.

[44] Article 2(1)(60) of the BRRD.

[45] Article 2(1)(59) and Art 40(2) of the BRRD.

[46] Article 40(1) of the BRRD.

the rights and assets transferred from the institution under resolution or provided by other sources.[47] Clearly, the reason for such a limitation is to avoid placing any undue financial burden on a publicly controlled institution. In any case, it is provided that any consideration paid by the bridge institution shall benefit: the owners of the shares or instruments of ownership, where the transfer has been effected by transferring shares or instruments of ownership issued by the institution under resolution from the holders of those shares or instruments; and the institution under resolution, where the transfer to the bridge institution has been effected by transferring some or all of its assets or liabilities.[48] The main purpose of the bridge institution is to ensure that essential financial services continue to be provided to the clients of the failing institution and that essential financial activities continue to be performed. The bridge institution should be operated as a viable going concern and be put back on the market when conditions are appropriate and within two years. If that is not possible or the institution is not viable, then it should be wound up.[49]

The asset separation tool is the mechanism through which a resolution authority transfers assets, rights or liabilities of an institution under resolution to an asset management vehicle.[50] In turn, an asset management vehicle is defined as a legal person that: is wholly or partially owned by one or more public authorities, which may include the resolution authority or the resolution financing arrangement, and is controlled by the resolution authority; and has been created for the purpose of receiving some or all of the assets, rights and liabilities of one or more institutions under resolution or a bridge institution.[51] The asset separation tool can only be applied together with another resolution tool.[52] As in the case of the sale of business tool and the bridge institution tool, the effectiveness of the asset separation tool arises from the transfer of assets and liabilities to the asset management vehicle taking place without having to obtain the consent of the shareholders of the institutions under resolution, or of any third party other than the asset management vehicle, and without having to comply with any procedural requirements under company or securities law.[53] The economic benefits which can result from the application of this tool arise from the consideration that the asset management vehicle is expected to manage the transferred assets with a view to maximising their value through their eventual sale or an orderly wind down.[54] This goal can be achieved on the grounds that the management of these assets can benefit from

[47] Article 40(3) of the BRRD.
[48] Article 40(4) of the BRRD.
[49] Recital 65 of the BRRD.
[50] Article 2(1)(55) of the BRRD.
[51] Article 42(2) of the BRRD.
[52] Article 37(5) of the BRRD.
[53] Article 42(1) of the BRRD.
[54] Article 42(3) of the BRRD.

a longer-term timeframe, and also because the asset management vehicle is not subject to the strict capital requirements which apply to banks. By so doing, the value of the transferred assets should be preserved to the benefit of the involved stakeholders. Accordingly, the BRRD provides some conditions to comply with in order for the asset management vehicle tool to be applied. Such resolution tool can be in fact employed only if: the situation of the particular market for those assets is of such a nature that their liquidation under normal insolvency proceedings could have an adverse effect on one or more financial markets; such a transfer is necessary to ensure the proper functioning of the institution under resolution or bridge institution; or such a transfer is necessary to maximise liquidation proceeds.[55] As to the consideration paid by the asset-management vehicle to buy assets and liabilities from the institution under resolution, the inherent price is to be determined by the resolution authority and can also have nominal or negative value.[56]

The bail-in tool is the mechanism through which a resolution authority exercises write-down and/or conversion powers in relation to liabilities of an institution under resolution.[57] The bail-in tool can be applied in order to recapitalise an institution under resolution to the extent sufficient to restore its ability to comply with the conditions for authorisation and to continue to carry out the activities for which it is authorised and to sustain sufficient market confidence. It can also be applied to convert to equity or reduce the principal amount of claims or debt instruments that are transferred: to a bridge institution with a view to providing capital for that bridge institution; or under the sale of business tool or the asset separation tool.[58] The application of the bail-in tool to the FOLF bank's liabilities requests the previous write-down or conversion of its capital instruments.[59]

[55] Article 42(5) of the BRRD.

[56] Article 42(6) of the BRRD; also, Art 42(7) of the BRRD states, in this regard, that 'any consideration paid by the asset management vehicle in respect of the assets, rights or liabilities acquired directly from the institution under resolution shall benefit the institution under resolution. Consideration may be paid in the form of debt issued by the asset management vehicle'.

[57] Article 2(1)(57) of the BRRD.

[58] Article 43(2) of the BRRD.

[59] As to the write-down or conversion of capital instruments, Art 37(2) of the BRRD states that 'where a resolution authority decides to apply a resolution tool to an institution and that resolution action would result in losses being borne by creditors or their claims being converted, the resolution authority shall exercise the power to write down and convert capital instruments immediately before or together with the application of the resolution tool'. In this regard, Art 60(1) of the BRRD provides that 'resolution authorities shall exercise the write down or conversion power in accordance with the priority of claims under normal insolvency proceedings, in a way that produces the following results: a) Common Equity Tier 1 items are reduced first in proportion to the losses and to the extent of their capacity and the resolution authority takes one or both of the actions specified in Article 47(1) in respect of holders of Common Equity Tier 1 instruments; b) the principal amount of Additional Tier 1 instruments is written down or converted into Common Equity Tier 1 instruments or both, to the extent required to achieve the resolution objectives set out in Article 31 or to the extent of the capacity of the relevant capital instruments, whichever is lower; c) the principal amount of Tier 2 instruments is written down or converted into Common Equity Tier 1 instruments or both, to the extent required to achieve the resolution objectives set out in Article 31 or to the extent of the capacity of the relevant capital instruments, whichever is lower'.

For this reason, the discussion on the bail-in tool below also encompasses references to the preliminary write-down and conversion of capital instruments that have to precede the application of resolution tools, causing losses to creditors or determining their claims to be converted. In this work, all these tools are referred to as bail-in since their way of working is substantially equivalent, although the bail-in tool *stricto sensu* only applies to liabilities.

The bail-in tool is certainly the most powerful, yet controversial, resolution tool.[60] Its main features and criticalities are discussed in the following paragraphs.

IV. Bail-in

Bail-in can be seen as one of the most effective ways to comply with the FSB's Key Attributes, requesting the management of a bank crisis to be conducted without using public funds, while maintaining financial stability. In other words, one of the main reasons for the introduction of the bail-in tool within the EU legal framework was to end, or at least reduce, the use of taxpayers' money in managing bank crises.[61] This was also one of the most important lessons learned from the global financial crisis of 2007–09, during and after which many EU Member States rescued their domestic banks with expensive public bail-outs.[62] The strategy to bail out banking and financial institutions caused the public finance of such Member States to significantly deteriorate, seriously impacting even the stock of their public debt.[63]

[60] See JH Sommer, 'Why bail-in? And how?' (2014) 20 *Economic Policy Review* 208, arguing that Wilson Ervin, a banker working for Credit Suisse, developed the concept of bail-in.

[61] This is underlined also in Recital 1 of the BRRD, where it is said that during the crisis Member States were forced to rescue banking institutions by using taxpayers' money; see on this I Kokkoris and R Olivares-Caminal, 'The Operation of the Single Resolution Mechanism in the Context of the EU State aid Regime' in JH Binder and D Singh (eds), *Bank Resolution: the European Regime* (Oxford, Oxford University Press, 2016) 316; see Ringe (n 2) 3, who defines as fundamental the objective of bail-in to avoid taxpayers' rescues of banking institutions; see also E Avgouleas and C Goodhart, 'Critical Reflections on Bank Bail-ins' (2015) 1 *Journal of Financial Regulation* 3, 4, arguing that bail-in aims to protect taxpayers by avoiding expensive public bailouts.

[62] Between 2008 and 2015, the EU Commission approved state aid measures for the financial sector (including guarantees, asset relief interventions, capital injections and liquidity measures) amounting to €4.966 trillion; see European Commission, 'State Aid Scoreboard 2016', available at www.ec.europa.eu/competition/state_aid/scoreboard/index_en.html.

[63] See European Central Bank, 'The Fiscal Impact of Financial Sector Support During the Crisis' (2015) ECB Economic Bulletin, Article 80, available at www.ecb.europa.eu/pub/pdf/other/eb201506_article02.en.pdf?fadae43a45a35a30cd17d3213277042d, stating that 'general government debt in the euro area increased by 4.8% of GDP over the period from 2008 to 2014 owing to financial sector assistance … The debt impact of financial sector support varied considerably across countries. Financial sector support led to a substantial increase in government debt of around 20% of GDP in Ireland, Greece, Cyprus and Slovenia. It also had a high impact in Germany, especially owing to measures taken at the onset of the crisis, and in Austria and Portugal, mainly as a result of more recent interventions. By contrast, government debt in Italy and France was hardly affected by financial sector support'.

Bail-in is conceptually the opposite of bail-out,[64] as the losses of an institution in crisis are not borne by taxpayers, but rather by its shareholders and creditors.[65] In this vein, bail-in has been described as a 'third way' – between the provision of liquidity by central banks to banks that are illiquid and the winding down of insolvent institutions – to handle a failing bank without public money.[66] Bail-in can also be understood as a mechanism to allow a FOLF institution to return to viability without relying upon taxpayers' money.[67]

Bail-in is undoubtedly the most powerful yet intrusive resolution tool, as well as the most relevant legal innovation introduced by the BRRD, as the other resolution tools (or instruments equivalent to them) were already known and commonly used, at least, in some jurisdictions around the globe.[68] The effectiveness of bail-in is in its ability to provide fresh value to the institution under resolution by eliminating shareholders' and creditors' rights. From this point of view, the write-down of capital instruments and liabilities and their conversion into capital can be regarded as provision of fresh value in terms of fewer debts to repay in the future.[69]

Still, although the introduction of bail-in has to be seen positively from a restructuring perspective, in some circumstances such a tool may be insufficient in resolving a bank, ie to achieve the resolution objectives. In such cases, the use of taxpayers' money is still likely to be needed. For this reason, it seems misleading to regard bail-in as the definitive replacement of bail-out.[70] Most likely the two tools will have to be jointly applied in order to successfully handle complicated bank crises. Yet, the new crisis management approach will have to be more mindful as to the position of taxpayers than in the past. And in this regard, bail-in is undoubtedly a significant improvement in that the write-down of capital and debt instruments of the FOLF bank and/or their conversion into capital mean there can be a reduction in the amount of external resources needed to handle its crisis.[71]

Yet, alongside arguments supporting the effectiveness and the importance of bail-in are also arguments against it, which demand caution when applying this

[64] See F Lupo-Pasini and RP Buckley, 'International Coordination in Cross-Border Bank Bail-ins: Problems and Prospects' (2015) 16 *European Business Organization Law Review* 208, arguing that a bail-out occurs when 'it is the government – usually the Treasury – that rescues the failing bank through the use of taxpayers' money'.

[65] Recital 5 to the BRRD states that 'the regime should ensure that shareholders bear losses first and that creditors bear losses after shareholders, provided that no creditor incurs greater losses than it would have incurred if the institution had been wound up under normal insolvency proceedings in accordance with the no creditor worse off principle as specified in this Directive'.

[66] See Ringe (n 2) 3.

[67] See C Bates and S Gleeson, 'Legal Aspects of Bank Bail-ins' (2011) 5 *Law and Financial Markets Review* 264.

[68] See JR LaBrosse, 'International Experience and Policy Issues in the Growing Use of Bridge Banks' in JR LaBrosse et al (eds), *Financial Crisis Management and Bank Resolution* (London, Informa Law from Routledge, 2009) 222.

[69] See n 22, 367.

[70] See Ringe (n 2) 19, pointing out that bail-in was perceived as a substitute to bail-out.

[71] See T Conlon and J Cotter, 'Anatomy of a bail-in' (2014) 14 *Journal of Financial Stability* 257, pointing out that the use of bail-in during the global financial crisis would have permitted to significantly reduce the amount of taxpayers' money needed to rescue failing banks.

intrusive resolution tool. The sections below discuss arguments both in favour of and against bail-in.

A. The Arguments Supporting the Application of the Bail-in Tool

The arguments in favour of bail-in rest primarily on its undebatable effectiveness as a restructuring tool, which could in turn reduce the need for public bail-outs. This line of thinking is enhanced by the consideration that there are very few reasons justifying the decision to make taxpayers bear the costs of rescuing banks. Such residual reasons would relate to the general interest of avoiding contagion[72] and the consequent financial instability that a bank's failure can potentially create through the so-called domino effect,[73] which could harm the public and thus taxpayers as well. Yet, it is worth noting that the position of shareholders and creditors is completely different from that of taxpayers. Shareholders decide to take up the risk of their company's failure. And if their company fails, they lose the money they have invested by buying shares. This is one of the founding principles of both company law and insolvency law.[74] Even for creditors, the argument is substantially equivalent. When an investor decides to lend money to a company by buying its bonds, they implicitly accept the so-called counterparty risk, ie that if the borrower fails, the investor foregoes the chance to get their money back.[75] On these grounds, making shareholders and creditors pay for the crisis of their bank is coherent and consistent with the general principles governing company law and insolvency law as well as their personal position in view of the risks they have freely chosen to take up.[76]

The relevance of bail-in results from the assumption that it could be used in an increasing number of resolution procedures, since other resolution tools in and of themselves might be insufficient to effectively resolve a bank. This argument can be derived from the conditions which have to be met in order to start resolution. These conditions relate to the institution being FOLF, the absence of

[72] Article 3 of the Commission Delegated Regulation (EU) 2016/860 of 4 February 2016 distinguishes between: direct contagion which is 'a situation where the direct losses of counterparties of the institution under resolution, resulting from the write-down of the liabilities of the institution, lead to the default or likely default for those counterparties in the imminent'; and indirect contagion which is 'a situation where the write-down or conversion of institution's liabilities causes a negative reaction by market participants that leads to a severe disruption of the financial system with potential to harm the real economy'.

[73] See M Bodellini, 'From Systemic Risk to Financial Scandals: the Shortcomings of U.S. Hedge Fund Regulation' (2017) 11 *Brooklyn Journal of Corporate Financial & Commercial Law* 432.

[74] Even more in general, Avgouleas and Goodhart (n 61) 3, argue that 'one of the key principles of a free-market economy is that owners and creditors are supposed to bear the losses of a failed venture'.

[75] In addition, Biljanovska (n 7) 121, argues that the mandatory involvement of shareholders and creditors in the losses can make them more active in controlling their bank.

[76] See n 22, 372.

credible private alternatives to solve the crisis[77] and the benefits in terms of public interest that the resolution is expected to bring. Importantly, the fact that the bank is failing or likely to fail entails that it:

- infringes or is likely to infringe in the near future the capital requirements required to obtain and maintain the authorisation;
- its assets already are or are likely to be in the near future less than its liabilities (which is balance-sheet insolvency);
- it already is, or is likely to be, in the near future unable to pay its debts (which can be balance-sheet insolvency and/or illiquidity); and/or
- extraordinary public financial support has been required.[78]

If a bank meets these conditions then arguably it is already in a very difficult position, since it has already lost (or it is about to lose) its capital adequacy and/or it already is (or is about to be) balance-sheet insolvent, having fewer assets than liabilities and/or is illiquid (or balance-sheet insolvent), being unable to pay its debts as they fall due and/or has requested public financial assistance.[79] Against this backdrop, the bridge bank tool, the asset separation tool and the sale of business tool, despite certainly being helpful, are unlikely to be sufficient, in that they mainly introduce some reorganisation measures, but do not provide substantial additional value or fresh financial resources. Although almost the same can be argued with regard to bail-in, which similarly does not provide fresh financial resources, the main difference is that the latter allows the clearing of the capital and reduces the liabilities of the FOLF bank by writing them down or converting them into capital, with the consequent effect of absorbing previous losses and recapitalising the institution. From a balance-sheet perspective, this is equivalent to an increase of the entity's assets.[80]

[77] These private sector measures include the early intervention powers of the authorities and the write down of Common Equity Tier 1 and/or the writedown and/or conversion of Additional Tier 1 and Tier 2 capital instruments according to Art 59 of the BRRD; in this regard see M Schillig, 'Bank Resolution Regimes in Europe: Recovery and Resolution Planning, Early Intervention, Resolution Tools and Powers' (2014) 24 *European Business Law Review* 89, stressing that 'Regulation (EU) No 575/2013 now requires that all Additional Tier 1 instruments must allow for a write down, or conversion into CET1 instruments, when the CET1 capital ratio of the institution falls below 5.125%'.

[78] Under Art 2(1)(28) of the BRRD, extraordinary public financial support is defined as 'State aid within the meaning of Article 107(1) TFEU, or any other public financial support at supra-national level, which, if provided for at national level, would constitute State aid, that is provided in order to preserve or restore the viability, liquidity or solvency of an institution or entity referred to in point (b), (c) or (d) of Article 1(1) or of a group of which such an institution or entity forms part'.

[79] See European Banking Authority, 'Guidelines on the interpretation of the different circumstances when an institution shall be considered as failing or likely to fail under Article 32(6) of Directive 2014/59/EU of the European Parliament and of the Council of 15 May 2014 establishing a framework for the recovery and resolution of credit institutions and investment firms (Bank Recovery and Resolution Directive)' [2014] OJ L173/190 3, available at www.eba.europa.eu/documents/10180/1085517/EBA-GL-2015-07+GL+on+failing+or+likely+to+fail.pdf/02539533-27ed-4467-b442-7d2fa6fcb3d3.

[80] See n 22, 373.

B. The Arguments against the Bail-in Tool

On the other hand, the arguments against bail-in do not concern its effectiveness as a resolution tool since, in that respect, it undoubtedly brings benefits to crisis management. Yet, some criticisms can arise from the way in which the bail-in tool has been introduced into the legal framework as well as from its capability to harm shareholders' and creditors' fundamental rights. In addition, there can also be crises where bail-in proves either insufficient or even counterproductive to effectively resolve a FOLF bank.

Thus, the main arguments against bail-in relate to its retroactive application and its interference with fundamental rights, on one hand, and its inability to always deliver on its goals, on the other. Both arguments are discussed in the following paragraphs.

i. The Retroactive Application of Bail-in and its Interference with Fundamental Rights

As to the way in which the rules governing the bail-in tool have been adopted at EU level, an important issue arises from the possibility to apply such tool also to (capital and debt) instruments issued before its introduction in the framework. Such retroactivity could ultimately penalise the position of investors who were not aware of the risk of their instruments being bailed in, having bought them before the adoption of the BRRD. The Italian *Commissione Nazionale per le Società e la Borsa* (Consob)[81] has been very critical on this point, highlighting that the legislative choice to make the bail-in tool retroactive is in contrast with several fundamental principles of law.[82] On these grounds, the Italian authority recommended amendment of the legal framework such that the bail-in tool can only apply to instruments issued after its introduction.[83]

With regard to the interference of the bail-in tool with property rights, it is worth noting that both Article 17 of the EU Convention of Fundamental Rights[84] and Article 1 of Protocol No 1 of the European Charter of Human Rights[85]

[81] Consob is the public authority responsible for regulating and overseeing the Italian financial markets.

[82] See Consob, 'Incontro Annuale con il Mercato Finanziario', Discorso del Presidente al Mercato Finanziario, Milan (8 May 2017) 8, available at www.consob.it/documents/11973/1102412/dsc2017.pdf/4b129aa8-b702-4f6f-91e8-94d38ede6114.

[83] ibid.

[84] It provides that: 'Everyone has the right to own, use, dispose of and bequeath his or her lawfully acquired possessions. No one may be deprived of his or her possessions, except in the public interest and in the cases and under the conditions provided for by law, subject to fair compensation being paid in good time for their loss. The use of property may be regulated by law in so far as is necessary for the general interest'.

[85] It provides that '1. Every natural or legal person is entitled to the peaceful enjoyment of his possessions. No one shall be deprived of his possessions except in the public interest and subject to the conditions provided for by law and by the general principles of international law. 2. The preceding

protect the right to own, use and dispose of possessions. The exception to this general principle is the possibility to deprive someone of their possessions when this is in the public interest, according to the provisions of law and subject to fair compensation.[86] Both shares in a company and creditor claims incorporated in debt instruments are treated as property rights.[87] The most critical aspect in this respect is that the application of the bail-in tool would harm shareholders' and creditors' fundamental rights without granting any compensation. However, the counterargument to justify the application of bail-in could be that, since the bank has been submitted to resolution being FOLF, both shares and debt instruments are likely to be valueless or almost valueless. And this also results from the consideration that if the bank had not been resolved (with the use of bail-in) then it should have been wound up with the risk that shareholders and creditors would lose even more.[88]

ii. The Self-Sufficiency of the Bail-in Tool

An additional key aspect to take into account relates to whether bail-in is really always sufficient and effective in and of itself (or in combination with the other resolution tools) to resolve banks – which means to achieve the resolution objectives – as well as to end public bail-outs, as the EU legislator would expect.[89] This aspect is important both when the aim is to resolve the bank as a going concern through an open bank bail-in[90] and when other resolution tools, such as asset separation, sale of business and bridge bank, are also applied along with the remaining parts of the failing institution being liquidated in a gone concern scenario. Even though the new system is grounded in the idea of bail-in being the alternative to bail-outs

provisions shall not, however, in any way impair the right of a State to enforce such laws as it deems necessary to control the use of property in accordance with the general interest or to secure the payment of taxes or other contributions or penalties'.

[86] See n 25, 118.

[87] See ECHR, *Sovtransavto Holding v Ukraine*, Appl No 48553/99 [2002] ECHR 621, 25 July, [92]; see ECHR, *Fomin and Others v Russian Federation*, Appl No 34703/04, [2013] ECHR, 26 February, [25].

[88] See Case C-526/14, *Kotnik and Others v Državni zbor Republike Slovenije*, EU:C:2016:570, [75], 'The scale of losses suffered by shareholders of distressed banks will, in any event, be the same, regardless of whether those losses are caused by a court insolvency order because no State aid is granted or by a procedure for the granting of State aid which is subject to the prerequisite of burden-sharing'. At [78] 'It follows from point 46 that the burden-sharing measures on which the grant of State aid in favour of a bank showing a shortfall is dependent cannot cause any detriment to the right to property of subordinated creditors that those creditors would not have suffered within insolvency proceedings that followed such aid not being granted'. At [79]: 'That being the case, it cannot reasonably be maintained that the burden-sharing measures, such as those laid down by the Banking Communication, constitute interference in the right to property of the shareholders and the subordinated creditors'.

[89] See Recital 67 of BRRD.

[90] See n 77, 90, 91, arguing that in such a case 'the bail-in tool may be exercised only if there is a realistic prospect that the application of bail-in in conjunction with other measures implemented in accordance with a business reorganisation plan by an administrator appointed for that purpose will achieve, not only the relevant resolution objectives, but will restore the institution to financial soundness and long term viability. Where these conditions are not fulfilled, resolution authorities may use any of the other resolution tools and the bail-in tool in order to capitalise a bridge institution (only)'.

(which should no longer take place), in the event of crises involving systemic banks as well as in systemic crises,[91] the two instruments will likely be jointly needed, as bail-in in and of itself (or in combination with the other resolution tools) may in some circumstances prove insufficient. Indeed, bail-in is an accounting operation (although detrimental for both shareholders and creditors, who are affected by the write-down and the conversion of debt into capital) which rebalances the ratio between assets and own funds plus liabilities by decreasing and/or wiping out the latter and/or converting some of them into capital. However, in practice it does not provide any fresh financial resource. Thus, if the FOLF bank is not only insolvent but also illiquid (which is often the case),[92] the insolvency problem can be solved with bail-in – provided that there are enough bail-in-able liabilities relative to the losses – but the liquidity issue cannot be tackled.[93] In the event of liquidity shortage, therefore, some forms of external financing and/or public intervention might also be necessary.[94]

Yet, in some extremely serious situations, even the bail-in of bail-in-able liabilities could prove to be ineffective to resolve the FOLF bank. This can happen when bail-in-able liabilities are not enough to absorb losses.[95] On these grounds, legislators and regulators introduced new provisions (concerning the minimum requirement for own funds and eligible liabilities (MREL)[96] and the total loss

[91] A definition of 'systemic crisis' is provided by Art 2(1)(30) of the BRRD, according to which it is 'a disruption in the financial system with the potential to have serious negative consequences for the internal market and the real economy. All types of financial intermediaries, markets and infrastructure may be potentially systemically important to some degree'.

[92] Often it is even difficult to distinguish between illiquidity and insolvency, particularly in crisis times; see JH Cochrane, 'Toward a run-free financial system' in M Neil-Baily and JB Taylor (eds), *Accross the great divide: new perspectives on the financial crisis* (Stanford, Stanford Hoover Institution Press, 2014) 197 and 205, pointing out that 'illiquidity and insolvency are essentially indistinguishable in a crisis', and additionally, illiquidity can easily bring also insolvency; see J Mitts, 'Systemic Risk and Managerial Incentives in the Dodd-Frank Orderly Liquidation Authority' (2015) 1 *Journal of Financial Regulation* 51, 52, who argues that banks that are considered illiquid often are even insolvent.

[93] See Ringe (n 2) 4, 7, who, more generally, argues that the capacity of the administrator to provide liquidity to the failing institution in order to keep the critical functions working is one of the critical elements of resolution. The author also points out that bail-in should be applied to both insolvent and illiquid institutions, but the current rules do not deal with the provision of liquidity as they only focus on the recapitalisation of FOLF banks.

[94] See n 22, 376.

[95] For this reason, Ringe (n 2) 14, correctly argues that banks must have enough bail-in-able liabilities otherwise bail-in cannot work.

[96] At EU level, Art 45 of the BRRD provides that 'member states shall ensure that institutions meet, at all times, a minimum requirement for own funds and eligible liabilities. The minimum requirement shall be calculated as the amount of own funds and eligible liabilities expressed as a percentage of the total liabilities and own funds of the institution'. The minimum requirement for own funds and eligible liabilities of each institution will be determined by the resolution authority, after consulting the competent authority, on the basis of a number of criteria. These requirements have been further specified by the European Banking Authority (EBA) in its Regulatory Technical Standards (RTS), see European Banking Authority, 'Opinion on the Commission's intention to amend the draft regulatory technical standards specifying criteria relating to the methodology for setting minimum requirement for own funds and eligible liabilities according to Article 45(2) of Directive 2014/59/EU' (2016) 1, available at www.eba.europa.eu/documents/10180/1359456/EBA-Op-2016-02+Opinion+on+RTS+on+MREL.pdf; in this regard see Ringe (n 2) 14, arguing that there was disagreement between EBA and the Commission on these RTSs.

absorbing capacity (TLAC))[97] obliging banks to issue minimum amounts of bail-in-able liabilities. Nonetheless, when losses are significant and difficult to stop – for instance in a systemic crisis scenario – even a predefined amount of bail-in-able liabilities could prove insufficient. Additionally, it has already become difficult and expensive for several banks (in particular for those established in countries where capital markets are not significantly developed) to issue bail-in-able liabilities.

But even more importantly, resolution tools – including bail-in – are meant to avoid the creation of financial instability and systemic risk, in that these are some of the resolution objectives. To this end, an excessive use of the bail-in tool can cause exactly the same consequences that resolution is supposed to avoid: contagion, financial instability and systemic risk.[98] This can happen, for instance, when a significant amount of bail-in-able liabilities are held by other banks and financial institutions. By writing them down, the insolvency problems of the FOLF bank are likely to be transmitted to the creditor banks and financial institutions. That is why the Financial Stability Board has urged global banks not to hold bail-in-able liabilities issued by global systemically important banks[99] (G-SIBs).[100] In the section entitled 'Limitation of Contagion' of the 'Principles on Loss-Absorbing and Recapitalisation Capacity for G-SIBs in Resolution', principle XII provides that 'Authorities should place appropriate prudential restrictions on G-SIBs' and

[97] The FSB published some principles for prescribing a certain amount of TLAC that global systemically important banks (G-SIBs) are required to hold; see Financial Stability Board, 'Principles on Loss-Absorbing and Recapitalisation Capacity for G-SIBs in Resolution' (2015) 3, available at www.fsb.org/wp-content/uploads/TLAC-Principles-and-Term-Sheet-for-publication-final.pdf; accordingly see International Monetary Fund, 'From Bail-out to Bail-in: Mandatory Debt Restructuring of Systemic Financial Institutions' (2012) 12 Staff Discussion Notes 22, available at www.imf.org/external/pubs/ft/sdn/2012/sdn1203.pdf.

[98] See n 22, 377.

[99] See Financial Stability Board, 'Policy Measures to Address Systemically Important Financial Institutions' (2011) 1 available at www.fsb.org/wp-content/uploads/Policy-Measures-to-Address-Systemically-Important-Financial-Institutions.pdf, arguing that 'SIFIs are financial institutions whose distress or disorderly failure, because of their size, complexity and systemic interconnectedness, would cause significant disruption to the wider financial system and economic activity. To avoid this outcome, authorities have all too frequently had no choice but to forestall the failure of such institutions through public solvency support. As underscored by this crisis, this has deleterious consequences for private incentives and for public finances'. The FSB and the Basel Committee on Banking Supervision have identified a group of 30 G-SIBs; see Basel Committee on Banking Supervision, 'Global Systemically Important Banks: Updated Assessment Methodology and the Higher Loss Absorbency Requirement' (2013) 1, available at www.bis.org/publ/bcbs255.pdf. In addition, the Basel Committee on Banking Supervision and FSB have created the category of domestic systemically important banks (D-SIBs), see Basel Committee on Banking Supervision, 'A Framework for Dealing with Domestic Systemically Important Banks' (2012) 1, available at www.bis.org/publ/bcbs233.pdf. In implementing these guidelines, the EU has adopted the definition of 'other systemically important institutions' (O-SIIs); see European Banking Authority, 'Guidelines on criteria to determine the conditions of application of article 131(3) of Directive 2013/36/EU (CRD) in relation to the assessment of other systemically important institutions (O-SIIs)' (2014) 1, available at www.eba.europa.eu/documents/10180/930752/EBA-GL-2014-10+%28Guidelines+on+O-SIIs+Assessment%29.pdf.

[100] Ringe (n 2) 16, points out that, due to the fact that banks hold a significant amount of each other's debt, the bail-in of liabilities held by other financial institutions can ease the contagion and spread systemic risk. For this reason, the FSB has drafted some new principles requiring the authorities to limit the amount of bail-in-able liabilities that banks can hold in other banks.

other internationally active banks' holdings of instruments issued by G-SIBs that are eligible to meet the Minimum TLAC requirement'. The rationale behind such principle is that to reduce the potential for a G-SIB resolution to spread contagion into the global banking system, it is crucial to strongly discourage internationally active banks from holding TLAC issued by G-SIBs.[101] Yet, the problem with such a measure is that it can be very difficult in practice to cut off the interlinkages among financial institutions. And, in turn, this can make it more expensive for banks to find appropriate forms of financing.[102]

Based on the same rationale, resolution authorities have also been given the powers to exempt some liabilities from being bailed in,[103] when this could endanger financial stability.[104] Nevertheless, if such exemptions are applied to a significant extent,[105] then some alternative resources have to be found to absorb

[101] See Financial Stability Board (n 97); see also TH Tröger, 'Regulatory Influence on Market Conditions in the Banking Union: the Cases of Macro-Prudential Instruments and the Bail-in Tool' (2015) 16 *European Business Organization Law Review* 588, arguing that 'once implemented, the bail-in instrument must not destabilise markets. In order to prevent knock-on effects, the bail-inable instruments have to be held outside the banking sector by investors with sufficient loss-bearing capacity (e.g., insurance companies, pension funds, high-net worth individuals, hedge funds). Under these conditions, a bank failure may become a non-disruptive event that does not imperil market participants' trust in the financial sector'.

[102] See n 22, 377.

[103] Under Art 44(3) of the BRRD, 'In exceptional circumstances, where the bail-in tool is applied, the resolution authority may exclude or partially exclude certain liabilities from the application of the write-down or conversion powers where: (a) it is not possible to bail-in that liability within a reasonable time notwithstanding the good faith efforts of the resolution authority; (b) the exclusion is strictly necessary and is proportionate to achieve the continuity of critical functions and core business lines in a manner that maintains the ability of the institution under resolution to continue key operations, services and transactions; (c) the exclusion is strictly necessary and proportionate to avoid giving rise to widespread contagion, in particular as regards eligible deposits held by natural persons and micro, small and medium sized enterprises, which would severely disrupt the functioning of financial markets, including of financial market infrastructures, in a manner that could cause a serious disturbance to the economy of a Member State or of the Union; or (d) the application of the bail-in tool to those liabilities would cause a destruction in value such that the losses borne by other creditors would be higher than if those liabilities were excluded from bail-in'.

[104] This is confirmed by Recital 4 to the Commission Delegated Regulation (EU) 2016/860 of 4 February 2016 specifying further the circumstances where exclusion from the application of write-down or conversion powers is necessary under Art 44(3) of Directive 2014/59/EU of the European Parliament and of the Council establishing a framework for the recovery and resolution of credit institutions and investment firms [2016] OJ L144/11, which provides that 'The decision to use the bail-in tool (or other resolution tools) should be taken to achieve the resolution objectives in Article 31(2) of Directive 2014/59/EU. In the same vein, those resolution objectives should also inform the decisions regarding the use of the tool, including the decision to exclude a liability or class of liabilities from the application of bail-in in a given case'.

[105] Article 8 of the Commission Delegated Regulation (EU) 2016/860 of 4 February 2016 states that 'when considering exclusions based on the risk of direct contagion pursuant to Article 44(3)(c) of Directive 2014/59/EU, resolution authorities should assess, to the maximum extent possible, the interconnectedness of the institution under resolution with its counterparties. The assessment referred to in the first subparagraph shall include all of the following: (a) consideration of exposures to relevant counterparties with regard to the risk that bail-in of such exposures might cause knock-on failures; (b) the systemic importance of counterparties which are at risk of failing, in particular with regard to other financial market participants and financial market infrastructure providers. When considering exclusions based on the risk of indirect contagion pursuant to Article 44(3)(c) of Directive 2014/59/EU,

previous losses and adequately recapitalise the bank. In such cases, the bail-in tool could prove not to be enough, depending on the size of losses to absorb as well as the amount of exempted liabilities. As a consequence, in such a scenario, the remaining options would consist of either the use of private external resources (even if it is rather unlikely that private players would decide to bear significant losses in order to rescue a failing bank) or the use of public resources.[106] The use of resolution funds' resources and the injection of public money are discussed in the next section.

V. Resolution Funds

With a view to ensuring the effective application of the resolution tools, the BRRD has also introduced some forms of external financing called 'resolution financing arrangements', also known as 'resolution funds'. Resolution funds are envisaged to be filled through mandatory contributions paid by banks.[107]

At Banking Union level, it was decided to create the Single Resolution Fund (SRF). In this regard, the SRM Regulation is complemented by an Intergovernmental

the resolution authority shall assess, to the maximum extent possible, the need and proportionality of the exclusion based on multiple objective relevant indicators. Indicators which may be relevant to the case include the following: (a) number, size and interconnectedness of institutions with similar characteristics as the institution under resolution, insofar as that could give rise to widespread lack of confidence in the banking sector or the broader financial system; (b) the number of natural persons directly and indirectly affected by the bail-in, visibility and press coverage of the resolution action, insofar as that has a significant risk of undermining overall confidence in the banking or broader financial system; (c) the number, size, interconnectedness of counterparties affected by the bail-in, including market participants from the non-banking sector, and the importance of critical functions performed by these counterparties; (d) the ability of the counterparties to access alternative service providers for functions which have been assessed as substitutable, given the specific situation; (e) whether a significant number of counterparties would withdraw funding or cease making transactions with other institutions following the bail-in, or whether markets would cease functioning properly as a consequence of the bail- in of such market participants, in particular in the event of generalised loss of market confidence or panic; (f) widespread withdrawal of short-term funding or deposits in significant amounts; (g) the number, size or significance of institutions which are at risk of meeting the conditions for early intervention, or meeting the conditions of failing or likely to fail pursuant to Article 32(4) of Directive 2014/59/EU; (h) the risk of a significant discontinuance of critical functions or a significant increase in prices for the provision of such functions (as evident from changes in market conditions for such functions or their availability), or the expectation of counterparties and other market participants; (i) widespread significant decreases in share prices of institutions or in prices of assets held by institutions, in particular where they can have an impact on the capital situation of institutions; (j) general and widespread significant reduction in short or medium term funding available to institutions; (k) significant impairment to the functioning of the interbank funding market, as apparent from a significant increase of margin requirements and decrease of collateral available to institutions; (l) widespread and significant increases in prices for credit default insurance or deterioration in credit ratings of institutions or other market participants which are relevant for the financial situation of institutions'.

[106] See n 22, 379.

[107] According to Art 102 of the BRRD, 'member states shall ensure that, by 31 December 2024, the available financial means of their financing arrangements reach at least 1% of the amount of covered deposits of all the institutions authorised in their territory. Member States may set target levels in excess of that amount'.

Agreement (IGA) between Member States participating in the SSM on the transfer and mutualisation of contributions into the SRF. The SRB manages the SRF and is responsible for its administration under the delegated acts adopted by the European Commission. The SRF is financed through contributions paid by the financial institutions, which are subject to the SRM. The target size of the Fund is at least one per cent of covered deposits in the banking system of the participating Member States. During the 10-year initial build-up period, the contributions of the financial institutions shall be raised at the national level and flow into 'national compartments', which shall be used only for the resolution of banks in the respective Member States. Thus, during the build-up period, the SRF consists of national compartments, which will be gradually merged. While the cost of resolving banks would mainly be covered by the national compartments, in the early years this national share would gradually decrease as the contributions from other countries' compartments increase.[108]

Yet, resolution funds should not be used to directly absorb the losses of the institution under resolution or to recapitalise it.[109] Such resources can be used on the following conditions: a contribution to loss absorption and recapitalisation equal to an amount not less than eight per cent of the total liabilities including own funds of the institution has been made through write-down, conversion or otherwise; and the resolution fund's contribution does not exceed five per cent of the total liabilities, including own funds of the institution.[110]

On top of this, the use of resources provided by resolution funds also needs to be authorised by the European Commission pursuant to the state aid regime.

The fact that resolution funds can provide resources only after a minimum amount (at least eight per cent of the total liabilities including own funds) of losses has been borne by shareholders and creditors and up to the limit of five per cent of the total liabilities including own funds of the institution is undoubtedly consistent with the general principles governing the new framework, according to which shareholders should bear losses first and creditors should bear losses after shareholders. These limitations should also reduce moral hazard on the grounds that external resources become available only after the mandatory involvement

[108] n 9, 10.

[109] According to Art 101 of the BRRD, 'the financing arrangements established in accordance with Article 100 may be used by the resolution authority only to the extent necessary to ensure the effective application of the resolution tools, for the following purposes: (a) to guarantee the assets or the liabilities of the institution under resolution, its subsidiaries, a bridge institution or an asset management vehicle; (b) to make loans to the institution under resolution, its subsidiaries, a bridge institution or an asset management vehicle; (c) to purchase assets of the institution under resolution; (d) to make contributions to a bridge institution and an asset management vehicle; (e) to pay compensation to shareholders or creditors in accordance with Article 75; (f) to make a contribution to the institution under resolution in lieu of the write down or conversion of liabilities of certain creditors, when the bail-in tool is applied and the resolution authority decides to exclude certain creditors from the scope of bail-in in accordance with Article 44(3) to (8); (g) to lend to other financing arrangements on a voluntary basis in accordance with Article 106; (h) to take any combination of the actions referred to in points (a) to (g)'.

[110] Article 44(5) of the BRRD.

of shareholders and creditors in bearing the losses and up to a certain amount.[111] Yet, the other side of the coin is that such limitations can end up preventing resolution funds from truly contributing towards effective resolution.

A. The Main Shortcomings of the Resolution Funds

Still, the design of resolution funds has two main shortcomings. The first is that in extremely serious situations it might be difficult to reach the goal of effectively resolving a bank while complying with such limitations, particularly by providing such a limited amount of resources. This can be the case when losses are high or when a significant amount of liabilities are exempted by resolution authorities from the application of bail-in, for example in light of possible negative effects on financial stability. In such cases, depending on the dimension of previous losses and the size of exempted liabilities, a proportional amount of external resources are likely to be necessary. And this amount could even exceed the limit of five per cent of the total liabilities including own funds which applies to the contributions that resolution funds can provide.

The second is that these arrangements will reach an amount of resources representing one per cent of the total covered deposits of all the institutions authorised by 2024.[112] It seems that even at the end of the transitional period they will not have a huge amount of resources to use.[113]

These two shortcomings can make it difficult for resolution funds to play a relevant role in case of resolution of very large banks, or when several banks are placed under resolution simultaneously.[114]

B. Lessons Learned from the First Resolution Cases

The weaknesses of resolution funds have been brought under the spotlight by some Italian cases. At the end of 2015, just before the entry into force of the bail-in rules, Banca delle Marche, Cassa di Risparmio di Ferrara, Banca Popolare dell'Etruria e del Lazio and Cassa di Risparmio della Provincia di Chieti (all of them being less

[111] See n 22, 380.

[112] Article 102 of the BRRD.

[113] Since 1 January 2016, euro-area countries participating in the Single Supervisory Mechanism (SSM) have been subject to the Single Resolution Mechanism (SRM) according to Regulation (EU) 2014/806, which provides for the establishment of a Single Resolution Fund (SRF). Pursuant to the provisions of the Regulation (EU) 2014/806, Member States must contribute their national funds to the SRF starting from 1 January 2016. SRF is initially subdivided into national compartments that are distinct for accounting purposes; over an eight-year transitional period the percentage allocated to the national compartments will be gradually reduced, while the pooled compartment will be increased until all the resources have been transferred to it. At the end of the transitional period, the SRF will have resources equal to 1% of covered deposits, corresponding to around €55 billion.

[114] See Ringe (n 2) 36.

significant banks) were resolved by the Bank of Italy.[115] The Bank of Italy, in its capacity as the Italian resolution authority, combined some resolution tools, such as separation of the assets and bridge bank, along with burden-sharing measures.[116] Interestingly, these four crises made it clear that resolution tools – even if helpful – might prove insufficient to effectively resolve banks, even when they are small and local. Fresh financial resources, which resolution tools are not able to provide, might also be necessary. As a consequence, fresh financial resources were eventually provided by the Italian resolution fund, which, after the separation of part of the toxic assets (mainly non-performing loans) from the good assets, sold the four banks at the beginning of 2017 to other two Italian banks (UBI Banca and Banca Popolare dell'Emilia Romagna) for only €1 each.[117]

In order to resolve the four banks (which had just €46.6 billion of aggregated total assets, €30.1 billion of aggregated net customer loans and €19.5 billion of aggregated deposits,[118] and represented only one per cent of the Italian-system-wide deposits),[119] the resolution fund employed €3.7 billion[120] – far more than the losses borne by shareholders and subordinated creditors, which amounted to €870 million.[121] In order to raise the resources to use, which were almost 70 per cent of the contributions that the Italian banking system is supposed to provide to the SRF by 2024 (€5.7 billion),[122] the Italian resolution fund had to borrow a significant amount of money from the three largest Italian banks (Unicredit, Intesa San Paolo and UBI Banca),[123] as the regular contributions from the banking system were not sufficient.[124]

Obviously, if bail-in had been applied with the write-down and/or conversion into capital of many more liabilities, the amount of money provided by the resolution fund would have been more limited. Still, these cases show that resolution tools, although important, may not be enough in and of themselves to resolve a bank even when the latter is small and local, and also make it clear that resolution

[115] The bail-in tool provisions entered into force on 1 January 2016.

[116] See Banca d'Italia (n 10), *passim*.

[117] See Reuters, 'Italy's UBI to buy rescued banks, raise cash in latest clean-up', 11 January 2017, available at www.reuters.com/article/italy-banks-ubi-ma-idUSL5N1F22FU?type=companyNews; and Reuters, 'Bank of Italy sells last of four small rescued banks to BPER', 2 March 2017, available at www.reuters.com/article/bper-banca-ma-carife-idUSI6N1FU02O.

[118] See European Commission, 'State aid: Commission approves resolution plans for four small Italian banks Banca Marche, Banca Etruria, Carife and Carichieti' Press release, Brussels 22 November 2015, *passim*, available at www.europa.eu/rapid/press-release_IP-15-6139_en.htm.

[119] See Banca d'Italia (n 10), *passim*.

[120] See Banca d'Italia, 'Annual Report of the National Resolution Fund', 28 April 2016, available at: www.bancaditalia.it/pubblicazioni/rendiconto-fondo-nazionale-risoluzione/2017-rendiconto-fondo-nazionale-risoluzione/en_Rendiconto_Fondo_nazionale_risoluzione_sul_2016.pdf?language_id=1.

[121] See Banca d'Italia, 'Questions and answers on the solution of the crisis at the four banks under resolution' (2016), available at www.bancaditalia.it/media/approfondimenti/2016/d-e-r-quattro-banche/index.html?com.dotmarketing.htmlpage.language=1.

[122] See n 120.

[123] ibid

[124] ibid, where it is underlined that 'for 2015, the ordinary contribution amounted to approximately EUR 588 million'.

funds are not well equipped as they do not even have enough resources to contribute to resolve small local banks.[125] At Banking Union level, the SRF is planned to reach €55 billion by 2024.[126] It is clear that such mechanisms are blunt swords.[127] And if this is the case for small and local institutions, these arguments look even more relevant in the event of crises involving very large banks and in systemic crises. In these scenarios, it is not credible that the use of bail-in (even in combination with other resolution tools) and resolution funds can always meet the resolution objectives.[128]

VI. The Provision of Public Funds in the Context of Resolution and the Interaction between the Resolution Regime and the State Aid Framework

In principle, it can be argued that from now on bail-in could and should be used in an increasing number of resolution procedures because it is the most effective tool. Yet, a problem arises when bail-in is not enough to achieve the resolution objectives (so, too, the resolution financing arrangements) or when the resolution authorities decide to exempt a significant amount of liabilities from being bailed in, for example to avoid the contagion of other institutions connected to the one in crisis.[129] In such cases, the use of public resources seems to be unavoidable.[130]

However, in this regard, the issue is that the state aid framework, at EU level, limits the possibility for a Member State to intervene in banks' resolution by using public money.[131] Indeed, Article 107 TFEU provides that any state aid is incompatible with the internal market, unless it qualifies as one of the exceptions set out

[125] See n 22, 381.

[126] However, on the grounds of these weaknesses, the recently passed reform of the European Stability Mechanism (ESM) has provided that in the event of the SRF being depleted, the ESM can act as a backstop and lend the necessary funds to the SRF to finance a resolution. To this end, the ESM will provide a revolving credit line. This is the common backstop; see European Stability Mechanism, 'What is the common backstop?', available at www.esm.europa.eu/content/what-common-backstop-0.

[127] See Ringe (n 2), arguing that the SRF is not a credible support for the resolution of a significant bank; see also JN Gordon and WG Ringe, 'Bank Resolution in the European: a Transatlantic Perspective on What It Would Take' (2015) 115 *Columbia Law Review* 1354, 1358.

[128] See n 22, 381.

[129] Recital 21 to the Commission Delegated Regulation (EU) 2016/860 of 4 February 2016 states that 'Preventing contagion to avoid a significant adverse effect on the financial system is a further resolution objective which may justify an exclusion from the application of the bail-in tool. In any event, exclusion on this basis should only take place where it is strictly necessary and proportionate, but also where the contagion is so severe that it would be widespread and severely disrupt the functioning of financial markets in a manner that could cause a serious disturbance to the economy of a Member State or of the Union'.

[130] See n 22, 382.

[131] See M Dewatripont, 'European Banking: Bailout, Bail-in and State Aid Control' (2014) 34 *International Journal of Industrial Organization* 40, recalling that the EU is 'the only jurisdiction in the world with State aid Control policies'.

in Article 107(2) TFEU, or has been approved by the Commission for one of the reasons laid down in Article 107(3) TFEU.[132] In relation to public support to banks, the main justification to allow public intervention, according to Article 107(3)(b) TFEU, is 'to remedy a serious disturbance in the economy of a member state'. As discussed in chapter four, the European Commission published a number of Communications identifying the criteria that have to be met to authorise the use of public money for the benefit of banks. The most relevant Communication, in this regard, is the 2013 Banking Communication,[133] which allows for the provision of public funds on the condition that burden-sharing measures apply[134] also to subordinated creditors and a restructuring plan is adopted and approved before obtaining the aid.[135] Accordingly, state aid measures can be given only if equity and subordinated debt-holders are involved in absorbing losses through the conversion and/or the write-down of their instruments. However, the Commission has also pointed that its main goal in the state aid authorisation process in the banking sector is to ensure financial stability.[136] And, for this reason, it has the power to exclude the application of burden sharing when this 'would endanger financial stability or lead to disproportionate results'.[137]

These state aid provisions have to be coordinated with the rules introduced in this regard by the BRRD.[138] The BRRD provides two different government financial stabilisation tools which can be used by Member States during the resolution of an institution: the public equity support tool[139] and the temporary public ownership tool.[140] They clearly entail the use of public money provided by the Member States concerned with a view to effectively resolving the bank under resolution. While the public equity support tool is a public recapitalisation of the bank under resolution, the temporary public ownership tool is a nationalisation of the bank in question which aims at providing confidence to stakeholders on the grounds

[132] See G Lo Schiavo, 'State Aids and Credit Institutions in Europe: What Way Forward?' (2014) 25 *European Business Law Review* 435, 438.

[133] Communication from the Commission of 30 July 2013 on the application, from 1 August 2013, of State aid rules to support measures in favour of banks in the context of the financial crisis (Banking Communication) [2013] OJ C 216/1.

[134] See n 132, 442, arguing that state aid provisions shall be limited to the minimum necessary amount and the beneficiary institution shall undertake the required level of own contribution in order to receive public support.

[135] See n 131, 42.

[136] See S Micossi, G Bruzzone and M Casella, 'Bail-in Provisions in State Aid and Resolution Procedures: Are They Consistent with Systemic Stability?' (2014) CEPS Policy Brief 4, available at www.ceps.eu/publications/bail-provisions-state-aid-and-resolution-procedures-are-they-consistent-systemic.

[137] See n 133, point 45.

[138] See I Kokkoris, 'State Aid Law v Single Resolution Mechanism: David v Goliath or vice versa' (2013) 10 *International Corporate Rescue* 392, 393.

[139] Article 57 of the BRRD states that 'member states may, while complying with national company law, participate in the recapitalisation of an institution … by providing capital to the latter in exchange for the following instruments, subject to the requirements of Regulation (EU) No 575/2013: (a) Common Equity Tier 1 instruments; (b) Additional Tier 1 instruments or Tier 2 instruments'.

[140] Article 58 of the BRRD states that 'Member States may take an institution … into temporary public ownership'. To reach this purpose, they 'may make one or more share transfer orders in which the transferee is: (a) a nominee of the Member State; or (b) a company wholly owned by the Member State'.

that a solvent institution, namely the state, is the new shareholder. However, both instruments can only be used as a last resort measure – after the other resolution tools have been applied[141] – with a view to transferring the holding in the resolved institution to the private sector as soon as commercial and financial conditions allow for it.[142]

A number of further conditions need to be met in order for these two tools to be employed. Accordingly, they can be implemented only: when the use of the resolution tools is not enough to avoid a significant adverse effect on the financial system; or when the application of the resolution tools do not suffice to protect public interest, where extraordinary liquidity assistance from the central bank has previously been given to the institution; or in relation to the temporary public ownership tool, when the application of the resolution tools does not suffice to protect the public interest, where public equity support through the equity support tool has previously been given to the institution. And additionally, before their use, it is requested that: a contribution to loss absorption and recapitalisation equal to an amount not less than eight per cent of total liabilities including own funds of the institution under resolution has been made by shareholders and creditors through write-down, conversion or otherwise; and the Commission has authorised the public intervention according to the Union state aid framework.[143]

The wording of Articles 57 and 58 of the BRRD suggests that, in order to apply these two tools, something more serious than the public interest requested to initiate resolution is required. Thus, these forms of public assistance can be given only in extremely severe situations when the crisis of a bank can undermine the financial stability of the system as a whole. This could be either the crises involving very large systemic banks or systemic crises. This interpretation would find further support in what is stated under Recital 57 to the BRRD, which provides that the Commission in evaluating the compliance of the government financial stabilisation tools with the state aid framework, in light of Article 107 TFEU,[144] should also assess whether 'there is a very extraordinary situation of a systemic crisis justifying resorting to those tools'.

[141] See n 101, 590, arguing that the fact that such stabilisation tools can be used only after the application of bail-in at least to 8% of the liabilities may have destabilising effects by accelerating 'the ride to Armageddon'. Interestingly, the author suggests that the extent to which bail-in is used should be subject to a systemic exception.

[142] See K Lannoo, 'Bank State Aid under BRRD and SRM' (2014) 13 *European State Aid Law Quarterly* 630, 632.

[143] Article 37(10) of the BRRD also adds that these tools can be used in the very extraordinary situation of a systemic crisis.

[144] Article 107(1) TFEU provides for a general prohibition of any aid granted by a member state: 'save as otherwise provided in the Treaties, any aid granted by a Member State or through State resources in any form whatsoever which distorts or threatens to distort competition by favouring certain undertakings or the production of certain goods shall, in so far as it affects trade between Member States, be incompatible with the internal market'. Article 107(2) and (3) of the TFEU regulate the exceptions to the prohibition of State aid. Article 107(2) provides that 'the following shall be compatible with the internal market: (a) aid having a social character, granted to individual consumers, provided that such aid is granted without discrimination related to the origin of the products concerned; (b) aid to make good the damage caused by natural disasters or exceptional occurrences; and, (c) aid granted to the economy of certain areas of the Federal Republic of Germany affected by the division of Germany,

While such an assessment is very difficult to make and will be necessarily based on the discretion of the Commission, an issue still remains. If the failure of the bank under resolution should not be able to lead to a systemic crisis, then the government financial stabilisation tools would not be available.[145] However, even in the event of crises of banks which are not seen as able to hit the whole system, it might be preferable to avoid their failures. The underlying reason could be that even the crisis of such banks can have a relevant impact on the territory where they operate. In other words, although such a crisis is unlikely to create systemic financial instability, yet it could harm the social and economic soundness of an entire territory, and its negative effects can radiate. A similar issue can arise if a number of banks were FOLF simultaneously, which is not simply a theoretical scenario.[146] Even in this case, it would be difficult to justify the application of the government financial stabilisation tools. However, if resolution funds are not sufficiently equipped, such a situation can become very serious and difficult to properly handle.

But even more importantly, what can make the use of government financial stabilisation tools inappropriate or not effective is that a significant amount of liabilities needs to be bailed in before their application. For the reasons already highlighted, such a measure can generate exactly the same consequences that resolution should prevent, namely financial instability and, in turn, systemic risk.[147]

VII. Impediments to Resolvability

For the resolution procedure to deliver on its objectives, impediments to resolvability – obstacles hindering the effective resolution of FOLF banks[148] – need

in so far as such aid is required in order to compensate for the economic disadvantages caused by that division. Five years after the entry into force of the Treaty of Lisbon, the Council, acting on a proposal from the Commission, may adopt a decision repealing this point'. Article 107(3) of the TFEU establishes that 'the following may be considered to be compatible with the internal market: (a) aid to promote the economic development of areas where the standard of living is abnormally low or where there is serious underemployment, and of the regions referred to in Article 349, in view of their structural, economic and social situation; (b) aid to promote the execution of an important project of common European interest or to remedy a serious disturbance in the economy of a Member State; (c) aid to facilitate the development of certain economic activities or of certain economic areas, where such aid does not adversely affect trading conditions to an extent contrary to the common interest; (d) aid to promote culture and heritage conservation where such aid does not affect trading conditions and competition in the Union to an extent that is contrary to the common interest; and, (e) such other categories of aid as may be specified by decision of the Council on a proposal from the Commission'.

[145] See n 22, 385.

[146] See S Micossi, G Bruzzone and M Cassella, 'Fine-Tuning the Use of Bail-in to Promote a Stronger EU Financial System' (2016) 136 CEPS Special Report, 3, available at www.ceps.eu/publications/fine-tuning-use-bail-promote-stronger-eu-financial-system.

[147] See n 22, 385.

[148] Elsewhere, I argued that impediments to resolvability can be grouped into two broad categories: 1) impediments resulting from the legal framework, ie exogenous impediments or architectural impediments (such as: a) the definition of 'resolvability', b) the involvement of different authorities in the resolution process, c) the concept of 'public interest', d) misalignments between the State aid framework

to be removed in advance. Despite both the BRRD and SRMR using the phrase 'impediments to resolvability' several times, there is no clear definition of the term. An insight in this respect is provided by Article 54(3) of the BRRD, concerning the removal of procedural impediments to bail-in, that states that

> member states shall ensure that there are no procedural impediments to the conversion of liabilities to shares or other instruments of ownership existing by virtue of their instruments of incorporation or statutes, including pre-emption rights for shareholders or requirements for the consent of shareholders to an increase in capital.

The BRRD builds on the wording 'impediments to resolvability' to emphasise that such impediments have to be removed. And to this end, the Directive provides the resolution authorities with specific powers.[149]

The Commission Delegated Regulation 2016/1075[150] classifies 'impediments to resolvability' into five categories: structure and operations; financial resources; information; cross-border issues; and legal issues.[151] For each category, the Commission Delegated Regulation identifies the main issues that resolution authorities are meant to consider when assessing the feasibility of a resolution strategy on the grounds that a successful resolution action also depends on whether there are impediments to resolvability and, if that is the case, if they can be successfully removed.[152]

A. The Process of Removing Impediments to Resolvability

On these grounds, addressing or removing impediments to resolvability is key to making banks resolvable.[153] Removing impediments to resolvability is accordingly regarded as a collaborative process involving the banks concerned, which are expected to work with the competent authorities and the resolution authorities.[154] Resolution authorities are to start this collaborative process by drawing up a

and the resolution regime, and e) the legal constraints in the provision of public financing); and, 2) impediments directly resulting from the institution and/or its group, ie endogenous impediments or impediments *stricto sensu*; see n 23, 48, 68.

149 Article 17(5) of BRRD.

150 Commission Delegated Regulation 2016/1075 has implemented the EBA Regulatory Technical Standards on the content of resolution plans and the assessment of resolvability of 19 December 2014.

151 Article 26(3) of Commission Delegated Regulation 2016/1075.

152 See M Bodellini and WP De Groen, 'Impediments to resolvability – what is the status quo?' (2021), In-depth analysis requested by the ECON Committee of the European Parliament, 10.

153 See M Lehmann, 'Impediments to resolvability of bank', In-depth analysis requested by the ECON Committee of the European Parliament (2019) 10, arguing that making banks resolvable 'denotes the process of moving away from governance practices and a financial industry structure in which banks are too big, too complex or too interconnected to fail without disrupting financial stability. In this sense, resolvable banks are the endpoint of a journey away from a financial sector in which taxpayer-funded bailouts were the norm'.

154 Accordingly, Art 10(5) of BRRD states that 'resolution authorities may require institutions to assist them in the drawing up and updating of the plans'; see also Art 8(8) of SRMR.

resolution plan for every bank, after consulting with the competent authority and the resolution authorities of the countries where significant branches are located.[155] Resolution plans have to be drafted and updated on an annual basis. The preparation of resolution plans is a key part of the process to remove impediments to resolvability in that impediments have to be firstly identified in the resolution plan.[156] Against this backdrop, resolution authorities should also identify the actions through which impediments can be addressed, when this is considered necessary and proportionate.[157]

Importantly, resolution plans are to list the actions that resolution authorities are to take in the event of institutions becoming FOLF.[158] As to the content of such plans,[159] the SRB divides the required information into several headings,[160] and the plan should also refer to the preferred resolution strategy, which can be either a multiple point of entry strategy, a single point of entry strategy or a combination of both.[161]

The resolvability assessment is an important component of the resolution plan[162] in that it aims at 'achieving the bank's preparedness for a potential resolution'.[163] The resolvability assessment identifies firstly the critical functions of the institution concerned and then accordingly explores the credibility and feasibility of a possible wind down under national insolvency proceedings.[164] The resolvability assessment focuses on seven dimensions: governance; loss absorption and

[155] Article 10(1) of BRRD.

[156] Articles 10(2) and 15 of BRRD and Art 8(6)(c) of SRMR.

[157] Article 10(2) of BRRD and Art 8(6)(c) of SRMR.

[158] Article 10(1) of BRRD and Arts 8(5) and 6 of SRMR.

[159] On the resolution plan content, see Art 10(7) of BRRD and Art 8(9) of SRMR. According to Art 22(1) of Commission Delegated Regulation 2016/1075, a resolution plan shall contain: '(1) a summary of the plan, including a description of the institution or group … (2) a description of the resolution strategy considered in the plan … (3) a description of the information, and the arrangements for the provision of this information, necessary in order to effectively implement the resolution strategy … (4) a description of arrangements to ensure operational continuity of access to critical functions during resolution … (5) a description of the financing requirements and financing sources necessary for the implementation of the resolution strategy foreseen in the plan … (6) plans for communication with critical stakeholder groups … (7) the conclusions of the assessment of resolvability … (8) any opinion expressed by the institution or group in relation to the resolution plan'.

[160] Namely: strategic business analysis; preferred resolution strategy; financial and operational continuity in resolution; information and communication plan; conclusion of the resolvability assessment; and opinion of the bank in relation to the resolution plan. See Single Resolution Board, 'Introduction to resolution planning' (2016) 19, 20, available at www.srb.europa.eu/system/files/media/document/intro_resplanning.pdf.pdf.

[161] See n 9, 23; see also n 153, 9.

[162] A detailed description of the assessment of resolvability is one of the elements to include in the resolution plan according to Art10(7)(e) of BRRD and Art 12(4) of BRRD in relation to groups.

[163] See Single Resolution Board, 'Expectations for banks' (2020) 6, available at www.srb.europa.eu/system/files/media/document/efb_main_doc_final_web_0_0.pdf.

[164] It is clearly stated that the resolvability assessment cannot assume any of the following: '(a) any extraordinary public financial support besides the use of the financing arrangements established in accordance with Article 100; (b) any central bank emergency liquidity assistance; (c) any central bank liquidity assistance provided under non-standard collateralisation, tenor and interest rate terms'; see Art 15(1) of BRRD and Art 16(1) of BRRD in relation to groups; see also Art 8(6) of SRMR.

recapitalisation capacity; liquidity and funding in resolution; operational continuity and access to financial market infrastructure services; information systems and data requirements; communication; and separability and restructuring.[165]

If, after consulting with the competent authority, the resolution authority comes to the conclusion that there are substantive impediments to resolvability, it has to inform the bank and the competent authority as well as the resolution authorities of the jurisdictions where significant branches are situated.[166] When the SRB is the resolution authority, it must 'prepare a report, in cooperation with the competent authorities, addressed to the institution or the parent undertaking analysing the substantive impediments to the effective application of resolution tools and the exercise of resolution powers'.[167]

If substantive impediments to resolvability have been identified, the institution in question is required within four months to propose to the resolution authority the measures to implement with a view to addressing or removing those impediments.[168] The resolution authority then assesses the proposed measures. If, after consulting the competent authority, the resolution authority is not convinced that the proposed measures are effective, it can require the institution to adopt alternative and proportionate measures, thereby notifying such measures[169] to the institution.[170] These 'measures range from additional information requirements to the cessation of activities',[171] and according to the European Banking Authority (EBA), can be grouped under three headings: structural measures concerning the organisational, legal and business structure of an institution; financial measures relating to its assets and liabilities; and products and additional information requirements.[172]

[165] n 163.

[166] Article 17(1) of BRRD.

[167] See Art 10(7) of SRMR, also stating that 'that report shall consider the impact on the institution's business model and recommend any proportionate and targeted measures that, in the Board's view, are necessary or appropriate to remove those impediments in accordance'.

[168] Article 17(3) of BRRD and Art 10(9) of SRMR. A tighter deadline (ie two weeks) is provided in relation to the proposal of measures concerning the compliance with the application of MREL to resolution entities; see also European Banking Authority, 'Guidelines on the specification of measures to reduce or remove impediments to resolvability and the circumstances in which each measure may be applied under Directive 2014/59/EU' (2014), 3 available at www.eba.europa.eu/sites/default/documents/files/documents/10180/933988/d3fa2201-e21f-4f3a-8a67-6e7278fee473/EBA-GL-2014-11%20%28Guidelines%20on%20Impediments%20to%20Resolvability%29.pdf?retry=1.

[169] See Art 17(5) of BRRD.

[170] Articles 17(3) and (4) of BRRD and Art 10(10) of SRMR; see also n 168, 3.

[171] n 163.

[172] See n 168, 3; additionally, see Art 17(4) of BRRD, also stating that 'in identifying alternative measures, the resolution authority shall demonstrate how the measures proposed by the institution would not be able to remove the impediments to resolvability and how the alternative measures proposed are proportionate in removing them. The resolution authority shall take into account the threat to financial stability of those impediments to resolvability and the effect of the measures on the business of the institution, its stability and its ability to contribute to the economy'.

The SRB has the power to instruct the NRAs to require banks under its direct remit to take such measures.[173] Yet, if possible, NRAs should apply the measures directly.[174] While resolution authorities have been given a significant amount of discretion in selecting the measures that they consider appropriate to remove impediments,[175] they are guided in this choice by the EBA's guidelines on measures to reduce or remove impediments to resolvability.[176]

B. Impediments to Resolvability in the Banking Union

In the SRB work programme 2020 it is outlined that the authority expected to adopt, by March 2021, 117 resolution plans covering all banking groups under its remit.[177] That goal has been achieved and now 'resolution plans are in place for all banks'.[178] This is certainly a meaningful step forward compared to the past.[179]

Still, having a resolution plan ready to be adopted, if needed, is not sufficient in and of itself to address the substantial concerns raised by the European Court of Auditors (ECA),[180] and a Member of the European Parliament (MEP),[181] as to the content of such plans and their compliance with the regulatory requirements.[182] In 2017, the ECA examined a sample of resolution plans and its final evaluation was that

> in none of the sampled documents did the SRB conclude categorically whether the bank could actually be resolved. While some chapters contained a brief summary of the assessment of resolvability, in most of them the summary was limited to a few of the identified potential impediments.[183]

[173] Article 10(11) of SRMR.

[174] ibid.

[175] See n 152, 13.

[176] See n 168, 3.

[177] See Single Resolution Board, 'Single Resolution Board work programme 2020' (2019) 4–6, available at www.srb.europa.eu.

[178] Single Resolution Board, 'Single Resolution Board work programme 2021–2023' 5, available at www.srb.europa.eu.

[179] Single Resolution Board, 'Annual report 2018' (2019) 9, available at www.srb.europa.eu.

[180] See European Court of Auditors, 'Special report no 23/2017: Single Resolution Board: Work on a challenging Banking Union task started, but still a long way to go' (20117) 23, available at www.eca.europa.eu/en/Pages/DocItem.aspx?did=44424.

[181] See S Giegold, (Verts/ALE), 'Question for written answer Z-00038/2019 to the Chair of the Single Resolution Board, Rule 141, Subject: Adoption of resolution plans and assessments of resolvability', 1, available at www.europarl.europa.eu/doceo/document/ECON-QZ-639806_EN.pdf.

[182] The SRB has already reacted to the observations made by the ECA saying that 'it should be pointed out that the ECA Special Report examined the state of play and resolution plans drafted by the SRB in 2016. Many of the Court's findings have been already addressed in the resolution plans which were prepared in 2017 or have been included as priorities in the multiannual planning and work programme published in December 2017'; see Single Resolution Board, 'Annual report 2017' (2018) 4–5, available at www.srb.europa.eu.

[183] See n 180.

Also, in replying to some questions asked by a MEP,[184] on 20 August 2019, the Vice-Chair of the SRB declared that

> certain banks may have to undertake considerable efforts to achieve resolvability, which must be phased-in over time. As long as banks are making credible progress towards this goal, categorically declaring a bank not resolvable may only slow down the progress in this regard. The SRB considers this approach an effective and promising way forward, which is in line with international practice. Only when banks do not respond and engage proactively with the SRB, formal measures will be necessary. Until today this has not been the case. For this reason, until now the SRB [has] not inform[ed] EBA about an institution not being resolvable in line with Article 10(3) SRMR. In this context it should be noted, that the notification to the EBA as such would not restore the resolvability of an institution.[185]

In this regard, elsewhere we argued that although the supportive approach adopted by the SRB in the process towards resolvability is certainly thoughtful, it is not clear whether there are still banks that in its view are not resolvable.[186] Thus, it remains uncertain whether impediments to resolvability have been identified and removed.[187] The Chair of the SRB declared in the work programme 2020 that 'work on the identification of impediments has also moved forward'. This is a positive outcome, but what still needs to be done is unknown and the SRB work programme 2020 outlines that in recent years, information resources and technology (IRTs) carried out the preliminary identification and analysis of potential impediments (as part of the resolvability assessment) and communicated the outcomes to banks, together with consequential working priorities. IRTs also conducted workshops with banks on the resolvability assessment, thereby confirming that that is an important factor for the removal of potential barriers to resolution.[188] The reference to 'step towards the removal of potential barriers' might be interpreted as the implicit admission that some institutions are still affected by such impediments, which therefore have not been removed yet.[189] If that was the case, then there would still be some banks that currently are not

[184] See n 181. The questions were: 1) for how many of the 127 banks within its remit has the SRB adopted final (phase four) resolution plans? 2) for how many of them has it concluded categorically by a specific reporting date whether the bank could actually be resolved? 3) For how many of them has it sent notifications of non-resolvability to the EBA?

[185] Single Resolution Board, 'Reply to written question Z-038/2019 by MEP Sven Giegold' (20 August 2019) 3, available at www.srb.europa.eu.

[186] See n 152, 15.

[187] M Grande, 'Resolution planning in practice', Presentation delivered at the Florence School of Banking and Finance (4 October 2017), available at www.srb.europa.eu, saying that examples of potential impediments identified by the SRB in 2016 are as follows: insufficient loss-absorbing capacity; operational continuity, such as continuity of access to FMIs; inability to provide information in time; execution of bail-in; funding during/post resolution; group structure (ie lack of a holding company); and cross-border issues.

[188] See n 177.

[189] See n 152, 15.

considered to be resolvable.[190] This conclusion would be consistent with what the Chair of the SRB stated in the SRB work programme 2019: 'making banks resolvable is a marathon not a sprint; it will take a number of years'.[191] It would also be in line with the content of the work programme 2021–23, where it is underlined that banks will have to 'build, under the SRB steer, the capabilities to become resolvable, gradually, by 2023 at the latest'.[192]

C. The Confidential Nature of Resolution Plans

Resolution plans have a confidential nature, thus their content is not publicly accessible. However, after Banco Popular was resolved in 2017, some parts of its resolution plan were published.[193] Interestingly, that resolution plan stated that there were several potential barriers to resolution, but none of them was considered to be substantive and therefore no formal procedure was launched to adopt specific measures for their removal.[194] Yet, the list of impediments is abridged, thereby making it impossible to analyse them and examine the approach taken by the SRB in determining that they were not substantive.

Elsewhere we argued in favour of the publication of a non-confidential and abridged version of such plans, on the grounds that this would not violate professional secrecy since there would not be any illegitimate disclosure of confidential information.[195] This is the approach already in place in the US, where the publication of these plans does not seem to negatively affect public confidence or market competition.[196] Importantly, in this respect, the FSB published a discussion paper recalling the relevance of public disclosure of information on resolution planning and the resolvability of institutions, and pointing to the benefits for investors and market discipline that such disclosure could provide.[197]

[190] See Financial Stability Board, 'Removing remaining obstacles to resolvability, report to the G20 on progress in resolution' (2015), *passim*, stating that at that point in time 'some G-SIB home authorities identified material impediments to the resolvability of the G-SIB or G-SIBs in their jurisdiction and stated that they would not consider the G-SIB or G-SIBs resolvable until these issues have been addressed'; particularly the impediments to resolvability identified at that time were related to: 1) funding and liquidity needs in resolution, 2) continuity of shared services that are necessary to maintain the provision of a firm's critical functions in resolution, 3) continued access to payment, settlement and clearing services, 4) capabilities to generate accurate and timely information in resolution, 5) implementation of the new TLAC standard, 6) making bail-in operational, 7) cross-border effectiveness of resolution actions'.

[191] See Single Resolution Board, 'Single Resolution Board work programme 2019' (2018) 3, available at www.srb.europa.eu.

[192] n 178, 8.

[193] See Banco Popular, Group resolution plan, Version 2016, available at -www.srb.europa.eu/system/files/media/document/2016_resolution_plan_updated_29_08_2019.pdf.

[194] ibid, 34–35.

[195] See n 9, 25.

[196] See C Russo, 'Resolution plans and resolution strategies: do they make G-SIBs resolvable and avoid ring fence?' (2019) 20 *European Business Organization Law Review* 1, *passim*.

[197] See Financial Stability Board, 'Public disclosures on resolution planning and resolvability', Discussion paper for public consultation, 3 June 2019, 2.

In the absence of public summaries of resolution plans, elsewhere we analysed the annual reports of banks under the remit of the SRB to find indications concerning impediments to resolvability.[198] The sample consisted of more than 400 annual reports drafted by 72 banks, representing approximately 60 per cent of the banks under the SRB's remit. The sample included 59 banking groups and 13 subsidiaries, and focused on the years 2015–20, thereby covering the whole period since the SRB has resumed its full legal mandate in 2016. The annual reports were analysed in respect of three types of information, namely: 'i) references to the crisis management framework or resolution; ii) indications of impediments or obstacles to resolvability; and iii) indications of impediments or obstacles to resolvability which are being addressed'.[199]

While, in most annual reports, banks referred to the crisis management framework or resolution,[200] only a few banks indicated the potential existence of impediments or obstacles to resolvability.[201] Most of these banks would rely upon a multiple point of entry strategy in the event of being resolved.[202]

On average, however, the annual reports of nearly every bank provide very limited explicit information on impediments or obstacles to resolvability and whether they have been assessed.[203] Yet, the SRB is well aware of the importance of disclosure on these aspects and recently pointed out that

> a more transparent assessment of resolvability is the next key milestone in the framework. That's why we have defined a heat-map on assessing resolvability, designed as a tool to monitor, benchmark and communicate on banks' progress towards full resolvability. An anonymised version of the heat-map according to various dimensions will be made public closer to the end of the phasing-in period of the guidance.[204]

[198] See n 152, 16, emphasising that 'the annual reports are required to cover all the aspects which are of material importance to the financial situation of the banks concerned. This means that when there are any significant changes to the bank in order to make the bank easier to resolve, this would be mentioned in the annual report'.

[199] ibid, 16.

[200] ibid, 16–17, highlighting that 'The share of banks making such a reference has grown slightly in the past few years from 63% in the annual reports covering the financial year 2015 to 69% in the annual reports for the financial year 2020. Among the different types of banks, the parent institutions relatively more frequently have such a reference. In most cases, the banks just refer to the BRRD and SRMR as part of the legislation they are subject to or note that they have a resolution plan'.

[201] ibid, 17, emphasising that 'in the period between 2015 and 2020, the share of banks in the sample mentioning impediments in their annual report ranged between 1 % and 6 %'.

[202] ibid, 17, saying that 'these are also almost exclusively 1 % to 3 % of the banks in the sample which indicated they have taken measures to address obstacles to resolution'. In this regard, it is stated in Banco Santander's 2020 annual report that: 'We continued to make progress with projects to improve resolvability, defining these lines of action: 1) Ensure a sufficient buffer of instruments with loss absorption capacity .... 2) Ensure information systems can quickly provide the high-quality information required in resolution. ... 3) Guarantee operational continuity in resolution situations.'

[203] ibid, 17.

[204] See S Laviola, 'SRB's new heat-map approach enhances resolvability assessment', 22 July 2021, available at www.srb.europa.eu/en/content/srbs-new-heat-map-approach-enhances-resolvability-assessment.

D. The Position of the SRB as to the Removal of Impediments to Resolvability and the Progress made by Banks within the Banking Union

The view of the SRB is that banks should proactively work to make themselves resolvable,[205] and accordingly the SRB expects that banks demonstrate that they are actually resolvable.[206] This view is based on the assumption that banks 'know their business structure and how to address possible impediments best',[207] and has been further reiterated with the publication of a guidance entitled 'Expectations for banks', where the SRB outlines that it expects that banks ensure an appropriate level of resolvability.[208] The guidance accordingly states that in achieving resolvability 'banks are expected to play an active role in the process of identifying and removing impediments; this is the most efficient way to progress towards resolvability'.[209] To this end, the guidance sets out the actions that banks should take to make themselves resolvable and provides guidelines on seven different dimensions that institutions should accordingly take into consideration.[210]

For most of these dimensions – liquidity and funding in resolution, operational continuity, IT systems and data requirements, and communication – banks do not publicly disclose information on a regular and comparable basis; loss absorption and recapitalisation are not considered as impediments to resolvability on their own.[211] Yet, some indicators that banks publish could help to identify progress toward resolvability, such as the complexity of the group structure measured by the number of consolidated entities and the amount of illiquid assets.[212] Applying the first indicator to 54 banks under the remit of the SRB, we found that overall the structures of the banks in the sample were somewhat simplified between 2015 and 2020.[213] The average number of consolidated entities indeed decreased from around 47 to 32 entities (−12.5 per cent). While the most significant decreases were in 2016 and 2020, between those years the average number of entities remained more or less the same.[214] Also, there seem to be some indications

[205] In this regard see n 161, 14, arguing that the SRB 'seems to deviate increasingly from the process for identification foreseen in the legislation, with more reliance on the industry in addressing impediments'.
[206] n 177.
[207] n 179, 5.
[208] n 163.
[209] ibid, 7, also stating that 'it is the SRB's task to set the direction and to ensure it actually happens'.
[210] n 163.
[211] See n 152, 18.
[212] ibid, 18.
[213] ibid, 18.
[214] ibid, 18, also adding that 'the reduction in the complexity of bank structures has been common across most groups and years … Looking at the period from 2016 to 2020, each year fewer than half of the banks reduced the number of consolidated entities and about one third kept the number of entities the same. During the course of the entire period just over half of the banks (54 %) decreased the number of entities, while about one third of the banks (31 %) increased the complexity. The remaining about 15 % of the banks kept the complexity unchanged'.

that banking groups and banks relying on a multiple point of entry strategy in particular simplified their structures.[215] Yet even before the adoption of the most recent initiatives by the SRB, several banks – Nordea, BBVA and Santander[216] – underwent a reorganisation of their groups on the grounds that resolvability could be more easily and effectively achieved with simplified organisational structures.

As to the second indicator, the assumption is that owning a huge amount of illiquid assets can turn out to be a challenge in resolution as they are (more) difficult to sell.[217] Banks with fewer illiquid assets thus can be seen (at least in principle) easier to resolve. The stock of illiquid assets has been measured on the basis of developments in the amount of Level 3 assets on the balance sheet.[218] This stock has slightly declined since 2015 for the 45 banks that reported Level 3 assets.[219] More precisely, while the amount of Level 3 assets remained fairly unchanged in 2016 and 2017, it subsequently decreased.[220] Overall, the stock of Level 3 assets declined from €655 billion to €631 billion in 2020 (down four per cent).[221] However, there are large differences across banks in the sample. Nearly half of them saw their stock of Level 3 assets fall between 2015 and 2020, and slightly more than half of them saw their Level 3 assets increase.[222] Overall, considering the stocks of illiquid assets, it can be inferred that most of the banks in the sample have not become easier to resolve.[223]

VIII. Resolution within the Banking Union

The decision to resolve Banco Popular Español SA in 2017 was the first resolution action taken by the SRB. On 6 June 2017, the ECB decided that the Spanish bank was FOLF and the following day, the SRB decided to submit the institution to resolution.[224]

The SRB and the Spanish National Resolution Authority considered that resolution action was in the public interest as it would protect all depositors and ensure financial stability in Spain and Portugal.[225] Banco Popular was in fact resolved on

[215] ibid, 19.
[216] ibid, 19.
[217] ibid, 19.
[218] The IFRS accounting framework considers three levels for the measurement of fair value, which aim to capture the exit price. This is relatively straightforward for identical assets and liabilities traded in active quoted markets (Level 1 assets), more difficult for prices that are observable for assets and liabilities (Level 2 assets), and most challenging for assets and liabilities for which no price is observed (Level 3 assets).
[219] See n 152, 10.
[220] ibid, 19.
[221] ibid, 19.
[222] ibid, 19.
[223] ibid, 19.
[224] See Single Resolution Board, 'Decision concerning the adoption of a resolution scheme in respect of Banco Popular Español S.A.' (2017) 7 June 2017, available at www.srb.europa.eu.
[225] ibid.

the assumption that its liquidation under Spanish law would have not been able to achieve the resolution objectives to the same extent as resolution. In the non-confidential version of the resolution plan of Banco Popular, the argument of the lack of credibility of the winding up under Spanish national insolvency law was grounded in the potential adverse effects that the liquidation could 'create for the real economy and the Spanish financial system due to its size, number of deposits and interconnections'.[226] In the press release published after the decision, the SRB mentioned that the use of the sale of business tool would allow to reach the resolution objectives and ensure financial stability in Spain and Portugal, where Banco Popular owned a subsidiary. Yet, no mention of Portugal was made in the resolution plan. Despite several references to the inability of Spanish insolvency proceedings to achieve the resolution objectives, no detailed explanation of where these deficiencies stood was provided. Nor were further details provided in the extended version of the resolution decision. While a longer description of the Spanish insolvency law was included, there was no detailed discussion as to why a possible liquidation under that law was not considered to be credible. This was merely justified by the likely 'adverse impact on the real economy and the financial system of Spain' and a 'material adverse effect on other institutions due to the high risk of contagion, through direct exposures and to the similarities of their business model'.

The resolution action taken by the SRB was based on a provisional valuation of assets and liabilities performed by Deloitte[227] and the resolution scheme combined write-down and conversion of capital instruments with the sale of business tool. Particularly, shares and Additional Tier 1 (AT1) instruments were written down, Tier 2 instruments were converted into shares and the new shares were sold to Santander for one euro.[228]

Although the resolution of Banco Popular was deemed a great success, it seems that its successful execution was primarily due to Santander deciding to purchase Banco Popular (for one euro), thereby taking on the considerable mismatch between assets and liabilities of the resolved entity. To comply with the capital requirements rules, in the following months in fact Banco Santander had to raise more than €7 billion to fill the gap.[229]

Even though Banco Popular's resolution is often described as a textbook case of how to resolve a FOLF bank (since no public funds were injected), the extent of litigation resulting from this decision has been substantial, with administrative review and claims brought before the Spanish courts, as well as the Court of Justice of the European Union and the International Centre for the Settlement

[226] ibid.
[227] See Deloitte, 'Hippocrates – Provisional Valuation Report', 6 June 2017, available at www.srb.europa.eu.
[228] See n 224.
[229] See n 9, 12.

of Investment Disputes (ICSID).[230] There were also complaints raised in front of the Spanish competition authority (Comision Nacional de los Mercados y Competencia). As to investor-state arbitration, in 2017 a group of Mexican investors explored litigation options over the failure of Banco Popular, which included a request for arbitration by ICSID presented by GBM Global, Sociedad Anonima de Capital Variable, Fondo de Inversion de Renta Variable et al, against the Kingdom of Spain for violation of the 2006 Bilateral Investment Treaty between Mexico and Spain.[231]

More recently, on 27 February 2022, the European Central Bank assessed that the Austrian bank, Sberbank Europe AG, and its subsidiaries in Croatia and Slovenia, Sberbank d.d. and Sberbank banka d.d. respectively, were failing or likely to fail due to a deterioration of their liquidity situation, likely connected to the start of the war in Ukraine.[232] The Austrian parent bank, Sberbank Europe AG, was fully owned by Sberbank of Russia, which is a Russian public joint-stock company whose majority shareholder is the Russian Federation (50 per cent plus one voting share). The ECB decided that the three banks were FOLF after determining that, in the near future, they would have been likely to be unable to pay their debts or other liabilities as they would fall due. Sberbank Europe AG and its subsidiaries experienced significant deposit outflows as a result of the reputational impact of geopolitical tensions. This led to a deterioration of their liquidity position. Importantly, in the view of the ECB, there were no available measures with a realistic chance of restoring this position at group level and in each subsidiary within the Banking Union.[233]

On the same day, the SRB confirmed that three banks were failing or likely to fail as a consequence of a rapid and significant deterioration of the banking group's liquidity situation. On these grounds, the SRB immediately applied a suspension of payments, enforcement and termination rights, known as a moratorium, to the three banks. The application of a moratorium determined that until 1 March 2022 at 23:59:59 all payment or delivery obligations pursuant to any contract to which the three banks were parties, including eligible deposits, were suspended (with

[230] See srb.europa.eu/en/content/banco-popular; see also F Della Negra and R Smith, 'The Banking Union and Union Courts: overview of cases as at 11 February 2019', available at ebi-europa.eu/publications/eu-cases-or-jurisprudence/.

[231] See n 9, 21.

[232] Sberbank Europe AG was a universal bank operating in some Banking Union Member States, EU Member States and third countries, either through branches or subsidiaries. It had 185 branches and more than 3,933 employees. Sberbank Europe AG reported €13.64bn total assets at consolidated level and €6.82bn in the Banking Union entities in Austria, Croatia and Slovenia (aggregated). The bank operated in the following sectors: corporate loans and global market services to large corporates; SMEs loans and account services to SMEs across Central and Eastern Europe; retail mortgage and consumer loans, deposits and account services to retail clients in all markets, including through its online branch in Germany.

[233] See European Central Bank, 'ECB assesses that Sberbank Europe AG and its subsidiaries in Croatia and Slovenia are failing or likely to fail', Press release, 28 February 2022, available at www.bankingsupervision.europa.eu/press/pr/date/2022/html/ssm.pr220228~3121b6aec1.en.html.

some exceptions as to payment and delivery obligations),[234] all secured creditors were restricted from enforcing security interests in relation to any of the assets of those institutions and all the termination rights of any party to a contract with the three banks were suspended.[235]

After the application of the moratorium, the SRB considered whether resolution action in respect of any of the three entities within the Banking Union was in the public interest. On 1 March 2022, it came to the conclusion that resolution was not necessary in the public interest in respect of the parent bank, Sberbank Europe AG, established in Austria, due to its characteristics and its specific financial and economic situation. The conclusion reached by the SRB was based on two main considerations: the functions performed by the Austrian bank, eg deposit-taking, lending activities and payment services, were not critical, since their discontinuance would have led neither to the disruption of services that were essential to the real economy of Austria nor to the disruption of financial stability in Austria or in other Member States; and the failure of the bank was not likely to result in significant adverse effects on financial stability in Austria or in other Member States.[236]

On the other hand, on the same day the SRB decided to adopt a resolution scheme in respect of both Sberbank d.d. and Sberbank banka d.d., the Croatian and Slovenian subsidiaries. With regard to Sberbank d.d., resolution action was considered necessary for the achievement of, and proportionate to, avoiding significant adverse effects on financial stability in that the winding up of the bank under normal insolvency proceedings would not meet the resolution objectives to the same extent. As a consequence, the SRB adopted a resolution scheme providing for the application of the sale of business tool. Thus, following a marketing procedure, the SRB decided to transfer all the shares issued by the Croatian bank to the Hrvatska Poštanska Banka.[237] As to Sberbank banka d.d., resolution action was considered necessary for the achievement of, and proportionate to: ensuring the continuity of the critical function of lending to small and medium sized enterprises (SMEs); and avoiding significant adverse effects on financial stability, also in that winding up of the bank under normal insolvency proceedings would have not met the resolution objectives to the same extent. As a consequence, the SRB adopted a resolution scheme providing for the application of the sale of business

[234] The exceptions related to: systems and operators of systems designated in accordance with Directive 98/26/EC; CCPs authorised in the Union pursuant to Art 14 of Regulation (EU) No 648/2012 and third-country CCPs recognised by ESMA pursuant to Art 25 of that Regulation; and central banks.

[235] See Single Resolution Board, 'SRB determines Sberbank Europe AG in Austria, and its subsidiaries in Croatia and Slovenia as failing or likely to fail', Press release, 28 February 2022, available at www.srb.europa.eu/en/content/srb-determines-sberbank-europe-ag-austria-and-its-subsidiaries-croatia-and-slovenia-failing.

[236] See Single Resolution Board, 'Notice summarising the decision taken in respect of Sberbank Europe AG', 1 March 2022, available at www.srb.europa.eu/system/files/media/document/20220103%20SRB%20Notice%20summarising%20the%20decision%20taken%20in%20respect%20of%20Sberbank%20Europe%20AG%20parent%20company.pdf.

[237] See n 236.

tool. Accordingly, following a marketing procedure, the SRB decided to transfer all the shares issued by the Slovenian bank to Nova Ljubljanska Banka d.d.[238]

Talking about these cases, the Chair of the SRB, stated that

> the three decisions taken today have one thing in common – protection. The decisions protect financial stability; and the decisions protect depositors up to an amount of €100,000 in Austria and with no limits in both Slovenia and Croatia. Today, we acted to protect the public interest and ensure financial stability. All of this has been done without having to use public funds, so not only are Sberbank's customers protected, the taxpayer is too. This was a complex, cross-border group and there has been excellent cooperation between authorities at EU and national level, which is even more vital in these times.[239]

IX. The UK Regime

The UK transposed the BRRD through the Banking Act 2009 as amended by the Financial Services Act 2012 and the Bank Recovery and Resolution Order 2016, with a view to ending the so-called too big to fail situations, thereby implementing mechanisms for orderly bank failure. The UK resolution regime applies to banks, building societies and certain investment firms incorporated in the UK, including the UK subsidiaries of foreign firms. However, in transposing the BRRD, the UK introduced some formal changes to the terminology used by the Directive, which concern the resolution objectives, the language relating to some key definitions as well as the 'no creditor worse off' principle.[240]

There are seven special resolution objectives mentioned by the UK Banking Act 2009, compared to the the five objectives of the BRRD.[241] These are:

(1) ensure the continuity of banking services in the UK and of critical functions;
(2) protect and enhance the stability of the financial system of the UK, including in particular by:
    (a) preventing contagion (including contagion to market infrastructures such as investment exchanges, clearing houses, recognised central securities depositories and central counterparties); and
    (b) maintaining market discipline;
(3) protect and enhance public confidence in the stability of the financial system of the UK;
(4) protect public funds, including by minimising reliance on extraordinary public financial support;

[238] See n 236.
[239] See n 36.
[240] See H Malek, J Potts and S Dzwig, *Bank Resolution – Key Issues and Local Perspectives* (London, Insol International, 2019) 163.
[241] The UK's objectives 3 and 7 are not mentioned in Art 31 of the BRRD, yet they reflect Recitals 50 and 53 to the BRRD.

(5) protect:
    (a) investors to the extent that they have investments covered by an investor compensation scheme; and
    (b) depositors to the extent that they have deposits covered by the Financial Services Compensation Scheme (FSCS) or another deposit guarantee scheme;
(6) protect client assets;
(7) avoid interfering with property rights in contravention of a Convention right (within the meaning of the Human Rights Act 1998).[242]

The Banking Act has introduced in the domestic framework each of the resolution tools set out in the BRRD. They are referred to as 'stabilisation options' and can be exercised through specified statutory powers:[243] private-sector purchaser (which is equivalent to the sale of business tool pursuant to the BRRD); bridge bank (which corresponds to the bridge institution pursuant to the BRRD); asset management vehicle (which is equivalent to the asset separation tool pursuant to the BRRD); bail-in; and temporary public ownership (which is one of the two government financial stabilisation tools regulated by the BRRD and discussed in section VI of this chapter).

In substantial terms, the Banking Act sets forth the same conditions for initiating resolution as provided under the BRRD: the bank is considered FOLF; no action other than resolution is expected to prevent the failure of the bank; resolution is considered in the public interest to achieve one or more resolution objectives; and the resolution objectives are not reachable to the same extent with the winding up of the FOLF bank.

The resolution process starts with the Prudential Regulation Authority (PRA),[244] in its capacity as the UK bank micro-prudential supervisor, deciding that a firm is FOLF.[245] In making such a decision, the PRA must consult with the Bank of England.[246] Accordingly, a firm is determined as FOLF if: there has been a failure to meet asset or management requirements that would justify the PRA cancelling the bank's permission to carry out regulated activities; assets are less than liabilities; the bank is unable to pay its liabilities; or extraordinary public financial support is required, but other than to remedy a serious disturbance in the economy of the UK.[247]

If a bank is determined as FOLF, the Bank of England must ascertain whether it is, or it is not, reasonably likely that action other than resolution will prevent its failure.[248] In making this decision, the Bank of England must consult with

[242] Banking Act 2009, s 4(3)-(9).
[243] See n 240, 167.
[244] Banking Act 2009, s 83A.
[245] Banking Act, s 7(2).
[246] Banking Act, s 7(5F).
[247] Banking Act, s 7(5C).
[248] Banking Act, s 7(3).

the PRA, the Financial Conduct Authority (FCA) and the Treasury.[249] Possible alternative actions include supervisory measures such as suspending dividends or management bonuses, financial restructuring or partial sale.

If the Bank of England is of the view that it is not reasonably likely that action other than resolution will prevent the failure of the firm, it can decide that using a stabilisation option is in the public interest to achieve a special resolution objective.[250] In making that decision, the Bank of England must consult with the PRA, the FCA and the Treasury.[251]

Linked to the previous condition, the Bank of England must also conclude that the special resolution objectives will not be achieved to the same extent by a winding up of the bank.[252] In making that decision, the Bank of England must consult with the PRA, the FCA and the Treasury.[253]

When all these conditions are met, then the FOLF institution is to be placed under resolution.

A. The Stabilisation Options

The stabilisation options are the resolution tools that the Bank of England can apply in the context of a resolution procedure with a view to achieving one or more resolution objectives.

The private-sector purchaser, as the sale of business tool in the EU framework, entails the transfer of all or part of a bank's shares or assets and liabilities to an authorised private purchaser.[254] The strength of this tool is that the transfer does not require the consent of the firm, nor the one of its shareholders, customers or counterparties.[255] The transfer usually takes place on the basis of the outcomes of an auction, thereby aiming to maximise the sale price.[256] Firms for which a partial transfer is deemed appropriate are usually those that have a single critical function relating to accounts customers use for everyday payments and cash withdrawals.[257] The tool is meant to be used for firms with between 40,000 and 80,000 transactional accounts, below the threshold for bail-in.[258] Through this tool, high-ranking deposits (including covered deposits) are expected to be transferred along with

[249] Banking Act, s 7(5G).
[250] Banking Act 2009, s 7(4).
[251] Banking Act, s 7(5H).
[252] Banking Act, s 7(5).
[253] Banking Act, s 7(5H).
[254] Banking Act 2009, s 11.
[255] Purple Book, 15, para 1.27.
[256] Banking Act 2009, s 11A(2).
[257] Purple Book, 16, box 1.
[258] A transactional account is one used at least nine times in the three months prior to an annual monitoring date, see Purple Book, 16, box 1.

high-quality assets to a private-sector purchaser or bridge bank. The rest of the firm is typically placed into an insolvency proceeding and thus liquidated.[259]

A bridge bank, as the bridge institution tool under the BRRD, is typically used if there is no private-sector purchaser immediately available.[260] The Banking Act, mirroring the BRRD, requests that the bridge bank is wholly or partly owned by the Bank of England, or controlled by the latter. It is to be created to receive the transfer of all or part of a bank's shares or assets and liabilities with a view to maintaining access to critical functions and later selling the business.[261] If, within two years of the initial transfer to the bridge bank, there has been no such transfer, the Bank of England must take steps to wind up the bridge bank.[262]

The asset management vehicle, as the asset separation tool in the EU framework, can only be used in conjunction with another resolution tool.[263] An asset management vehicle is wholly or partly owned by the Bank of England or controlled by it, and created for the purpose of buying assets from a firm or bridge bank.[264] The conditions to use the asset management vehicle are: a normal liquidation of the assets would adversely affect financial markets; the transfer is necessary to ensure the proper functioning of the transferring bank or bridge bank; or it would maximise recoveries.[265] The asset management vehicle is expected to manage the transferred assets with a view to maximising their value by sale or winding down over a longer timeframe.[266]

As in the EU framework, bail-in is the write-down or conversion of liabilities into capital.[267] According to the Purple Book, the Bank of England considers bail-in appropriate for the largest firms, with balance sheets of not less than £15–25 billion, which are too large to split up or sell to a private purchaser.[268] These include all global systemically important banks and domestic systemically important banks established in the UK.[269]

The Bank of England's preferred strategy for the majority of global systemically important banks is the single point of entry (SPOE) bail-in. Under the SPOE strategy, bail-in is typically applied to the top-level financial holding company of the group as the latter has normally issued shares and debt instruments to the market. This approach ensures that the subsidiary operating companies remain fully functional.[270] They can also be recapitalised in the case of significant losses

[259] Purple Book, 16, box 1.
[260] Banking Act 2009, s 12 and Purple Book, 25, para 2.20.
[261] Banking Act 2009, s 12(1A).
[262] Banking Act 2009, s 12(3A)-(3D).
[263] Banking Act, s 12ZA and s 8ZA(2).
[264] Banking Act, s 12ZA(2).
[265] Banking Act, s 8ZA(3); Purple Book, 25–6, para 2.25.
[266] Banking Act 2009, s 12ZA(4).
[267] Banking Act, s 12A.
[268] Purple Book, 16, box 1.
[269] Purple Book, 24, box 3.
[270] See n 240, 170.

by triggering the internal group instruments they have issued to the parent company.[271] The multiple point of entry strategy, on the contrary, might prove suitable for some global systemically important banks operating in some jurisdictions through intermediate holding companies that are managed and funded in local markets.[272]

The temporary public ownership, which in the EU framework is a government financial stabilisation tool, rather than a resolution tool, is regarded as a last resort measure.[273] The requirements to apply this tool are not only the conditions for resolution; in addition the Treasury will consider temporary public ownership to resolve or reduce a serious threat to the UK financial system, or to protect the public interest where the Treasury has provided financial assistance.[274] The Treasury must consult the PRA, the FCA and the Bank of England before making such decision.[275]

B. The Resolution Procedure

The resolution of a bank usually takes place outside normal market hours over the 'resolution weekend', although an actual weekend may not be required for smaller institutions, or where there has been extensive advance planning. Several resolution powers given to the Bank of England do not request the sanction of the courts, thereby relying only upon statutory instruments.[276] In the view of the Bank of England, once an institution has been submitted to resolution, there are three phases: the stabilisation phase, during which the Bank of England is meant to decide how to use the resolution tools to preserve critical structures by restoring solvency;[277] the restructuring phase, which is expected to address the causes of the institution's failure and restore viability;[278] and the exit from resolution phase, in which the Bank of England's role ends.[279]

The Banking Act has transposed several safeguards introduced by the BRRD which are crucial to protect the public. These safeguards relate to: continuity obligations to preserve facilities and services that the use of resolution tools might otherwise disrupt;[280] 'no shareholder or creditor worse off' principle, under which the latter cannot be worse off than they would have been in an insolvency

[271] Purple Book 22, para 2.8, and 24, box 3.
[272] See n 240, 170.
[273] See Banking Act 2009, ss 9 and 13 and Purple Book, 17, para 1.38.
[274] Banking Act, s 9(1)-(3).
[275] Banking Act, s 9(4).
[276] See n 240, 171.
[277] Purple Book, 21, paras 2.2 and 2.4.
[278] Purple Book, 21, para 2.2.
[279] See n 240, 171.
[280] Banking Act 2009, ss 63–70.

proceeding;[281] and a contribution to loss absorption and recapitalisation equal to an amount not less than eight per cent of total liabilities including own funds of the institution under resolution has been made by shareholders and creditors through write-down, conversion or otherwise before the use of public funds can take place.[282] Also, Treasury consent is required if the use of a resolution tool is likely to have implications for public funds:[283] contractual counterparties cannot terminate agreements purely because a firm has been placed under resolution, so long as the firm continues to perform its substantive obligations;[284] netting and set-off provisions and collateral arrangements shall be respected;[285] the Bank of England can suspend contractual payment and delivery obligations, and termination rights, for two days;[286] and, if the Treasury notifies the Bank of England that the use of a resolution tool would contravene one of the UK's international law obligations, the Bank of England cannot exercise that tool.[287]

X. The US Regime: The Orderly Liquidation Authority

The widespread adoption of the banking holding company (BHC) structure by American banking groups has also shaped the US crisis management framework and, accordingly, failing BHCs are not placed into a receivership, as is the case with insured depository institution (IDIs). If BHCs end up in a crisis, either they are liquidated or they undergo a reorganisation under the US Bankruptcy Code, or they are submitted to the Orderly Liquidation Authority (OLA) under the Dodd-Frank Act. The *discrimen* between the two available options (liquidation and reorganisation vis-à-vis OLA) is grounded in the systemic nature of the

[281] Purple Book, 17, para 1.35, also providing that the shareholders and creditors who are worse off in resolution than in insolvency are to be compensated by the Treasury, which in turn will recover from industry. It has been argued in this regard that the 'no creditor worse off' principle under the Banking Act is difficult to reconcile with the BRRD. Indeed, the Banking Act does not appear to limit the freedom of the resolution authority to take resolution actions so long as adequate after-the-event compensation is paid, whereas the BRRD can be interpreted as imposing the 'no creditor worse off' principles as an express limitation on the resolution authority's freedom of action; see S Gleeson and R Guynn, *Bank Resolution and Crisis Management: Law and Practice* (Oxford, Oxford University Press, 2016) paras 13.49-13.55. It remains an open question whether the UK approach potentially allows for 'over-bailing-in' creditors with compensation after the event, and whether this is compatible with the BRRD. In practice, however, this issue is unlikely to arise because, in deciding whether to use the bail-in tool, the Bank of England and PRA are bound to have regard to the 'no creditor worse off' principle as well as the need to balance the burdens on the taxpayer and the industry as a whole under special resolution objectives 2, 3, 4 and 7; see n 240, 171.

[282] Purple Book, 17, para 1.38.

[283] Banking Act 2009, ss 78–79.

[284] Banking Act, s 48Z.

[285] Banking Act, s 48P.

[286] Banking Act, ss 70A and 70C.

[287] Banking Act 2009, ss 76–77.

BHC concerned. In this vein, should the BHC in crisis be systemically important, then it will be submitted to OLA. While liquidation or reorganisation under the US Bankruptcy Code are the default option, OLA is the residual solution to apply when there are concerns that the BHC's bankruptcy could pose a systemic threat.[288]

When a BHC is handled in the context of the procedures under the Bankruptcy Code, a bankruptcy trustee is appointed with the main function to oversee the bankruptcy estate. To this end, a public liquidation or reorganisation proceeding is initiated before a bankruptcy court staffed with specialist judges. The BHC's creditors can challenge pre-bankruptcy transfers and are given the right to vote on reorganisation plans. Counterparties under qualified financial contracts (QFCs),[289] such as swaps and repurchase agreements, have the right to immediately terminate their contracts as well as to seize collateral when the debtor files for bankruptcy.[290]

Yet, a strong argument has been advanced against this process on the grounds of it being inappropriate for BHCs and other diversified financial conglomerates.[291] Its inappropriateness would result from the long timeframe and the uncertainty concerning pre-bankruptcy contracts and transfers, which could in turn negatively affect public confidence thereby leading to runs on the banks of the group.[292]

The 2008 Lehman Brothers bankruptcy is a clear example of this. This episode, along with the government rescue of AIG, led the US Congress to introduce OLA under the Dodd-Frank Act for non-bank firms whose bankruptcy is seen as able to pose systemic risks.

The objective of OLA, as stated in the Dodd-Frank Act, is to avoid the binary choice between disruptive bankruptcy and taxpayer bail-out, on one hand, and to create an incentive-compatible process suited to large financial conglomerates, on the other. With a view to reaching this twofold objective, OLA represents a hybrid process which, to a certain extent, combines the characteristics of the Federal Deposit Insurance Corporation (FDIC)-style receivership with the ones of corporate bankruptcy.[293]

The expected effectiveness of OLA rests on the flexibility and discretion given to the FDIC, which in substantial terms acts as the receiver of BHCs, thereby

[288] See M Bodellini, 'Old Ways and New Ways to Handle Failing Banks across the Atlantic' (2021) 2 *Journal of Comparative Law* 589.

[289] The category of QFCs covers most derivatives, repurchase agreements and a range of other short-term funding instruments that get similarly special treatment in bankruptcy in light of the need to maintain market liquidity.

[290] See n 288, 590.

[291] See A Gelpern and N Véron, 'An Effective Regime for Non-viable Banks: US Experience and Considerations for EU Reform' Study requested by the ECON Committee of the European Parliament, Economic Governance Support Unit (EGOV) – Directorate-General for Internal Policies of the Union (2019) 28.

[292] See n 288, 590.

[293] See H Scott and A Gelpern, *International Finance: Transactions, Policy, and Regulation* (New York, Foundation Press, 2018), *passim*.

mirroring to a certain extent the receivership of IDIs. In so doing, the objectives of preserving continuity of systemically important activities (including payment services, clearing and consumer activities), while preserving the value of the firm and minimising the spill-over effects potentially resulting from the firm's failure, are expected to be achieved.[294] Yet, it has been argued that the requirements of liquidating the BHC, while penalising the management and ruling out any losses to taxpayers, can ultimately make achieving continuity more complicated.[295]

OLA has to date never been applied, so it is impossible to ascertain whether reaching its objectives is actually feasible. OLA can apply to a number of different financial companies, such as BHCs, broker-dealers, insurers, systemically important non-bank firms designated for enhanced federal supervision, and other firms predominantly engaged in financial activities.[296] IDIs, however, are not among the institutions that can be placed under OLA. Financial companies that will be submitted to OLA, should they meet the requested conditions, are not identified in advance. Indeed, the decision on the procedure to adopt is to be made when the crisis materialises.[297] As a consequence, neither the firm nor its creditors know until the beginning of the resolution process whether the institution concerned will be subject to OLA or to bankruptcy.[298] OLA applies when the Secretary of the Treasury, in consultation with the President, and two-thirds of the serving members of each of the Federal Reserve and FDIC boards independently determine that: the firm is in default or in danger of default; its failure and resolution under other available authority, such as bankruptcy, 'would have serious adverse effects on the financial stability in the United States'; the effect of OLA on creditors would be appropriate in light of the threat to financial stability; and no viable private sector alternative is available to prevent the default.[299]

By building on some of the qualifying features of the IDI resolution process, OLA gives to the FDIC broad discretion in managing the process, including the power to treat differently creditors who are similarly situated in the creditor ranking. Also, with the exception of QFCs, the FDIC has the power to cherry-pick the contracts (including financial contracts) to keep in force.[300] On the other hand, the characteristics imported from the bankruptcy process include a recovery floor on the basis of which creditors must receive no less than the amount they would have

[294] See n 288, 590.

[295] See n 291, 29.

[296] See J Deslandes, C Dias and M Magnus, 'Liquidation of Banks: Towards an "FDI"' for the Banking Union?' In-depth analysis (2019) 3.

[297] See n 288, 591.

[298] See n 291, 29, also arguing that it is possible for a firm to be systemically important in death, even if it had not been recognised as such in life.

[299] See n 288, 591.

[300] See US Treasury, 'Orderly Liquidation Authority and Bankruptcy Reform. Report to the President of the United States', February 2018, available at home.treasury.gov/sites/default/files/2018-02/OLA_REPORT.pdf, where the Treasury proposed to limit and clarify this authority as well as to shift substantially from public to private funding for the resolution process.

received in a bankruptcy liquidation and a more favourable treatment of contingent claims as well as certain contracts.[301]

The Dodd-Frank Act has also provided for the establishment of an Orderly Liquidation Fund (OLF), which has borrowing authority from the US Treasury, although the Secretary of the Treasury must approve the FDIC borrowing for the OLF.[302]

The FDIC has gradually developed its main strategy for resolving systemically important firms under OLA, namely the Single Point of Entry (SPOE) resolution strategy. With the SPOE strategy, the FDIC is to intervene at the holding company level, thereby preserving operating subsidiaries as going concerns. Such a strategy is expected to maintain continuity of functions for the operational subsidiaries as well as the franchise value of the group.

Thus, loss-absorbing capital and liabilities at the holding company level, consistent with the total loss-absorbing capacity (TLAC) requirements, are to be used to ensure the survival of the subsidiaries. Relying on this, the FDIC is meant to establish a bridge financial company to take over most of the holding company's assets, including its shares in the operating subsidiaries.[303] The bridge financial company will be capitalised through haircutting shareholders and creditors of the holding company, with the latter thereby becoming the new shareholders of the bridge company that will eventually be sold.[304]

Clearly, the effectiveness of OLA very much depends on the availability of a sufficient amount of TLAC at the holding company level. However, this factor is sometimes regarded with scepticism.[305] Such scepticism is caused by the nature of TLAC investors and their capability to absorb losses without triggering contagion.[306] Industry critics and policy-makers have also criticised the FDIC's broad discretion as OLA receiver and its ability to treat similarly situated creditors in a different way (subject to the liquidation recovery floor) with limited scope for judicial review.[307]

XI. Concluding Remarks

The FSB Key Attributes of Effective Resolution Regimes for Financial Institutions, drafted in response to the global financial crisis of 2007–09, have been implemented

[301] See n 288, 591.

[302] See n 291, 31, also underscoring that the 'borrowing authority from the Treasury is limited to 10 percent of the book value of total consolidated assets of the firm in receivership during the 30-day period after the FDIC's appointment and to 90 percent of the fair (market) value of the firm's total consolidated assets thereafter'.

[303] See n 296, 4.

[304] See n 291, 31.

[305] See SJ Lubben and AE Wilmarth, 'Too Big and Unable to Fail' (2017) 69 *Florida Law Review* 1205.

[306] See n 288, 592.

[307] n 300, *passim*.

in many jurisdictions across the world. The new paradigm they have introduced is to resolve systemic financial institutions in an orderly manner without taxpayer exposure to loss from solvency support, while maintaining continuity of their vital economic functions. Hence, such a new paradigm is now part of the resolution regime of several countries and should help reduce the use of taxpayers' money in managing bank crises, which often occurred during the global financial crisis and, to a certain extent, even later.

According to the FSB Key Attributes, the resolution regime is meant to apply to any financial institution that could be systemically significant or critical in the event of failure. Building on the peculiarities of their banking systems, the three jurisdictions examined in this chapter (the EU, UK and US) have introduced new procedures dedicated to systemic institutions. These procedures are called 'resolution' in the EU and UK, and OLA in the US, and the designated resolution authorities are respectively the SRB, the Bank of England and the FDIC. They have all been given intrusive powers to successfully handle systemic failing institutions. As recommended by the FSB Key Attributes, such new procedures are activated when a firm is no longer viable or likely to be no longer viable, and has no reasonable prospect of returning to viability. The underlying assumption is that the new regime should enable a timely and early entry into resolution before a firm becomes balance-sheet insolvent, and before the equity has been fully wiped out.

According to the FSB Key Attributes, the main way to reach the twofold objective of successfully resolving financial institutions without using taxpayers' money, while maintaining financial stability, is to rely upon banks' internal resources. These are the resources which have already been provided by shareholders and creditors, who should thereby contribute to loss-absorption and recapitalisation. This can be done through the application of the resolution tools, particularly bail-in in the EU and UK, and through the so-called SPOE strategy in the US.

There is no doubt that the introduction of a new regime with a special administrative procedure, like resolution and OLA, tailored to the peculiar structures of systemic institutions, has been a significant step forward in effectively managing crises. The strength of the new regime results from the effectiveness of resolution tools, particularly bail-in and the US equivalent, namely SPOE strategy. By making shareholders and creditors bear previous losses, bail-in and the SPOE strategy can in fact help counteract moral hazard and bring about market discipline.[308] Also, they can limit the amount of taxpayers' money which will be used in the future to handle systemic institutions in crisis.

Yet, this does not necessarily mean that bail-outs (and more generally the use of public money in bank crises) will completely disappear.[309] If the assumption is that every effort has to be made in order to avoid banks' failures and their

[308] See A Gardella, 'Bail-in and the Financing of Resolution within the SRM Framework' in D Busch and G Ferrarini (eds), *European Banking Union* (Oxford, Oxford University Press, 2015) 373.

[309] Accordingly see n 25, 138, arguing that 'although bail-in will alleviate the burden on taxpayers substantially, it will not make public interventions obsolete'.

submission to insolvency proceedings when there exists a risk that they can create financial instability, then bail-outs will occur again, as sometimes they can be less costly than financial instability.[310] In fact, while bail-in and SPOE strategy are certainly effective and efficient instruments, there could still be cases where they may not be able in and of themselves to effectively resolve a FOLF institution reaching the objectives that resolution and OLA are meant to achieve. If an institution can be resolved with bail-in and the SPOE strategy, it means that it is not facing an 'incurable' crisis, since it already has a reasonable amount of internal resources (ie bail-in-able and TLAC-eligible liabilities) which can be written down and/or converted into capital without creating financial instability. On the other hand, an institution might sometimes be FOLF and its internal resources – *rectius* its bail-in-able and/or TLAC-eligible liabilities – could be insufficient to take it out of its crisis without amplifying the issue. That is the reason why, while bail-in and the SPOE strategy are certainly helpful, they may still need to be combined with the use of external resources. The same argument can be made when it is deemed appropriate to exempt a relevant number of liabilities from being bailed in, as such a strategy could transmit losses to other institutions thereby generating financial instability. Such external resources in the event of relatively limited-size banks being FOLF can be provided in the EU by resolution funds, provided that they are given more contributions. By contrast, in the case of crises involving very large banks and even more so in systemic crises, it is hard to find effective alternatives to the use of public money, as resolution funds, by nature, cannot have the same financial power as sovereigns, since they receive only limited contributions from the industry.[311] On these grounds, it is likely that bail-outs will continue to be performed in the future although with different forms to those seen in the past, and in combination with bail-in. To this end, the EU framework introduced the public equity support tool and the temporary public ownership tool, which represent new forms of bail-out that can be used only after the application of bail-in to a minimum amount of liabilities. In the US it seems that the amount of resources available in the context of OLA is larger than in the EU. However, this does not automatically mean that they will always be sufficient for OLA to be effective. Therefore, the possibility to make use of public funds cannot be *ex ante* ruled out.

In conclusion, it can be argued that bail-in and SPOE strategy cannot definitively replace bail-outs, but by properly combining the two tools, even in serious crises, a significant amount of taxpayers' money can be saved. And this represents considerable progress given the available solutions within the legal frameworks that were in place on both sides of the Atlantic before and immediately after the global financial crisis.

[310] See n 131, 37; see also n 146, 16, 17, calling for 'a Treaty-compatible scheme' enabling EU Member States to recapitalise solvent banks with public money on a precautionary and temporary basis in light of the difficulties that the European banking sector is still experiencing.

[311] Accordingly see M Schillig, 'Bank Resolution Regimes in Europe – Part I. Recovery and Resolution Planning, Early Intervention' (2014) 24 *European Business Law Review* 102, arguing that where such resolution funds turn 'out to be insufficient, only taxpayers can provide the necessary cash'.

6

Deposit Guarantee Schemes

I. Introduction

Deposit guarantee schemes (DGSs) represent one of the major players within the banking system safety net.[1] Their existential function consists of protecting covered depositors in the event of their bank being placed into liquidation and closed down. In such cases, by promptly reimbursing covered depositors, DGSs ensure that the stability of the system is preserved, thereby avoiding the crisis of one bank being transmitted to other institutions, which would lead to a number of other crises.[2]

The paramount importance of this function arises from the ontological vulnerability of banks, which can face liquidity crises at any point in time.[3] Such a risk is embedded in the banks' business model and way of operating, as they take deposits from the public and use them to extend loans. However, while deposits are withdrawable on demand, loans have typically longer-term maturity. This creates the so-called maturity mismatch between assets and liabilities, which can prompt liquidity issues, should several depositors, for whatever reason, decide to withdraw their deposits at the same time. This in turn results from the bank having invested deposits to make loans, with the consequence that the bank no longer has those funds available and therefore will need to sell its (liquid and illiquid) assets to meet depositors' requests. While the sale of liquid assets is typically easy and fast, the sale of illiquid assets is not always feasible and sometimes can only take place at discounted prices, thereby causing losses to the bank, which can even affect its capital solidity. In this way, liquidity crises can easily turn into solvency crises. In addition, banks are also prone to (in)solvency issues which can manifest in the event of a considerable number of borrowers defaulting on the loans they were given. Several defaults in succession would cause proportionally high losses

[1] See International Association of Deposit Insurers, 'Public Policy Objectives for Deposit Insurance Systems – Guidance Paper' (2020) 3, where it is outlined that 'A deposit insurance system may not be effective if it does not have clear, relevant and well-defined objectives that point to the broad functions it serves within the safety-net framework'.

[2] See accordingly A Arda and M Dobler, 'The Role for Deposit Insurance in Dealing with Failing Banks in the European Union' (2022) 22/2 IMF Working Paper.

[3] See M Bodellini, 'The optional measures of deposit guarantee schemes: towards a new bank crisis management paradigm?' (2021) 1 *European Journal of Legal Studies* 342.

that can wipe out the bank's capital, leading to insolvency. Against this background, DGSs play a key function as they should reassure insured depositors that their deposits will be returned even in the event of their bank going into a crisis and being liquidated. On these grounds the very presence of DGSs should disincentivise insured depositors from running on their bank in the event of issues.

The global financial crisis of 2007–09 highlighted a number of significant policy lessons for deposit insurance systems. 'The evolution of the crisis showed the importance of maintaining depositor confidence in the financial system and the key role that deposit protection plays in maintaining that confidence'.[4] Those lessons had important implications for the International Association of Deposit Insurers (IADI), which accordingly in 2014 revised its Core Principles for Effective Deposit Insurance Systems, published in 2009.[5] The Core Principles are a framework supporting effective deposit insurance practices that can be used by jurisdictions all over the world to design their internal regime on deposit insurance.[6] Interestingly, in addition to the key function of depositors' pay-out (principle 15), the Core Principles also deal with the early detection and timely intervention of DGSs (principle 13) as well as failure resolution (principle 14), which are discussed extensively below.

On this basis, this chapter analyses the functions of DGSs, mostly focusing on the so-called optional measures as well as on the restrictions limiting their implementation, and discusses some reform proposals to facilitate the involvement of DGSs in bank crises.[7]

II. The Functions Performed by Deposit Guarantee Schemes in Bank Crises

Despite having performed for decades a key role as safety net players,[8] DGSs were initially regulated at EU level only in 1994, when the first European Directive

[4] International Association of Deposit Insurers (IADI), 'IADI Core Principles for Effective Deposit Insurance Systems' (2014).

[5] Since its establishment in 2002, the mission of IADI has been to contribute to the enhancement of deposit insurance effectiveness by promoting guidance and international cooperation.

[6] The 16 IADI Principles relate to the following aspects. Principle 1: public policy objectives. Principle 2: mandate and powers. Principle 3: governance. Principle 4: relationships with other safety-net participants. Principle 5: cross-border issues. Principle 6: deposit insurer's role in contingency planning and crisis management. Principle 7: membership. Principle 8: coverage. Principle 9: sources and uses of funds. Principle 10: public awareness. Principle 11: legal protection. Principle 12: dealing with parties at fault in a bank failure. Principle 13: early detection and timely intervention. Principle 14: failure resolution. Principle 15: reimbursing depositors. Principle 16: recoveries.

[7] On the role of DGSs in bank crises see also International Association of Deposit Insurers, 'Five emerging issues in deposit insurance', IADI Policy Briefs no 4 (September 2021) *passim*.

[8] In this regard see International Association of Deposit Insurers (IADI), 'Governance of Deposit Insurance Systems – Guidance Paper' (2009) 7, where it is outlined that 'Deposit insurance systems can be structured in a number of different ways. Many deposit insurers are structured as separate government agencies or state-owned enterprises, while others are structured as government

on DGSs was adopted.[9] The most relevant legal innovation introduced by that Directive was to render it mandatory for every bank to be a member of a scheme.[10] Indeed, this became a required condition for obtaining the authorisation and then exercising the banking activity. The rationale for this was grounded in the important function DGSs are expected to perform, along with the other safety net players, in ensuring trust and confidence in the system.[11]

The EU legislation on DGSs was then revised in 2009,[12] with the increase and harmonisation of the coverage limit to €100,000 per deposit.[13] In 2014, the so-called Deposit Guarantee Schemes Directive (DGSD) was adopted in the context of the creation of a new European-wide regulatory and supervisory architecture: the Banking Union.[14] According to the DGSD, DGSs have four functions to perform, two of which are mandatory, and two of which are optional, in that Member States are allowed to decide whether their DGSs are also empowered to perform them in addition to the mandatory functions.[15] Thus, the four functions of DGSs, according to the DGSD, are: the pay-box function (mandatory); resolution financing (mandatory); the implementation of alternative measures aimed at preventing a bank's failure (optional); and the provision of financial means in the context of liquidation aimed at preserving the access of depositors to their covered deposits (optional).[16]

departments or departments of central banks or supervisory authorities. Others still are run by the private sector, usually by industry associations of deposit-taking institutions. Whatever the governance structure, they all share a common framework that consists of (1) a higher authority from which the deposit insurer receives its mandate or other authority (e.g., legislature, ministry or treasury department, industry association) and to which it is accountable; (2) the presence of a governing body (e.g., board of directors or supervisory board); and (3) a management team'.

[9] Directive 94/19/EC of the European Parliament and of the Council of 30 May 1994 on deposit-guarantee schemes [1994] OJ L135/5

[10] See M Bodellini, 'Alternative forms of deposit insurance and the quest for European harmonised deposit guarantee scheme-centred special administrative regimes to handle troubled banks' (2020) 2–3 *The Uniform Law Review*, 238.

[11] See S Ingves, 'Remarks Given at IADI Conference on Designing an Optimal Deposit Insurance System', Basel 2 (2017) 1, available at www.bis.org/speeches/sp170602.pdf.

[12] Directive 2009/14/EC of the European Parliament and of the Council of 11 March 2009 amending Directive 94/19/EC on deposit-guarantee schemes as regards the coverage level and the payout delay [2009] OJ L68/3.

[13] Importantly in this regard see International Association of Deposit Insurers (IADI), 'Enhanced Guidance for Effective Deposit Insurance Systems: Deposit Insurance Coverage – Guidance Paper' (2013) 3, where it is stated that 'Traditionally, the scope and level of deposit insurance coverage have been set so as to balance the deposit insurer's objectives of financial stability and depositor protection with incentives for depositors to exercise market discipline to limit bank risk taking and moral hazard'. Accordingly, 'The target deposit insurance coverage limit should be determined on the basis of a detailed analysis of the depositors (deposits) at risk of loss. Deposit insurance coverage limits should be set, given the policy objectives, so that most individual retail depositors in insured institutions that are at risk of being resolved are fully protected, while leaving a significant portion of the value of deposits unprotected'.

[14] Directive 2014/49/EU of the European Parliament and of the Council of 16 April 2014 on deposit guarantee schemes (Deposit Guarantee Schemes Directive) [2014] OJ L173/149.

[15] Article 11 of DGSD.

[16] The book will refer to the two optional measures under Art 11(3) and (6) of the DGSD as optional measure(s), optional intervention(s) or optional function(s), interchangeably.

The pay-box function is performed in the context of a liquidation with the aim of protecting the covered depositors of a failing bank by reimbursing them when the latter is placed into liquidation and then closed down. When that is the case, covered depositors are reimbursed by the DGS up to the covered amount. The pay-box function is considered the primary function of a DGS, as it gives to covered depositors the certainty that their deposits are protected up to the insured amount.[17] Such certainty is an effective safeguard to maintain financial stability and prevent bank runs.[18] After paying out the covered deposits, the DGS is entitled to subrogate to the covered depositors' rights in the assets liquidation process, benefiting from the same preference ('super priority') given to covered depositors by Article 108 of the BRRD.[19] As a result of giving to DGSs the same preference assigned to covered depositors in the liquidation creditor ranking, the former will more likely recover a relevant part (if not all) of the amount paid to reimburse covered depositors.[20] However, this preference does not come without any consequences, in that it could end up affecting the DGS's ability to perform the other three functions, as discussed in the following paragraphs.[21]

The second function relates to resolution financing. DGSs are in fact expected to finance the resolution of a FOLF bank according to a number of conditions laid down in Article 109 of the BRRD, thereby performing the role of loss absorber to the benefit of covered depositors.[22] In particular, the DGS is meant to contribute to resolution financing to the extent that it would have suffered a loss resulting from reimbursing depositors should such bank have been placed into liquidation. Accordingly, should the bail-in tool be applied, the DGS would be requested to provide the bank under resolution with resources equivalent to the amount by

[17] According to Art 11(1) of DGSD the financial means of a DGS shall be primarily used in order to repay depositors pursuant to this Directive.

[18] See n 13, 3, holding that 'Most depositors, if not adequately protected, will indiscriminately run from both sound and weak banks. Consequently, low coverage limits – level and scope – can create incentives for pre-emptive depositor runs that can undermine financial stability'.

[19] According to Art 108(1) of BRRD, 'Member States shall ensure that in their national laws governing normal insolvency proceedings: (a) the following have the same priority ranking which is higher than the ranking provided for the claims of ordinary unsecured creditors: (i) that part of eligible deposits from natural persons and micro, small and medium-sized enterprises which exceeds the coverage level provided for in Article 6 of Directive 2014/49/EU; (ii) deposits that would be eligible deposits from natural persons and micro, small and medium-sized enterprises were they not made through branches located outside the Union of institutions established within the Union; (b) the following have the same priority ranking which is higher than the ranking provided for under point (a): (i) covered deposits; (ii) deposit guarantee schemes subrogating to the rights and obligations of covered depositors in insolvency'.

[20] See International Association of Deposit Insurance, 'Depositor Preference and Implications for Deposit Insurance' (2020) 4 *IADI Briefs* 3, outlining that 'The introduction of depositor preference is mostly supported by the argument that it enhances recoveries by uninsured depositors and the DI and thus lowers costs for these parties'.

[21] See n 10, 239.

[22] According to Art 11(2) of DGSD the financial means of a DGS shall be used in order to finance the resolution of credit institutions in accordance with Art 109 of BRRD. The resolution authority shall determine, after consulting the DGS, the amount by which the DGS is liable.

which covered deposits would have been written down in the hypothetical event of applying the bail-in tool to them (virtual bail-in); should the other resolution tools be applied, similarly, the DGS would be required to disburse an amount equivalent to the losses that such covered depositors would have suffered.[23] Still, exercising this function is now rendered more unlikely by the introduction of the depositor preference, determining that the DGS would make a contribution only when all the other liabilities ranked below covered deposits are not enough to absorb the incurred losses.[24]

The third function, which is optional, consists of the DGS intervention at the early stages of a crisis to prevent it from escalating further. It can be exercised by providing different forms of support,[25] but needs to meet some criteria in order to be performed,[26] particularly the 'least cost principle', under which it cannot end up being more costly for the DGS than the amount it would have paid to reimburse depositors had the bank undergone a liquidation with depositors' pay-out.[27]

The fourth function, which is also optional, is the DGS provision of financial support in the context of a liquidation with a view to preserving access of depositors to their covered deposits.[28] Such financial support can be granted in different ways, but its final objective must be to allow depositors to keep on accessing their deposits.[29] Even these interventions, like the previous ones, need to comply with

[23] See n 10, 239.

[24] See S Gleeson and R Guynn, *Bank Resolution and Crisis Management* (Oxford, Oxford University Press, 2016) *passim*.

[25] These measures are contemplated also by principle 13 of the IADI Principles for Effective Deposit Insurance Systems (Early detection and timely intervention), stating that 'The deposit insurer should be part of a framework within the financial system safety net that provides for the early detection and timely intervention and resolution of troubled banks'; see n 4, 36.

[26] According to Art 11(3) of DGSD, the following conditions need to be met: '(a) the resolution authority has not taken any resolution action under Article 32 of BRRD; (b) the DGS has appropriate systems and procedures in place for selecting and implementing alternative measures and monitoring affiliated risks; (c) the costs of the measures do not exceed the costs of fulfilling the statutory or contractual mandate of the DGS; (d) the use of alternative measures by the DGS is linked to conditions imposed on the credit institution that is being supported, involving at least more stringent risk monitoring and greater verification rights for the DGS; (e) the use of alternative measures by the DGS is linked to commitments by the credit institution being supported with a view to securing access to covered deposits; (f) the ability of the affiliated credit institutions to pay the extraordinary contributions in accordance with paragraph 5 of this Article is confirmed in the assessment of the competent authority'.

[27] See G Boccuzzi and R De Lisa, 'The Changing Face of Deposit Insurance in Europe: from the DGSD to the EDIS Proposal' in G Bracchi, U Filotto and D Masciandaro (eds), *The Italian banks: which will be the 'new normal'?* (Rome, Edibank, 2016) *passim*.

[28] According to Art 11(6) of DGSD, Member States may decide that the available financial means may also be used to finance measures to preserve the access of depositors to covered deposits, including transfer of assets and liabilities and deposit book transfer, in the context of national insolvency proceedings, provided that the costs borne by the DGS do not exceed the net amount of compensating covered depositors at the credit institution concerned.

[29] These measures are contemplated also by principle 14 of the IADI Principles for Effective Deposit Insurance Systems, stating that 'Resolution and depositor protection procedures are not limited to depositor reimbursement. The resolution authority/ies has/have effective resolution tools designed to help preserve critical bank functions and to resolve banks. These include, but are not limited to, powers to replace and remove senior management, terminate contracts, transfer and sell assets and liabilities, write down or convert debt to equity and/or establish a temporary bridge institution'; see n 4, 37.

the 'least cost principle', and therefore they cannot end up being more expensive for the DGS than the amount it would have paid to reimburse depositors had the bank been submitted to a liquidation with depositors' pay-out.[30]

III. The Interplay between the Legislation on DGSs and the State Aid Regime

At EU level, further complexity affecting DGSs' intervention arises from the interplay between the state aid regime and the DGSD provisions on the optional measures that the latter can be empowered to perform according to the national rules of the Member States where they are established.[31] In this regard, the European Commission Banking Communication 2013 provides that, while the performance of the pay-box function does not qualify as provision of state aid measures,[32] when a DGS grants funds in the context of a bank's liquidation or at an early stage to prevent the bank's failure, such interventions might constitute state aid.[33] A number of elements are considered to ascertain whether the state aid regime is complied with. Particularly, for these interventions to be deemed legitimate, regardless of the private nature of the resources granted, such resources shall not be under the state's control and the decision to intervene shall not be imputable to the state.[34] If this is not the case, the intervention will be considered as state aid and will need to be authorised by the European Commission, on the condition that burden-sharing measures apply too.

Such provision is particularly critical because a bank receiving extraordinary public financial support would be consequently considered as FOLF under Article 32 of BRRD. This in turn would clearly compromise the DGS's attempt to prevent its failure.[35]

[30] See C Gortsos, 'The role of deposit guarantee schemes (DGSs) in resolution Financing' (2019) 37 *European Banking Institute Working Paper Series* 67.

[31] See n 10, 241.

[32] Pursuant to the Communication from the Commission of 30 July 2013 on the application, from 1 August 2013, of state aid rules to support measures in favour of banks in the context of the financial crisis ('2013 Banking Communication') [2013] OJ C216/1 ('European Commission Banking Communication 2013'), para 63, first part, 'Interventions by deposit guarantee funds to reimburse depositors in accordance with Member States' obligations under Directive 94/19/EC on deposit-guarantee schemes do not constitute State aid'.

[33] Pursuant to the European Commission Banking Communication 2013, para 63, second part, 'However, the use of those or similar funds to assist in the restructuring of credit institutions may constitute State aid'.

[34] Pursuant to the European Commission Banking Communication 2013, para 63, third part, 'Whilst the funds in question may derive from the private sector, they may constitute aid to the extent that they come within the control of the State and the decision as to the funds' application is imputable to the State'.

[35] See C Brescia Morra, 'The New European Union Framework for Banking Crisis Management: Rules versus Discretion' (2019) 3 *European Company and Financial Law Review* 365.

Importantly, in this regard, the European Commission has over time changed its position on the qualification of the DGSs' optional measures as a state aid. While, before 2015, the Commission was of the view that DGSs' optional measures were allowed on the grounds that they did not qualify as a provision of state aid, this interpretation changed in 2015 in the Banca Tercas case. The position of the European Commission both before and after the Banca Tercas case is explored in the next section, after a discussion on the key contributions provided over time by DGSs in successfully managing bank crises.

IV. The Key Contributions of DGSs in Handling Bank Crises

DGSs have been crucial in the successful handling of bank crises.[36] The two optional measures under Art 11(3) and (6) of the DGSD have been frequently implemented by the DGSs of some EU Member States and have often proven to be effective.[37] This has been, for example, the case in Italy. The effectiveness of the two Italian administrative bank crisis management procedures (ie special administration and compulsory administrative liquidation, discussed in chapters three and four) was in fact due in many cases to the availability of the domestic DGSs to provide financial help through one of the two available optional measures.[38] Italy has had in place for long time rules allowing its DGSs to perform both optional functions,[39] and interestingly these measures were carried out much more often than the pay-box function, being considered more effective by the authorities involved and the DGSs themselves.[40]

[36] See International Association of Deposit Insurers, 'Banking resolution: expansion of the resolution toolkit and the changing role of deposit insurers' (2021) 3 IADI Policy Briefs 2.

[37] See European Forum of Deposit Insurers, 'EFDI State of Play and Non-Binding Guidance Paper. Guarantee Schemes. Alternative Measures to Pay-out for Effective Banking Crisis Solution' (2019) 4, stating that according to a survey recently conducted on its members '14 DGSs out of 37 (8 private and 6 public) provide for "preventative measures" *ex* Art. 11.3 DGSD in their Statute … 17 DGSs (6 private and 11 public) provide for "possible interventions in liquidation" *ex* Art. 11.6 DGSD in their Statute'; see also European Banking Authority, 'Opinion of the European Banking Authority on Deposit Guarantee Scheme Funding and Uses of Deposit Guarantee Scheme Funds' (2020) 76, available at www.eba.europa.eu/sites/default/documents/files/document_library/Publications/Opinions/2020/EBA%20Opinion%20on%20DGS%20funding%20and%20uses%20of%20DGS%20funds.pdf, stating that according to a similar survey, 'Fourteen respondents from fourteen Member States reported that the use of measures under Article 11(3) was allowed in their jurisdiction'.

[38] See n 10, 237.

[39] See G Boccuzzi, 'Towards a new framework for banking crisis management. The international debate and the Italian model' (2011) *Quaderni di Ricerca Giuridica della Consulenza Legale della Banca d'Italia* 234.

[40] Similarly see A Carstens, 'Deposit insurance and financial stability: old and new challenges' Keynote address, 17th IADI Annual General Meeting and Annual Conference on Deposit insurance and financial stability: recent financial topics, Basel (2018) 3, arguing that the deposit insurer may require a wider range of instruments, beyond conventional liquidation actions which are 'needed to protect deposits as well as to manage and sell the bank's assets in a way that minimises the cost to the deposit insurance funds and maximises value for creditors'.

In Italy several crises were resolved due to the decision of DGSs to either help restructure the bank in trouble (which was sometimes placed into special administration) or fund the acquisition of (some parts of) the bank placed under compulsory administrative liquidation. The first optional measure was performed by financing (in several ways) the bank in trouble, often in the context of a special administration, with a view to preventing the situation from escalating and becoming an irreversible crisis. The support of the bank in trouble occurred mostly by funding its acquisition, recapitalising it, providing guarantees, purchasing shares, and/or taking on the negative balance between liabilities and assets to transfer. The second optional measure was implemented by providing different forms of financial support in the context of a compulsory administrative liquidation with a view to preserving access of depositors to their deposits, in this way maintaining financial stability. Such support took place mainly by funding the acquisition of the troubled bank by another bank, purchasing shares and/or taking on the negative mismatch between liabilities and assets to transfer.[41]

In terms of decision-making, the choice to support the crisis management was made by the members of the DGSs, namely all banks participating in the schemes. The main reason for accepting to jointly take on onerous financial burdens was grounded in the understanding that otherwise the whole banking system (and therefore, possibly, each bank) would have been negatively affected both in economic terms and in reputation terms, potentially also harming the confidence of the public in the stability of the system. Yet, DGSs always conducted a cost-benefit analysis of their interventions, where the points of reference to compare were the cost of the optional measure and the hypothetical cost that they would have had to bear in reimbursing covered depositors had their deposits not been transferred to another bank. This preventive assessment is known as the 'least cost' test or principle. If such assessment showed that the cost of depositors' pay-outs would have been higher than the amount required for the restructuring, or than the funds to employ in the liquidation procedure to preserve depositors' access to their deposits, then the optional intervention could take place.[42]

In Italy there are two DGSs, which were originally created on a voluntary basis as private law consortia between the end of the 1970s and the mid-1980s. The first one is the cooperative mutual banks' DGS (*Fondo di Garanzia dei Depositanti del Credito Cooperativo*) which was set up in 1978 by the Italian cooperative mutual banks (*banche di credito cooperativo*) and is meant to intervene with regard to banks belonging to that category. The second one is the main Italian DGS (*Fondo Interbancario di Tutela dei Depositi*), which was set up in 1986 by the Italian banks (along with some foreign banks' branches) other than the cooperative mutual banks.[43] The structure of both DGSs was changed in 1997 to align to the newly

[41] See n 10, 237.

[42] The cost of depositors' pay-out was calculated also in light of the amount that the DGS expected to recover from the insolvency proceeding after subrogating to the depositors' rights.

[43] See n 39, 220.

introduced duty for each bank to become members of a scheme.[44] Interestingly, at the time of their establishment, the pursued objective was to set up two proactive (and somehow reactive) system-wide tools, funded directly by banks, to be employed in the event of crises, on the assumption that it is in the interest of the whole banking system to prevent, or at least mitigate, the negative effects of crises. Accordingly, over time their main function has been to play a relevant role in resolving bank crises investing resources provided by the other banks.[45] This strategy has been then defined as system-wide-driven intervention(s).

From 1988 to 2018, the main Italian DGS (*Fondo Interbancario di Tutela dei Depositi*) intervened 12 times; in eight cases, the intervention was conducted to allow for the application of the transfer of assets and liabilities tool in the context of a liquidation, thereby avoiding an inefficient atomistic liquidation with depositors' pay-out; in two cases, the intervention supported banks placed into special administration, and in only two cases, the DGS simply reimbursed covered depositors in the context of a liquidation.[46] Since 2018 the Italian DGS has intervened a few more times by significantly recapitalising *Cassa di Risparmio di Genova* and *Banca Popolare di Bari*, both placed into special administration.[47] In line with such approach, between 1997 and 2015 the cooperative mutual bank's DGS (*Fondo di Garanzia dei Depositanti del Credito Cooperativo*) intervened 80 times and only once reimbursed covered depositors.[48]

Despite the satisfactory outcomes resulting from these optional measures, in 2015 the European Commission changed its approach as to the compliance of DGSs' optional interventions with the state aid rules. The following paragraphs discuss the Commission's position before 2015 when DGSs' optional measures were not considered in contrast with the state aid regime and the new position taken in the Banca Tercas case in 2015, where the Italian DGS optional intervention was qualified as an illegitimate state aid.

A. The Sicilcassa Crisis and the Position of the European Commission before 2015

A position holding that DGSs' optional interventions were compliant with the state aid framework was taken by the European Commission in the Sicilcassa case in the late 1990s.

[44] See F Baldi, M Bredice and R Di Salvo, 'Bank-Crisis Management Practices in Italy (1978–2015). Perspectives on the Italian Cooperative Credit Network' (2015) 44 *The Journal of European Economic History* 142; see n 39, 220.

[45] See n 10, 238.

[46] See Fondo Interbancario di Tutela dei Depositi, 'FIDT's Interventions, Interventions Report' (2020), available at www.fitd.it/Cosa_Facciamo/Interventi.

[47] Reuters, 'Italy in talks with EU over Popolare Bari rescue' (2020) *passim*.

[48] See n 44, 144–45.

Sicilcassa was a regional bank operating mainly in Sicily. In the early 1990s, a Bank of Italy inspection showed that the Sicilian bank had an extremely high number of non-performing loans. This, coupled with high operating costs, harmed both profitability and capital adequacy. On these grounds, the Bank of Italy requested Sicilcassa to reorganise with a view to merging with another more sound and solid bank. The required transactions, however, did not take place and in 1995 the Bank of Italy carried out another inspection, which revealed that the bank was in financial distress and facing serious risks for its stability. The bank was not considered able to resolve those issues on its own and thus on 7 March 1996 was placed into special administration. The administrators appointed by the Bank of Italy performed an assessment of the bank's situation, which brought up further credit losses exceeding its capital of about €979 million. Depositors and customers lost confidence in the bank, and this in turn triggered a liquidity crisis. The administrators proposed a reorganisation plan, which included a significant recapitalisation to be funded by other banks. This was considered insufficient and no other bank showed any interest in taking part. Sicilcassa was therefore placed into compulsory administrative liquidation and a relevant amount of its assets, together with almost all of its liabilities and the business organisation (staff, contracts and branches) were transferred to Banco di Sicilia. Bad loans were left within the entity under liquidation. The negative gap between assets and liabilities transferred to Banco di Sicilia was compensated by support amounting to almost €500 million provided by the Italian DGS and through a capped collateralised loan with favourable interest rate extended by the Bank of Italy.[49]

The European Commission opened the procedure for infringement of the state aid regime, focusing particularly on the intervention of the DGS to cover losses as well as on the capped collateralised loan with favourable interest rates given by the Bank of Italy. The European Commission reached the conclusion that the contribution of the DGS to cover the mismatch between assets and liabilities transferred to Banco di Sicilia did not qualify as state aid because the scheme was composed of a majority of private banks. Furthermore, the autonomy and independence of the DGS was recognised by excluding the existence of any public control over the intervention. Accordingly, the participation without voting rights of a Bank of Italy representative to the DGS's meetings was deemed irrelevant.[50] With regard to the capped collateralised loan granted by the Bank of Italy, the European Commission held that, despite constituting a state aid, it was compatible with the Treaty due to the restructuring measures implemented by the bank and the strict conditions posed by the Commission itself.[51]

[49] See n 39, 234.

[50] See A Vignini, 'State Aid and Deposit Guarantee Schemes. The CJEU Decision on Tercas and the role of DGSs in banking crises. The role of the CJEU in shaping the Banking Union: notes on Tercas (T-98/16) and Fininvest' (2019) 85 *Quaderni di Ricerca Giuridica della Consulenza Legale della Banca d'Italia* 18.

[51] European Commission, Decision of 10 November 1999 conditionally approving the aid granted by Italy to the public banks Banco di Sicilia and Sicilcassa (2000/600/EC) [2000] OJ L256/21, *passim*.

B. The Banca Tercas Crisis and the New Position of the European Commission after 2015

The position previously held by the Commission in the Sicilcassa case changed in 2015 when another Italian bank, Banca Tercas, ended up in a crisis.

Banca Tercas was a small-sized Italian bank mostly operating in a limited area (Abruzzo) in the southern part of the country. The bank had been placed into special administration by the Bank of Italy in 2012.[52] In October 2013, Banca Popolare di Bari advanced its availability to recapitalise Banca Tercas, thereby offering to become its main shareholder, on the condition that the Italian DGS would disburse €280 million to absorb previous losses, cover the negative equity and buy the impaired assets. After some negotiations between the parties involved and in light of the authorisation released by the Bank of Italy on 7 July 2014, the DGS undertook the planned intervention. On 27 July 2014, Banca Popolare di Bari subscribed to an increase of capital amounting to €230 million and on 1 October 2014 the special administration ended.[53]

On 2 March 2015, however, the European Commission informed Italy of the opening of the infringement procedure according to Article 108(2) TFEU.[54] The Commission argued that the measures implemented by the Italian DGS qualified as a state aid pursuant to Article 107 TFEU and Article 63 of the European Commission Banking Communication 2013. This interpretation was eventually confirmed in the final decision made on 23 December 2015 on the basis of the alleged public nature of the resources owned by the scheme, the public mandate exercised by the Italian DGS in the operation, and the role played by the Bank of Italy in the approval of the intervention.[55]

The Commission claimed that, despite the private nature of the contributions to the DGS, 'resources that remain under public control and are therefore available to the public authorities constitute State resources'.[56] In this vein, the Commission argued that the 'imputability to the State of an aid measure taken by a *prima facie* independent body which does not itself form part of the State can be inferred from a set of indicators arising from the circumstances of the case'.[57] In the opinion of the European Commission, the Italian DGS would exercise the public mandate of protecting depositors, not only when reimbursing them in the context of a liquidation, but also through the power to engage 'in other

[52] See Banca d'Italia, 'Banca Tercas – Cassa di Risparmio della Provincia di Teramo. Nomina degli organi dell'amministrazione straordinaria' *Italian Official Gazzette* (2012), available at www.bancaditalia.it.

[53] See n 10, 244.

[54] European Commission, Decision on the State aid SA.39451 (2015/C) (ex 2015/NN) implemented by Italy for Banca Tercas, Brussels, C (2015) 9526, 23 December 2015 [2015] OJ, *passim*.

[55] ibid, *passim*.

[56] ibid, para 113.

[57] ibid, para 116.

types and forms of intervention', as provided by the Italian legislation and under direction of the Bank of Italy. The Bank of Italy's control over the DGS was, in turn, inferred by the powers that the authority could exercise, such as the authorisation of the DGS's interventions and the approval of its statute. This interpretation was, in the view of the Commission, further supported by the Bank of Italy's participation to the DGS's meetings through one of its officials as an observer, regardless of the latter not having voting rights.[58] Additionally, the functions performed by the special administrator(s), appointed by the Bank of Italy, were regarded as an additional indicator of public control.[59] Also, moving from the mandatory participation in the DGS for every Italian non-mutual bank and the control exercised by Bank of Italy over the scheme, the Commission came to the conclusion that the latter has a public mandate in that its actions are 'subject to public policy objectives that are specific, fixed and defined by public authorities and controlled by them, notably the public policy objectives of protecting depositors'[60] and preserving the stability of the financial system.[61]

Based on these considerations, the intervention was qualified as the provision of an unlawful state aid measure primarily because the rescue strategy did not include the application of burden-sharing measures.[62] As a consequence, Italy was requested to recover the illegitimately provided aid.

C. The Consequences of the New European Commission Position and the Reaction of the Italian Banking System

The new position of the European Commission with regard to the qualification of DGSs' optional interventions as state aid significantly harmed the Italian banking system, which at that time saw a number of banks facing complicated crises.[63]

[58] ibid, paras 129–31.

[59] See n 50, 17.

[60] n 54, para 140.

[61] ibid para 141.

[62] The other two reasons were that: Italy did not present a restructuring plan, so the Commission was not able to evaluate if the aided entity could return to long-term viability; and no measures were implemented that would have sufficiently limited the distortion of competition created by the aid.

[63] The health of the Italian banking system was in that period very serious; according to a survey published by Mediobanca on the basis of the 2015 balance sheets, there were 114 banks with an amount of non-performing loans from two to eight times the value of their regulatory capital; see Mediobanca, 'Focus on the Italian banking system' (2015) *passim*, available at www.mbres.it/en/publications/leading-italian-companies; see also International Monetary Fund, 'A strategy for resolving Europe's problem loans' (2015) 19 Staff Discussion Note 9, available at www.imf.org/external/pubs/ft/sdn/2015/sdn1519.pdf, pointing out that NPLs are a serious problem for many financial institutions, which is particularly common in countries that rely mainly on bank financing, such as the euro area. Large amounts of NPLs in the banks' balance sheets reduce their profitability, by increasing funding costs and tying up the capital. This in turn negatively impacts credit supply and ultimately the growth of the

Between 2014 and 2015 four small-sized banks were in a serious situation of distress and had already been placed into special administration, namely Cassa di Risparmio di Ferrara, Banca delle Marche, Banca Popolare dell'Etruria and Cassa di Risparmio di Chieti.[64] Originally, the plan to handle them provided to set up a DGS intervention in line with the consolidated strategy. Yet, the newly established position of the European Commission, arising from the Banca Tercas case, no longer allowed it to put in place those measures. As a consequence, the four banks were resolved by the Bank of Italy at the end of 2015 with the support provided by the Italian resolution fund, as discussed in chapter five.[65]

In contrast, in 2015 the Cooperative Mutual Banks' DGS, in handling the crisis of Banca di Romagna Cooperativa, put in place an intervention that the Commission considered compliant with the state aid regime. Banca di Romagna Cooperativa was placed under compulsory administrative liquidation and the DGS supported the transfer of its assets and liabilities to Banca Sviluppo, upon the condition that both shareholders and subordinated creditors were made bear the previous losses through burden-sharing measures.[66]

Yet, after the decision requesting Italy to recover the aid granted in the Banca Tercas case, a solution aligned to the new position of the Commission had to be found in order to properly manage that crisis. The Italian DGS decided to set up a scheme to be voluntarily funded by the Italian banks.[67] The voluntary nature of the banks' participation enabled the scheme and its intervention to be considered compliant with the European Commission's new interpretation of the state aid regime. With regard to Banca Tercas, the Voluntary Scheme replicated the same intervention that the DGS was meant to perform in the first place, thereby paving the way for the recapitalisation eventually carried out by Banca Popolare di Bari, that, in so doing, acquired the control of Banca Tercas.

Since its creation, the Voluntary Scheme has intervened also in favour of Cassa di Risparmio di Cesena, Cassa di Risparmio di Rimini and Cassa di Risparmio di San Miniato (cumulatively disbursing €784 million) and Cassa di Risparmio di Genova (disbursing €318 million).[68]

entire economic system; in Italy the NPLs' problem is particularly serious as their value in 2015 was around €360 billion, ie 17% of all loans; see N Jassaud and K Kang, 'A strategy for developing a market for nonperforming loans in Italy' (2015) 15 International Monetary Fund Working Paper, *passim*.

[64] See M Bodellini, 'To Bail-In, or to Bail-Out, that is the Question' (2018) 19 *European Business Organization Law Review* 380.

[65] See M Bodellini, 'Greek and Italian "lessons" on bank restructuring: is precautionary recapitalisation the way forward?' (2017) 19 *Cambridge Yearbook of European Legal Studies* 151.

[66] European Commission, 'State aid: Commission approves liquidation aid for Italian bank Banca Romagna Cooperativa. European Commission' Statement 15/5409 (18 July 2015) *passim*.

[67] The Voluntary Scheme was established with a separate management, but relies on the DGSs' administrative bodies. The Scheme is financed by a group of banks representing 84.4% of the DGSs' member banks and 96.1% of the DGSs' covered deposits (31 December 2017).

[68] Information on the Voluntary Intervention Scheme is available at www.fitd.it/Schema_volontario/Lo_schema_volontario_di_intervento.

V. The General Court of the European Union and the Court of Justice of the European Union Judgments in the Banca Tercas Case

Despite the emergency solution implemented through the creation of the Voluntary Scheme, Italy, Banca Popolare di Bari and the Italian DGS, with the intervention of the Bank of Italy, challenged the European Commission's decision in the Banca Tercas case, bringing a legal claim before the General Court of the European Union for its annulment. The claim was based on the alleged infringement of Article 107 TFEU for the erroneous reconstruction of facts concerning the public nature of the resources employed, the imputability to the state of the contested measures, the granting of a selective advantage and the assessment of the compatibility of the alleged state aid with the internal market.[69] On 19 March 2019, the General Court of the European Union, in the judgment given in the Joined Cases T-98/16, T-196/16 and T-198/16, annulled the European Commission's decision taken in 2015 for a number of reasons.[70]

With regard to the nature of the resources employed, the Court stated that, while it is irrelevant that the aid is granted by public or private bodies established by the state with the mandate to do so, the state's control over an undertaking's activities cannot be automatically presumed. On the contrary, when the aid is granted by a private body with autonomous powers over the use of its resources, as in the case of the Italian DGS, the Commission faces an even greater burden of proof as to the existence of a public control over the use of such resources and the imputability to the state of the entity's activities. Thus, the Commission must adequately prove that the state has the power to exercise a dominant influence when granting the aid, but also that this dominant influence has been effectively exercised in the adoption of the contested measure.[71] Accordingly, the Court examined whether the Commission met such a more pervasive burden of proof, focusing on the scope of the public mandate entrusted to the Italian DGS, the autonomy of the DGS in deciding as to the measures to implement and the use of state's resources.[72]

As to the first aspect, the Court held that the DGS was not exercising any public mandate, since such alternative measures, which are never mandatory, were adopted by the DGS only with a view to avoiding the more costly financial consequences resulting from the reimbursement of covered depositors.[73] This argument found further evidence in that the DGS intervened after having ascertained that

[69] See n 50, 17.

[70] General Court of the European Union, Italian Republic and Others *v* European Commission, Joined Cases T-98/16, T-196/16 and T-198/16, Luxembourg, 19 March 2019.

[71] ibid, paras 69–70.

[72] ibid, para 90.

[73] ibid, para 97.

such measures complied with the least-cost principle, as they were deemed to be less expensive than a depositors' pay-out.[74]

With regard to the second aspect, the Court pointed that the Italian DGS is a private consortium of banks, which acts on behalf and in the interest of its members. The banks' representatives sit on its governing bodies and are appointed by the banks themselves in their capacity as DGS members.[75] The Court emphasised that the authorisation released by the Bank of Italy to provide the financial support does not constitute a suitable indicator to prove the imputability of the measure to the state.[76] Similarly, the Court contrasted the argument that the Bank of Italy could exercise control over the DGS activities by attending its meetings through one of its officials as an observer with no voting rights.[77]

In relation to the third aspect, the Court came to the conclusion that the DGS's intervention was based on the free willingness to do so of its members, which autonomously decided to empower the DGS to put in place those alternative measures and to finance the assistance granted to Banca Tercas, pursuing their own private interest to avoid the more expensive pay-out of covered depositors.[78] In this regard, in the view of the Court, the Commission failed to prove that the disbursed resources were under the control and at disposal of the Italian public authorities.[79]

All these elements and considerations led the Court to annul the Commission's decision.[80] Nonetheless, the European Commission appealed against the judgment of the General Court before the European Court of Justice.[81] On 2 March 2021, the Court of Justice of the European Union dismissed the appeal brought by the Commission against the judgment of the General Court, stating that the General Court correctly held that the measures put in place by the Italian DGS did not constitute state aid because they were not imputable to the Italian state.

VI. The Current Legal Constraints to DGSs' Optional Interventions in Bank Crises

Although the General Court of the European Union (and then the Court of Justice of the European Union) overturned the European Commission's decision in the

[74] ibid, para 104
[75] ibid, para 113.
[76] ibid, para 120.
[77] ibid, para 121.
[78] ibid, para 159.
[79] ibid, para 161.
[80] ibid, para 162.
[81] www.curia.europa.eu/juris/document/document.jsf?text=&docid=216205&pageIndex=0&doclang=EN&mode=lst&dir=&occ=first&part=1&cid=8873673; the appeal states: 'The Commission considers that the judgment under appeal is based on incorrect legal considerations and distortion of the facts, which irremediably invalidate its findings and the operative part of the judgment'.

Banca Tercas case, there are still some provisions in force potentially preventing the DGSs from successfully carrying out optional measures. In this regard, a combination of different rules, with a different underlying rationale and adopted in different periods, are able to make the DGS optional measures very difficult (if not impossible) to implement. These provisions are the state aid rules, particularly the European Commission Banking Communication 2013, paragraph 63, and the depositor preference pursuant to Article 108 of BRRD, which extends also to DGSs when subrogating to depositors' rights in the insolvency proceedings, combined with a narrow reading of the least-cost principle.

A. The Constraints Resulting from Qualifying DGSs Optional Measures as a State Aid

The first issue arises from the Banking Communication 2013 provision stating that when a DGS provides funds in the context of a bank's liquidation and at an early stage to prevent the bank's failure, the intervention is compatible with the state aid regime (irrespective of the private nature of the resources) only if the disbursed resources are not under the state's control and the decision to intervene is not imputable to the state. If this is not the case, the intervention is qualified as a state aid and can be implemented only once authorised by the Commission, on the condition that burden-sharing measures are implemented. The required application of the burden-sharing mechanism, in turn, creates further coordination issues since the DGS as such typically does not have any power to apply such mechanism.[82]

Qualifying DGSs' optional measures as state aid gives rise to further issues in that a bank receiving extraordinary public financial support is consequently determined as FOLF under Article 32 of BRRD.[83] This in turn would compromise the DGS's attempt to prevent the bank's failure. Against this backdrop the European Banking Authority has stated clearly that 'there may be merit in clarifying in the EU framework that the use of DGS funds for failure prevention would not in itself trigger the determination that the institution was failing or likely to fail'.[84]

[82] See European Forum of Deposit Insurers (n 37) 5, arguing that this 'reflects an asymmetry with the resolution authorities powers'; therefore 'considering that Article 11.3 already states that "the DGS shall consult the resolution authority and the competent authority on the measures and the conditions imposed on the credit institution" it might be appropriate to provide for an explicit pro-active role in this regard in favour of the DGS when packaging the entire intervention, also in order to clarify the roles and responsibilities of each player involved'.

[83] See n 64, 373.

[84] See European Banking Authority, 'Opinion on Deposit Guarantee Scheme Funding and Uses of Deposit Guarantee Scheme Funds' (2020), EBA/OP/2020/02, 80, also suggesting that 'The wording of Article 11 of the DGSD should be clarified to ensure that measures mentioned in Article 11(3) are referred to as "preventive measures" and those in Article 11(6) are referred to as "alternative measures", because currently the measure under Article 11(3) is referred to as an "alternative measure", which could create confusion about the purpose of such measures'.

The Banca Tercas case is considerably important in this respect since it shows the European Commission's interpretation of its Banking Communication 2013 rules. The European Commission held that a privately funded and managed consortium, such as the Italian DGS, granted state aid measures to Banca Tercas on the grounds that its intervention was allegedly influenced and directed by the public authorities. This interpretation of the facts has been criticised and eventually the Commission's decision has been overruled by the General Court and by the Court of Justice of the European Union.[85] While the decision of the General Court (then confirmed by the Court of Justice) is very important in that it sheds some light as to the legitimacy of the Italian DGS intervention, in order to clarify the legal regime in force and avoid uncertainties potentially giving rise to litigation, a review of the Banking Communication 2013 rules on DGS's optional measures appears to be needed.[86]

The importance of such a review is supported by a number of considerations. From a systematic perspective, the need to amend those provisions can be inferred from the essence of the Financial Stability Board Key Attributes of Effective Resolution Regimes for Financial Institutions, which set the goals of the new crisis-management regime. If the main objective of the new system is, as highlighted by the Key Attributes, to handle a bank's crisis without using public money while avoiding harm to financial stability,[87] then it is illogical, if not counterproductive, to render the use of private resources, like the ones of the Italian DGS, more complicated.[88] This point is made even more clear by the consideration that managing a bank's crisis without public money while keeping financial stability is a very difficult objective to achieve.[89] Importantly, this argument also holds true if a public authority (such as the bank supervisor or the Ministry of Finance) decides to exercise moral suasion on the banking system participants, namely the banks, to implement an effective solution in the interest of the whole system.[90] Moreover, in any case, the use of private resources, by default, cannot be qualified as a state aid, since the logical underlying assumption is that such an aid is granted by disbursing

[85] See S Maccarone, 'La sentenza del Tribunale europeo sul caso Tercas' (2019) 3 *Bancaria*, *passim*.

[86] Accordingly see European Banking Authority, 'Opinion on Deposit Guarantee Scheme Funding and Uses of Deposit Guarantee Scheme Funds' (2020), EBA/OP/2020/02, 81, stating that 'Subject to the outcome of the Commission's appeal in the *Tercas* case, the EBA invites the Commission to consider if there is a need to amend the Banking Communication and the potentially different consequences for DGSs depending on their legal status and/or governance structure'.

[87] Financial Stability Board, 'Key Attributes of Effective Resolution Regimes for Financial Institutions' (2014) 1, stating that the implementation of the Key Attributes 'should allow authorities to resolve financial institutions in an orderly manner without taxpayer exposure to loss from solvency support, while maintaining continuity of their vital economic functions'.

[88] See n 10, 249.

[89] See B Biljanovska, 'Aligning Market Discipline and Financial Stability: a More Gradual Shift from Contingent Convertible Capital to Bail-in Measures' (2016) 17 *European Business Organization Law Review* 105, 106, arguing that 'market discipline and financial stability cannot be achieved simultaneously'.

[90] n 10, 249.

state resources, rather than private resources.[91] Thus, in a context where public intervention is rightly discouraged, any possible privately funded solution should be facilitated instead.[92]

The proposed revision of the Banking Communication 2013 should accordingly ensure that the optional functions performed by those DGSs that collect private resources, are privately managed and comply with the least-cost principle do not qualify as a state aid. This would in turn resolve the friction between Article 11 of the DGSD, paragraph 63 of the Banking Communication 2013 and article 32 of the BRRD, stating that the provision of extraordinary public financial support would make the bank concerned FOLF. Thus, if DGSs' optional measures no longer qualified as a state aid, their implementation, which would not cause the recipient bank to be considered as FOLF, could successfully take place.

B. The Constraints Resulting from the Extension of the Depositor Preference to DGSs

The second issue arises from the introduction of the depositor preference by the BRRD, which extends to DGSs once subrogating to depositors' rights in the insolvency proceedings. This rule, coupled with a strict application of the least-cost principle, can end up making every DGS optional intervention very difficult (if not impossible) to implement. In this vein, optional interventions are allowed only to the extent that the DGS does not disburse more money than the amount it would have had to pay to reimburse covered depositors in the context of a liquidation with depositors' pay-out.[93] Yet, due to the depositor preference, which also applies to DGSs, it is unlikely that the latter will be called to bear losses at all. This could happen only in those scenarios where losses are so high that all the other liabilities ranked below deposits are not sufficient for their absorption. Even if, by only focusing on the bank crisis in question, the DGS concerned might appear

[91] Similarly see International Monetary Fund, 'Euro Area Policies: Financial System Stability Assessment' (2018) 226 IMF Country Report 28, arguing that 'Deposit and asset transfers funded by DISs could likewise be granted a presumption of compliance when provided on a "least cost" basis according to agreed open procedures and subject to European-level oversight, thus minimizing competition concerns'.

[92] See n 10, 250.

[93] On this see European Banking Authority, 'Opinion on Deposit Guarantee Scheme Funding and Uses of Deposit Guarantee Scheme Funds' (2020), EBA/OP/2020/02, 81, stating that 'There is a need to provide more clarity on how to assess that: the costs of the measures do not exceed the costs of fulfilling the statutory or contractual mandate of the DGS (as per Article 11(3)); the costs borne by the DGS do not exceed the net amount of compensating covered depositors at the credit institution concerned (as per Article 11(6)). There is also a need for more clarity on what kind of costs should be taken into account in the abovementioned assessments (only direct or also indirect costs – and what costs constitute indirect costs), particularly because the current lack of clarity poses the risk that different authorities will take different approaches to the least cost assessment; such clarifications should be made in a legal product that provides sufficient legal certainty for DGSs'.

better off thanks to the depositor preference rule, in that it will recover all (or a relevant part of) the resources employed to reimburse covered depositors, this is still not necessarily the best possible outcome from a system-wide perspective.[94] The best possible outcome from such a perspective would be the overall cheapest and safest solution for all the stakeholders involved.[95] Still, due to the depositor preference rule, it will be almost impossible for DGSs to provide any support aimed at preventing the bank's failure as well as to finance measures in the context of liquidation. As a result, typically only a liquidation with depositors' pay-out would be implementable and this could cause the destruction of more value, thereby negatively affecting both the other unsecured creditors and potentially the banking system as whole should financial stability be affected. This argument is based on the grounds that a disorderly atomistic liquidation where banking activity is immediately interrupted and business lines are not transferred to other institutions can trigger a crisis of confidence, causing massive shifts of deposits across banks. In extremely serious situations, this can even lead to deposit runs. Should the first crisis also spread to other banks, then the costs for the DGS resulting from depositors' pay-out could end up being much higher than initially foreseen.[96]

Undoubtedly, such outcomes would be neither beneficial for the system nor in the interest of the DGS itself. Since the interests of the DGS reflect the interests of its members, which in turn are the banks that are part of the banking system, I argued elsewhere that the interests of the DGS are the interests of the banking system.[97] On these grounds, the least-cost principle could be revised to take into account the general interests of the banking system as a whole and not just the cost paid by the DGS in implementing the optional measures concerned. On these grounds, the cost of the optional measures should be compared not only with the cost of depositors' pay-out but also with the amount of direct and indirect costs for the banking system – and potentially for the real economy – arising from a piecemeal liquidation.[98] This means, in other words, that disregarding the

[94] See A De Aldisio, G Aloia, A Bentivegna, A Gagliano, E Giorgiantonio, C Lanfranchi and M Maltese, 'Towards a framework for orderly liquidation of banks in the EU' Notes on Financial Stability and Supervision of Banca d'Italia No 15 (August 2019) 6, who demonstrate that even when an optional measure implemented by the DGS ends up being more expensive for it than the depositors' pay-out, such a strategy is typically more effective from a system-wide perspective.

[95] See European Forum of Deposit Insurers (n 37) 25.

[96] See n 94, 9.

[97] See n 10, 251.

[98] See European Forum of Deposit Insurers (n 37) 6, stating that in the context of the measures pursuant Art 11(6) of DGSD, 'the "least cost evaluation" is recommended to consider a comprehensive range of elements, including the direct (financial, operational, etc.) and indirect costs (missing return on liquidity, increasing cost of funding, etc.) of pay-out, adequate haircuts on the expected recovery side, and also contagion and reputation risks which may lead to further reimbursements; on the other side, the costs of "interventions in liquidation" for the DGS, entailing refundable or recoverable disbursements and guarantees, are proposed to be calculated to the extent of expected losses estimated at the date of the intervention; in case of shortfall between assets and liabilities to be transferred, clearly also the related cost to be covered by the DGS in favour of the acquiring bank has to be considered'.

indirect costs for the banking (and possibly the economic) system would lead to a partial result, that as such would be unable to identify the best possible solution to adopt.

This interpretation seems to be supported by the rationale which lies behind the DGSD, which also introduces and regulates DGSs optional measures. In this vein, it would be illogical to regulate these functions, while having in place other rules which in effect hinder their implementation. But even more significantly, the Financial Stability Board Key Attributes of Effective Resolution Regimes mandate to resolve FOLF banks without using public money while avoiding negative systemic effects.[99] Given that the resources disbursed by DGSs are those paid by banks, their capacity to handle crises in forms different from depositors' pay-out should be facilitated on the grounds that there might otherwise be a risk that either taxpayers' money could be needed or the whole system might be harmed. Accordingly, the incentive should be moved from enabling only (often inefficient) piecemeal liquidations (with depositors' pay-out) to allowing also more system-wide effective DGS optional measures.[100] The counterargument to this could be that a system-wide-driven determination of the least-cost principle would be either arbitrary and inaccurate, or practically impossible to make (or both). However, it has been argued that, even though calculating indirect costs would not be easy, still on the basis of previous experiences such costs can be material and therefore a methodology to assess them could be developed.[101] At any rate, should such a broader application of the least-cost principle aimed at taking into account the overarching interest(s) of the system be regarded as practically unfeasible, then more radical solutions could be introduced. These would be either the increase of the coverage threshold for covered deposits or the removal of the extension to DGSs of the depositor preference in the exercise of their subrogation rights within insolvency proceedings.[102] By rendering depositors' pay-outs more costly, both options would impact on the least-cost test and accordingly make it easier for DGSs to also perform the optional measures. Since the interests of the system and the interests of DGSs are aligned, DGSs should not be inclined to raise any opposition to such a legislative amendment.

[99] See n 87, 1.

[100] See n 10, 252.

[101] Still, see n 94, 9, which says that 'even if it is more difficult to quantify these costs than it is to quantify direct costs, experience shows that they can indeed be material, as the history of crises is full of contagion episodes. It would not be overly difficult to identify a methodology to estimate these additional costs'; on this see also European Forum of Deposit Insurers, 'Cost-Benefit Analysis and Least-Cost Calculation for Decision Making Process of Deposit Guarantee Schemes' State of Play and Non-Binding Guidance Paper (2021) *passim*.

[102] ibid, 8, arguing that 'to broaden the number of cases in which the DGS may carry out alternative interventions, the super-priority rule could be eliminated for subrogated DGSs (it could still be applied to insured depositors)'.

VII. Deposit Insurance in the US

The key feature of the US bank crisis management regime consists of the centralisation of functions in the hands of the FDIC, which acts both as deposit insurer and as receiver. While such a centralisation of functions could potentially give rise to conflicts of interest, it also brings a number of synergies which are often said to make the system more efficient.

The FDIC manages the DIF that is funded in advance with risk-based contributions provided by IDIs. Additionally, the DIF has a borrowing facility of US $100 billion available with the US Treasury and there is also in place a note purchase agreement for US $100 billion with the Federal Financing Bank, which is a specialised government entity under the Treasury.[103]

As deposit insurer, the FDIC is meant to pay out insured depositors using the resources of the Deposit Insurance Fund (DIF). The standard insurance amount is US $250,000 per depositor, per insured bank, for each account ownership category.

After paying out insured depositors, the FDIC is entitled to subrogate to their rights in the distribution process. As a result of this, the FDIC typically becomes the largest and one of the most senior creditors of the receivership.[104] Unlike in the EU, however, the US framework provides for a general depositor preference regime, according to which all insured and uninsured deposits ranks equally. As a consequence, when subrogating to the insured depositors' right in the distribution process, the FDIC ranks *pari passu* with the other uninsured depositors.

Yet, in addition to paying out to depositors, the FDIC has also developed a number of methods to successfully deal with failing banks, thereby using several transaction methods to transfer assets and liabilities from failing banks to other private players. Interestingly, these transactions can be successfully implemented because the FDIC can dispose of the deposit insurance resources.[105] This is particularly the case for purchase and assumption (P&A) transactions, whose goal is to find another institution willing to take over some or all of the assets and liabilities of the failed bank.[106] Such transactions, which are often regarded as one of the most effective ways to manage crises, clearly show how important it is to have the option of employing the deposit insurer's resources to implement strategies different from depositors' pay-out and possibly more effective than it from a system-wide perspective.

[103] See Federal Deposit Insurance Corporation, 'FDIC Annual Report 2018', available at www.fdic.gov/about/strategic/report/2018annualreport/2018ar-final.pdf.

[104] See A Gelpern and N Véron, 'An Effective Regime for Non-viable Banks: US Experience and Considerations for EU Reform' Study Requested by the ECON committee of the European Parliament, Economic Governance Support Unit (EGOV) – Directorate-General for Internal Policies of the Union (2019) 19.

[105] M Bodellini, 'Old Ways and New Ways to Handle Failing Banks across the Atlantic' (2021) 2 *Journal of Comparative Law* 584.

[106] See n 104, 22.

The FDIC Improvement Act (FDICIA) of 1991 has significantly restricted the FDIC discretion to design the crisis management strategy by mandating it to use the resolution method which is least costly for the DIF. Also, according to the FDICIA, the FDIC is now requested to: develop a more rigorous cost-assessment methodology, projecting losses to the DIF on a present-value basis, using a realistic discount rate; documenting its reasoning and assumptions; and undergoing annual reviews of its resolution practice by the Government Accountability Office (GAO). The introduction of this reinforced least-cost criterion has led to a substantial decrease in the number of whole-bank P&A transactions and, as a result, to a relevant increase of the losses suffered by uninsured depositors.

VIII. A Limited-Scope Reform Proposal to Allow DGSs to Play a Leading Role in Bank Crises

The Italian and US experiences clearly underline the importance of involving DGSs in bank crisis management, and allowing them to implement measures other than depositor pay-outs.

On these grounds, a number of structural reform proposals to amend the EU regime have been advanced with a view to enabling DGSs to play a leading role in bank crises by also performing optional measures. Accordingly, the enlargement of the Single Resolution Board (SRB)'s powers to allow it to handle the failure of every bank established in the Banking Union regardless of their systemic or not-systemic nature has been discussed, along with the creation of a European DGS to be managed by the SRB, that accordingly would be empowered to execute the transfer of covered deposits of failing banks to an acquirer, as well as to apply other resolution-like tools. The adoption of a European bank-specific insolvency regime has also been taken into consideration.[107]

While the first two solutions appear more effective and are potentially able to remove those inconsistencies currently affecting the design of the Banking Union, there still seems to be very little political willingness to move towards radical architectural reforms. The inability to reach a political agreement on the creation of an EDIS, as the third pillar of the Banking Union, is a clear indicator of how complicated it is to create centralised mechanisms which are meant to collect resources from Member States, to use on a cross-border basis depending on the current needs. Nonetheless, the adoption of a European harmonised special administrative regime dedicated to those FOLF banks which cannot be resolved and based

[107] See F Restoy, 'How to improve crisis management in the banking union: a European FDIC?' CIRSF Annual International Conference 2019 on 'Financial supervision and financial stability 10 years after the crisis: achievements and next steps' (Lisbon, 2019) 5, available at www.bis.org.

on a leading role of DGSs could be a remarkable intermediate step. Such a regime could, in turn, lead progressively towards the adoption of more comprehensive solutions thereby creating over time a more resilient legal framework. Indeed, if this regime proves effective, the next step – to centralise at Banking Union level the decision-making process, the administration of common financial resources and the application of national tools, mirroring the resolution procedure – could become politically acceptable. Such a step, in other words, could help to gradually complete the Banking Union by building some solid foundations for the creation of an EDIS also empowered (either directly or through the SRB) to implement optional interventions, possibly converting over time the EU dual-track regime into a single-track regime, as discussed in chapter four.[108]

[108] See n 10, 253.

7

The Legacy of the COVID-19 Crisis

The Non-Performing Loan Problem

I. Introduction

The crisis provoked by the COVID-19 pandemic is different from the global financial crisis of 2007–09. Whereas the latter was a crisis arising out of the financial system, which eventually ended up seriously harming the real economy, the COVID-19 crisis has its origins in the real economy, and has been mostly caused by lockdowns and the measures on containment and social distancing adopted in countries around the globe.[1] Such measures, whose objective was to slow down the propagation of the virus, have significantly harmed both demand and supply of goods and services, and only a few economic activities and sectors (eg e-commerce and internet services) have benefited from the changed landscape.[2]

Nonetheless, the COVID-19 crisis is expected to hit the banking system too.[3] The banking system is notoriously heavily reliant on the real economy, so if the latter struggles, the former will be negatively affected as well. Those businesses whose activities have been stopped or limited since 2020 because of the containment measures have already shown their inability to repay loans and credit lines previously granted. Likewise, individuals losing their jobs will be unable to repay their mortgages when the extensive relief programmes activated by national governments are removed. In both cases, such insolvency issues will be transmitted to credit institutions. Should such a situation replicate several times, a risk exists to trigger another financial crisis of systemic relevance.[4]

[1] See WG Ringe, 'COVID-19 and European banks: no time for lawyers' in C Gortsos and WG Ringe (eds), *Pandemic Crisis and Financial Stability* (Frankfurt, European Banking Institute, 2020) 43.

[2] See C Hadjiemmanuil, 'European economic governance and the pandemic: Fiscal crisis management under a flawed policy process' in C Gortsos and WG Ringe (eds), *Pandemic Crisis and Financial Stability* (Frankfurt, European Banking Institute, 2020) 175.

[3] See M Bodellini and P Lintner, 'The impact of the Covid-19 pandemic on credit institutions and the importance of effective bank crisis management regimes' (2020) 9 *Law and Economics Yearly Review* 182.

[4] See M Draghi, 'We face a war against coronavirus and must mobilise accordingly' *Financial Times* (25 March 2020), where the former President of the European Central Bank and current Italian Prime Minister argues that the pandemic has already provoked a spiral of economic consequences that will inevitably lead to a serious recession, with the risk of it eventually 'morphing into a prolonged depression, made deeper by a plethora of defaults leaving irreversible damage'.

The sharp deterioration of borrowers' risk profile will also discourage banks from lending,[5] and this will exacerbate and likely prolong the economic crisis.[6] Such criticalities will also cause a surge of non-performing loans (NPLs), and this is regarded as a very serious issue on the grounds that several banks had not managed yet to offload previously accumulated stocks of those 'bad' assets when the pandemic began in early 2020.[7] Accordingly, the ECB observed that due to the COVID-19 crisis, many companies struggled to keep operating. Several companies as a consequence will not survive the crisis and many households will be unable to repay their loans. As a result, an increase in NPLs is unavoidable as not all loans will be paid back in full.[8] Also, cleaning up banks' balance sheets in the current market conditions might prove a very difficult challenge.[9]

Such weaknesses are further exacerbated by the structural low profitability of the commercial banking business model (particularly) in Europe.[10] Banks' low profitability derives from a number of different factors, such as interest rates having been close to zero (and even negative) for long time, along with an excess of capacity, with several institutions having too many branches and staff, which increases their operating costs. Against this background, banks' ability to make profits will be key for the banking sector to emerge from the crisis as well as to effectively support the economic recovery.[11]

However, banks are, on average, more and better capitalised than they used to be around the time of the global financial crisis of 2007–09. Due to the regulatory initiatives adopted in the aftermath of that crisis, banks have been required to raise their

[5] See LS Morais, 'The EU fiscal response to the COVID-19 crisis and the Banking sector: risks and opportunities' in C Gortsos and WG Ringe (eds), *Pandemic Crisis and Financial Stability* (Frankfurt, European Banking Institute, 2020) 300.

[6] See C Brescia Morra, 'Lending activity in the time of coronavirus' in C Gortsos and WG Ringe (eds), *Pandemic Crisis and Financial Stability* (Frankfurt, European Banking Institute, 2020) 392.

[7] C Gortsos, 'The application of the EU banking resolution framework amidst the pandemic crisis' in C Gortsos and WG Ringe (eds), *Pandemic Crisis and Financial Stability* (Frankfurt, European Banking Institute, 2020) 367, however points out that the rate of non-performing loans during the last years has, on average, significantly decreased mainly because of the introduction of the Council Action Plan of July 2017 on Non-Performing Loans and the accommodating macroeconomic conditions. Yet, the existing stock of NPLs resulting from the global financial crisis or the subsequent fiscal crisis in the Euro Area still varies significantly among Member States.

[8] European Central Bank, 'What are non-performing loans (NPLs)?', available at www.bankingsupervision.europa.eu/about/ssmexplained/html/npl.en.html, stressing that to minimise this increase of NPLs, 'even in difficult times, banks should only lend to customers who are likely to pay back. It has also reminded banks to keep a close eye on the risks to identify and tackle non-performing loans early on'.

[9] The increase of NPLs in banks' balance sheets is closely observed by supervisors; in this regard it has been reported that the European Central Bank has been assessing the usefulness of creating a Euro-Area bad bank in charge to manage huge portfolios of NPAs; see M Arnold and J Espinoza, 'ECB pushes for Euro Zone bad bank to clean up soured loans' *Financial Times* (19 April 2020).

[10] See Bank for International Settlements, 'Effects of Covid-19 on the banking sector: the market's assessment' (2020) *BIS Bulletin* 5.

[11] See n 3, 182.

capital, by issuing more loss-absorbing instruments, as discussed in chapter three.[12] Importantly, this increased amount of capital has already allowed supervisors and regulators to temporarily reduce banks' buffers with a view to helping them extend loans.[13]

Against this backdrop, what remains to be seen is whether the increased amount of capital that banks hold will be sufficient to absorb those losses resulting from the surge of COVID-19-related NPLs. Should this not be the case, then alternative strategies will have to be designed to effectively tackle the NPL problem. Among them, asset management companies (AMCs) could play a key role. This chapter further analyses the NPL problem and then discusses the use of AMCs as a tool to adopt with a view to addressing the problem.

II. Non-Performing Loans

The definition of 'non-performing loans' is a critical one since there exist different interpretations as to when a problem loan is to be classified (or reclassified) as non-performing.[14]

When the borrower is financially healthy and pays regularly the agreed instalments as scheduled, the loan is said to be performing. Yet, a risk always exists that the borrower stops being able to repay the loan within the agreed timespan. When this is the case, or when this is likely to happen, then the bank must classify the loan as 'non-performing'. NPLs are often also called 'bad loans'.

On these grounds, the common element stressed by several definitions of 'non-performing loans' relates to the borrower's failure to pay either the principal or interests. The key aspect is that a loan becomes non-performing if the borrower has failed to pay either the principal or interests over the last 90 days.[15] Accordingly, the ECB defines a loan as 'non-performing' 'when there

[12] See M Bodellini, 'The long "journey" of banks from Basel I to Basel IV: has the banking system become more sound and resilient than it used to be?' (2019) 20 *ERA Forum*, *passim*; see also International Monetary Fund, 'Global Financial Stability Report, October 2018: A Decade after the Global Financial Crisis: Are We Safer?' (2018), available at www.elibrary.imf.org/view/IMF082/253199781484375594/25319-9781484375594/ch02.xml; see Financial Stability Board, 'Implementation and Effects of the G20 Financial Regulatory Reforms, 3rd Annual Report' (2017), available at www.fsb.org/wp-content/uploads/P030717-2.pdf.

[13] See European Central Bank, 'ECB Banking Supervision provides temporary capital and operational relief in reaction to coronavirus', Press release (12 March 2020), available at www.bankingsupervision.europa.eu/press/pr/date/2020/html/ssm.pr200312-43351ac3ac.en.html. On 16 April 2020, the European Central Bank also temporarily relaxed the capital requirements for market risk, see European Central Bank, 'ECB Banking Supervision provides temporary relief for capital requirements for market risk', Press release (16 April 2020), available at www.bankingsupervision.europa.eu/press/pr/date/2020/html/ssm.pr200416~ecf270bca8.en.html.

[14] Until early 2015, under application of the EBA Implementing Technical Standard (ITS) on non-performing exposures and forbearance, there was still no EU definition of NPLs.

[15] See P Baudino, J Orlandi and R Zamil, 'The identification and measurement of non- performing assets: a cross- country comparison' Financial Stability Institution (FSI), Insights on Policy Implementation No 7 (2018).

are indications that the borrower is unlikely to repay the loan, or if more than 90 days have passed without the borrower paying the agreed instalments'.[16]

A clear and unambiguous definition of 'non-performing loans' is crucial, as when the conditions under such definition are met, then the loan concerned should be classified as non-performing and this in turn triggers the application of specific accounting rules.[17] The definition should then be fair and well-balanced. In this regard, it has been observed that should such definition be over-accommodating, a risk exists not to capture loans that are problematic with sufficient evidence that payments are unlikely to be resumed. By contrast, if the definition is under-accommodating, the number of loans classified as 'non-performing' would be higher, with negative repercussions for banks.[18] On these grounds, banks need to look closely at the loans they have extended and identify at an early stage those ones that are at risk of becoming non-performing. This process is called 'recognition of non-performing loans'.[19]

NPLs negatively affect banks from different perspectives. First of all, they impact on banks' profitability in that the profits that banks make through lending are reduced. Also, to face the losses caused by the reclassification of loans as non-performing, banks are required to book provisions, that is to set aside resources to cover the losses they expect to incur.[20] As a consequence, such money can no longer be used to extend new loans or to absorb other losses. This further reduces banks' earnings and weakens their capital solidity. A bank that has accumulated too many NPLs is no longer in a position to properly finance its borrowers. When such issue acquires systemic proportions, it can possibly affect the economy as a whole.[21]

[16] n 9; also explaining that non-performing loans can materialise 'when an individual loses their job and therefore cannot repay their mortgage as agreed, or when a company experiences financial difficulties'.

[17] D Singh, *European Cross-Border Banking and Banking Supervision* (Oxford, Oxford University Press, 2020) 103, in this regard outlines that banks are also allowed to cease the classification of loans as non-performing if they are no longer impaired or in default and if, according to the bank's judgement, the debtor is now expected to repay the loan.

[18] ibid, 101, also arguing that 'in view of this, the definition of NPLs is likely to lead to potential conflicts of interest that both the bank and the supervisor will need to be aware of when exercising judgement about the likelihood of bank's failure. In the latter case, the supervisor may forebear to an extent that it is hoped that an economic recovery will reduce the overall number of NPLs without any formal supervisory intervention'.

[19] n 8.

[20] n 17, 105, stressing that 'the provision for expected losses will impact, nonetheless, a bank's Tier 1 capital, since the level of provision in the judgement of the banks will reduce the value of the gross loan portfolio on the asset side of the balance sheet'.

[21] See n 8, which in this regard also emphasises that 'first and foremost, banks should avoid extending overly risky loans from the outset. They should follow sound lending criteria and properly assess the creditworthiness of borrowers to ensure that loans are only granted to customers who are likely to repay them. It is also important to have a proper monitoring system in place so that the bank detects at an early stage when a borrower is facing financial difficulties. Then the bank still has tools available to remedy the situation. In some cases, simply advising the client about his or her finances can be enough to prevent the loan from becoming non-performing'.

The accounting regime concerning loan loss provisioning has been revised in the aftermath of the global financial crisis, with IAS 39 being replaced by IFRS 9. This reform is expected to lead to a change of paradigm, moving from a system based on the concept of incurred losses to one based on the concept of expected future losses. In other words, while the previous regime had a backward-looking approach under which loan loss provisions were set too late on the basis of historical data, the new regime has a more proactive approach with loan loss provisions set in advance in light of forecasts grounded in expected losses. This clearly differs from the previous regime, in that banks do not have to wait for the occurrence of a given event to record losses and accordingly book provisions.

III. How to Tackle the Non-Performing Loan Problem: Asset Management Companies

The NPL issue is further exacerbated in the current economic environment affected by the COVID-19 provoked crisis (and potentially by the war in Ukraine), as banks will likely struggle to sell such assets on the market. It will be difficult for banks to find third parties willing to pay a price reflecting their book value. In the best-case scenario, NPL operators might offer to buy these assets at a discounted price; this would however cause banks to record losses, which will be increasingly higher depending on the price discount relative to the NPLs' book value.

Against this backdrop, from a system-wide perspective one of the most effective tools to employ with a view to tackling the NPL problem is the AMC. These are typically special purpose vehicles, either privately or publicly owned, which sometimes benefit from both private and public capital and funding. By focusing on the management of specific assets (including NPLs), AMCs can rely upon high-level skills and developed specialised expertise, also taking advantage of economies of scale and scope and synergies that in turn might lead towards value-maximisation.

Asset management companies have been extensively used to manage and dispose of NPLs during previous crises and, particularly in the aftermath of the global financial crisis of 2007–09 and the eurozone debt crisis of 2010–12, they proved to be an effective instrument in this respect. At least 12 EU Member States (including the UK) utilised AMCs to face those crises.[22] On these grounds, in 2020, Andrea Enria, Chair of the Supervisory Board of the European Central Bank (ECB), during a public hearing before the Committee on Economic and Monetary Affairs (ECON) of the European Parliament, reiterated his previously advanced

[22] See E Avgouleas, R Ayadi, M Bodellini, B Casu, WP De Groen and G Ferri, 'Non-performing loans – new risks and policies? What factors drive the performance of national asset management companies?' Policy Paper drafted for the European Parliament (2021) 9.

proposal to address the NPL problem through the use of AMCs.[23] More specifically, Enria stated that either a European AMC or a network of national AMCs should be established. This proposal is based on the assumption that when the COVID-19 economic relief measures, implemented in many EU Member States, are lifted, a new wave of distressed bank loans will emerge. Enria argued also that within a network of national AMCs, mechanisms to avoid loss mutualisation among Member States could be designed, if that were the political will. Yet, in his view, common funding of national AMCs and harmonised pricing would be crucial to ensuring a level playing field within the Banking Union, thereby preserving the competitiveness of Member States' banking systems.[24]

Likewise, in December 2020, building on the AMC blueprint drafted in 2018,[25] the European Commission published an Action Plan which lists AMCs among the main tools to be used in tackling the expected surge of NPLs caused by the COVID-19 crisis. The Commission stated that a new generation of NPLs is expected to emerge in the near future, especially after the expiration of the various memoranda signed between banks and their creditors.[26] Accordingly, for coordination purposes, the Commission suggested the creation of an EU-wide network of national AMCs collaborating with each other, thereby benefiting from synergies and economies of scale gained from the exchange of best practices and experiences, as well as data-sharing.[27]

Past experience on the use of AMCs to manage NPLs has shown that they have both advantages and disadvantages. The following paragraphs will discuss these, and focus on AMC design and the legal framework in force. The effectiveness of AMCs in fact significantly depends on the type of NPLs to transfer, the price at which they buy NPLs from banks, their capital and funding structure, and their governance and control arrangements.

A. Advantages of AMCs

In principle, AMCs involved in crisis management with a view to removing bad assets from bank balance sheets are an effective way to tackle the accumulation of

[23] See Committee on Economic and Monetary Affairs of the European Parliament, Public Hearing with Andrea Enria, Chair of the Supervisory Board of the European Central Bank, Brussels, 27 October 2020, *passim*; such proposal had been previously presented in an article published in the Financial Times, see A Enria, 'ECB: the EU needs a regional 'bad bank'', *Financial Times*, 26 October 2020.

[24] See n 22, 11.

[25] See European Commission, 'Commission Staff Working Paper, AMC Blueprint, Accompanying the document, Communication from the Commission to the European Parliament, the Council and the European Central Bank, Second Progress Report on the Reduction of Non-Performing Loans in Europe' (Brussels, 14 March 2018) SWD(2018) 72 final, 5, where it is stressed that AMCs could produce a particularly effective result in relation to NPLs concerning commercial real estate and large corporate exposures.

[26] See European Commission, 'Communication from the Commission to the European Parliament, the Council and the European Central Bank, Tackling non-performing loans in the aftermath of the COVID-19 pandemic' (Brussels, 16 December 2020) COM(2020) 822 final.

[27] ibid.

NPLs. This argument looks even more evident when the involvement of AMCs is compared with decentralised management of distressed loans at individual bank level.[28] This results from several benefits arising from centralised management of NPLs entrusted to AMCs.

Such benefits consist of: increased efficiency and effectiveness in managing NPLs by bridging the intertemporal valuation gap, pooling expertise and reducing funding costs; ability to clean up bank balance sheets, thereby reducing uncertainty about financial strength and increasing the ability of banks to continue lending; contribution in promoting and developing secondary markets for NPLs, which in turn could ensure value maximisation.

Centralisation of NPL management at the level of AMCs is effective in solving the creditors' coordination problem and this can in turn enhance secondary markets by making them more liquid.[29] Also, AMCs can reach higher levels of efficiency as they can focus on single-asset classes and accordingly benefit from expertise and skills specific to distressed debt management and workouts; this is not always the case with banks as they typically lack the ability to develop sophisticated in-house debt-restructuring skills.[30]

From a system-wide perspective, AMCs purchasing large portfolios of NPLs from several banks could: push banks to recognise losses, thereby contributing to rapid restoration of confidence in the banking system; improve asset quality and liquidity; strengthen the banking system, through the exit of non-viable banks and restructuring of viable banks; benefit from economies of scale and bargaining power, which may contribute to more efficient asset sales; and allow banks to focus on financial intermediation rather than asset-recovery.[31]

Building on these considerations, it can be argued that an AMC scheme that helps banks clean up their balance sheets by offloading distressed assets can boost credit growth. Through burden sharing with banks' shareholders, this type of intervention can also avoid the risk of creating moral hazard. Accordingly, a comprehensive structure for a pan-European AMC has been proposed with virtually ring-fenced country subsidiaries to ensure burden-sharing without debt mutualisation. This could resolve a number of governance, valuation and transparency issues that might otherwise affect a decentralised solution involving the uncoordinated actions of several national AMCs.[32]

[28] See D Klingebiel, 'The use of asset management companies in the resolution of banking crises: cross-country experience' World Bank (2000) *passim*; CW Calomiris, D Klingebiel and L Laeven, 'Seven Ways to Deal with a Financial Crisis: Cross-Country Experience and Policy Implications' (2012) 24 *Journal of Applied Corporate Finance* 8, 22.

[29] See E Bolognesi, P Stucchi and S Miani, 'Are NPL-backed securities an investment opportunity?' (2020) 77 *The Quarterly Review of Economics and Finance* 327, 339.

[30] See n 22, 14.

[31] See C Cerruti and R Neyens, 'Public asset management companies: a toolkit' World Bank (2016), *passim*.

[32] See E Avgouleas and C Goodhart, 'Utilizing AMCs to Tackle the Eurozone's Legacy Non-Performing Loans, Non-Performing Loans' (2017) 83.

B. Disadvantages of AMCs

There are three key disadvantages relating to the use of AMCs in managing NPLs:

- The first disadvantage is that transferring a loan from a bank to an AMC may cause a loss of information and thus knowledge concerning that debtor. Such loss could potentially affect the ongoing restructuring should that debtor need additional credit lines to finalise a successful turnaround. This issue might be even more critical for highly information-intensive loans, such as those granted to small and medium-sized enterprises and households.[33]
- The second disadvantage might arise from the lack of a clear AMC mandate as well as from inconsistencies in adhering to it, as this could reduce their effectiveness. The main issue in this respect is that AMCs should not be treated as a permanent warehouse of NPLs, but should focus on working out the acquired NPLs in an efficient manner over a predefined timeline according to a precise mandate.[34]
- The third disadvantage concerns the price paid to buy NPLs. An excessively high price can indeed cause public losses, while excessively low prices could cause banks to suffer large losses that can lead them toward insolvency. In this respect, AMCs should not operate on the assumption that they will disburse public money by offering excessively generous acquisition prices, as that would impair their functioning.[35]

IV. Types of NPLs to Transfer

In terms of types of loans to transfer, while AMCs enjoy economies of scale which increase depending on the size of the purchased portfolios, some NPL classes are deemed not to be suitable for centralised management. In the view of the European Commission, for example, while commercial real estate loans, corporate loans and loans granted for property development are assets which can be effectively managed by AMCs, retail loans, small business loans and loans to the public sector have rarely been worked out effectively by AMCs.[36]

Also, a heterogeneous mix of NPLs can impair the process by making the management and disposal of these assets less effective. Homogeneity of the transferred NPLs for centralised management and disposal is therefore a key factor for the success of AMCs.

[33] See n 22, 16.
[34] ibid, 16.
[35] ibid, 16.
[36] See n 25, 45.

Accordingly, the AMC's mandate should identify the most suitable NPL mix and perimeter, which the AMCs should then adhere to.

V. Transfer Price

A second key element for the effective functioning of AMCs relates to the price at which NPLs are sold. The most critical issue in this regard is that information asymmetries tend to create a relevant divergence between the prices that investors are willing to pay and the prices that banks want to collect from the sales, thereby making the NPL market a typical example of a 'market for lemons'.[37] Such information asymmetries increase the costs of undergoing a reliable due diligence and, as a consequence, only those few investors who have the resources to absorb such costs are willing to operate on the NPL market. These inefficiencies also affect market liquidity, which is rather scarce due to the very limited number of operators purchasing NPLs. Illiquidity, in turn, further lowers the NPL market price.

As to transfer pricing, while one of the main reasons for establishing AMCs is to raise the market price of NPLs, effective and efficient methods to assess their value as well as the value of the attached collateral should still be developed and applied to avoid over-optimistic transfer prices that would consequently cause AMCs to suffer losses in the future.

The transfer price is crucial since, should it be higher than the book value, banks would not be negatively affected, but AMCs would likely end up suffering losses (or lower gains) at a later stage. Loss-making AMCs, after having lost their capital, might have to be liquidated in the context of insolvency proceedings in the jurisdiction where they have been set up, thereby leading to those fire sales that they were expected to avoid in the first place or causing additional losses for the guarantors, that in most cases are the governments.[38] On the other hand, should the transfer price be too low, banks will need to undergo a recapitalisation, which is not always an available option. Should a necessary recapitalisation fail, then a crisis management procedure might need to be activated.

The identification of the transfer price should thus be grounded in a transparent and market-based due diligence process to be performed by an independent third party with specific experience in asset valuation. At EU level, the legal framework uses as a proxy the so-called 'real economic value', which refers to the long-term economic value of the assets concerned, on the basis of underlying cash flows over a long time horizon.[39] However, this is a very loosely defined proxy, that might

[37] See GA Akerlof, 'The Market for "Lemons": Quality Uncertainty and the Market Mechanism' (1970) 84 *The Quarterly Journal of Economics* 488.

[38] See n 22, 19.

[39] The concept of real economic value was introduced by the Impaired Assets Communication of 2009 and is defined as the 'underlying long-term economic value of the assets, on the basis of underlying cash flows and broader time horizon'. n 25, 50 also states that the real economic value 'is an

be difficult to use for the transfer of assets with uncertain cash flows or uncertain market value.[40]

In the EU, the transfer price acquires even further relevance as it is also instrumental to ascertaining whether NPL transfers comply with the state aid regime. This aspect becomes crucial when the AMC concerned is publicly supported. In this regard, the Commission defines an AMC supported by state aid as one 'that is partially or fully publicly-owned (or even privately owned but with actions that are imputable to the State, or benefiting from a State guarantee), buying assets at a transfer price higher than the estimated market value'.[41] If a publicly supported AMC buys NPLs at a price exceeding the estimated market value, then the transaction would involve the provision of state aid, whose size will amount to the difference between the transfer price and the estimated market value.[42] In these circumstances, for the transaction to take place the Commission's authorisation is required. The Commission's authorisation, in turn, will be released if a number of conditions laid down in the Commission Impaired Asset Communication 2009 are met: transfer price not exceeding the real economic value;[43] losses resulting from the write-down of NPLs from their net book value to the transfer price not to be covered by the impaired asset aid; and valuation of impaired assets to be conducted by independent experts and validated by the competent authority on the basis of the valuation provisions set out in the Communication.[44]

Further to these conditions, the requirements for the provision of a restructuring aid, according to the Commission's Banking Communication of 2013[45] and the Restructuring Communication of 2009,[46] also have to be fulfilled. Such additional conditions are: restoring the bank's long-term viability; limiting state aid to the minimum necessary through burden sharing and own contribution; and limiting distortions of competition.[47]

estimation of the asset value by disregarding the additional haircuts which private investors require because of the lack of information and because of the temporary illiquidity of those assets. If markets are efficient and liquid, the real economic value of assets equals the assets' market price. However, if markets are seized up by lack of information and illiquidity, the real economic value usually exceeds the (estimated) market price'.

[40] See n 22, 19.

[41] See n 25, 4, 9.

[42] In this regard see n 25, 9, where it is underlined that a diagnostic exercise should be performed, through an Asset Quality Review (AQR) and a Stress Test, with a view to helping 'the authorities to determine an appropriate transfer price, which typically lies between the (estimated) market value and the real economic value of the concerned assets'.

[43] See n 25, 50.

[44] See Communication from the Commission of 26 March 2009 on the treatment of impaired assets in the Community financial sector ('Impaired Assets Communication') [2009] OJ C 72/1.

[45] Communication from the Commission of 30 July 2013 on the application, from 1 August 2013, of State aid rules to support measures in favour of banks in the context of the financial crisis ('Banking Communication') [2013] OJ C 216/1.

[46] Communication of the Commission of 19 August 2009 on the return to viability and the assessment of restructuring measures in the financial sector in the current crisis under the State aid rules ('Restructuring Communication') [2009] OJ C195/9.

[47] See n 22, 20.

A. Transfer Price, State Aid Regime and Crisis Management

Depending on the price, as well as conditions, under which a publicly supported AMC purchases NPLs from credit institutions, different scenarios can occur as to the application of the state aid regime and the crisis management regime. While some of these scenarios would be fully or partially outside the scope of the state aid and the crisis management frameworks, others could actually trigger their application. Accordingly, purchases of NPLs can take place: without state aid; through an asset separation tool in a resolution procedure; with state aid in the context of national insolvency proceedings; and with state aid through a precautionary recapitalisation.[48]

When publicly supported AMCs buy NPLs from credit institutions at the prevailing market price of the assets concerned, no provision of state aid is involved since AMCs would act as market-based operators. Accordingly, the transaction would remain outside the scope of application of both the state aid regime and the BRRD-SRMR regime.

In the case in which a FOLF credit institution has been placed into resolution, the resolution authority can apply, inter alia, the asset separation tool. Such tool is substantially an AMC involved in the procedure with a view to buying some of the assets (typically NPLs) of the institution under resolution.[49] In this context, additional support might be needed in order for the AMC to be able to purchase such assets. Against this backdrop, financial means can be provided either by the Single Resolution Fund (SRF) or by the national resolution fund. Yet, such financial means would be qualified as state aid, therefore the intervention would be subject to the state aid rules, requiring authorisation from the Commission. Also, this support can be given when it is considered necessary for the efficient application of resolution tools; nonetheless, in this respect, a number of strict conditions need to be met. Thus, a minimum contribution to loss absorption and recapitalisation of at least eight per cent of total liabilities including own funds by shareholders and creditors of the entity in resolution, if losses are indirectly passed on to the SRF, is requested. Also, the upper limit for contributions by the fund is capped at five per cent of the total liabilities including own funds of the entity under resolution.

If a FOLF credit institution has been submitted to insolvency proceedings under national law, the domestic resolution authority might decide to transfer the bank's NPLs to an AMC. Even in this case, public support might be needed to enable the transfer of NPLs to take place. Against this background, the Banking Communication 2013 allows Member States, under certain conditions, to provide a liquidation aid with a view to facilitating the exit of non-viable institutions from the market in an orderly manner to avoid negative effects on financial stability, as

[48] See n 25.

[49] The asset separation tool is regulated under Art 42 of the BRRD.

discussed in chapter four.[50] The conditions to meet in order for such liquidation aid to be validly granted are: limitation of liquidation costs; limitation of competition distortions; and burden-sharing. Additionally, the transfer of NPLs from a credit institution to a publicly supported AMC is also to be assessed against the Impaired Assets Communication of 2009.[51] In this regard, however, the full liquidation and related dissolution of the institution concerned permit that the NPLs transfer price can be also set above the loans' real economic value, on the grounds that the residual entity will be facing constraints that limit distortions of competition and will eventually exit the market.[52]

Interestingly, a solvent and non-FOLF credit institution can also benefit from public financial support[53] without being consequently determined as FOLF, when the aid is granted in the context of a so-called precautionary recapitalisation and the ensuing requirements are met. This means that if NPLs are transferred to a publicly supported AMC relying on extraordinary public financial support, with a view to remedying a serious disturbance in the economy of a Member State and preserving financial stability, such transaction can qualify as a precautionary recapitalisation, and as a result the bank concerned would not be considered FOLF. Yet, several requirements need to be met for a precautionary recapitalisation to be conducted. Firstly, a precautionary recapitalisation can take place only in order to remedy a serious disturbance in the economy of a Member State and preserve financial stability. Also, it is confined to solvent institutions that are not FOLF. The recapitalisation needs to be of a precautionary and temporary nature and is conditional on final approval by the Commission under the EU state aid framework. The intervention must be proportionate to remedy the consequences of the serious disturbance of the economy and the public resources should not be used to offset losses that the institution has incurred or is likely to incur in the near future. Also, the amount of public funds provided should be limited to injections necessary to address a capital shortfall established in national, EU-wide or SSM-wide stress tests, AQR reviews or equivalent exercises conducted by the ECB, the European Banking Authority (EBA) or national authorities and, where applicable, confirmed by the competent authority.[54]

[50] On liquidation aid see para 65 of the Communication from the Commission of 30 July 2013 on the application, from 1 August 2013, of State aid rules to support measures in favour of banks in the context of the financial crisis ('Banking Communication') [2013] OJ C216/1; in this regard see R Lastra, C Russo and M Bodellini, 'Stock Take of the SRB's activities over the past years: What to Improve and Focus On?' Policy Paper Drafted for the European Parliament (2019) *passim*.

[51] See n 22, 19.

[52] On the provision of liquidation aid in the crises of Banca Popolare di Vicenza and Veneto Banca, see M Bodellini, 'To bail-in, or to bail-out, that is the question' (2018) 19 *European Business Organization Law Review* 373 *passim*.

[53] Pursuant to Art 3(1)(29) SRMR and Art 2(1)(28) BRRD, 'extraordinary public financial support' refers to State aid within the meaning of Art 107(1) TFEU or any other public financial support at supra-national level, which, if provided at national level, would constitute state aid, that is provided in order to preserve or restore the viability, liquidity or solvency of an entity or of a group of which such an entity forms part.

[54] Article 32(4) of the BRRD.

Precautionary recapitalisations have been conducted so far with a view to increasing the capital of solvent institutions that had previously failed a stress test in the so-called adverse scenario.[55] Nonetheless, such tool might also be applied to allow for the transfer of NPLs to a publicly supported AMC, on the condition that the publicly supported intervention pursues the same objective as a capital injection and the specific state aid conditions for impaired asset measures are complied with.[56] If such conditions are met, a bank's impaired assets can be purchased by a publicly supported AMC at a transfer price that exceeds the estimated market value of the NPLs. Yet, the transfer price cannot exceed the NPLs' real economic value. By so doing, the final outcome of purchasing NPLs in the context of a precautionary recapitalisation would be substantially equivalent to an increase of capital. While with a direct injection of capital, assets can then be sold at market prices on the grounds that the public intervention has already ensured that the bank maintains its capital position despite the loss arising from assets' sale, with an impaired asset relief measure, the bank can sell NPLs at a price higher than market price (but not exceeding the real economic value), hence its capital position is preserved by reducing the upfront loss.[57]

B. The COVID-19 Pandemic and the Temporary Framework of the Commission on State Aid

Owing to the COVID-19 pandemic, the Commission has decided to relax the rules on the provision of state aid with a view to facilitating and favouring an economic recovery. In this vein, the Commission has adopted the Temporary Framework for State aid measures to support the economy in the current COVID-19 outbreak,[58] which also deals with precautionary recapitalisation.[59] Under the new framework, if credit institutions need extraordinary public financial support in the form of liquidity, recapitalisation or impaired asset measures as a consequence of the COVID-19 outbreak, it would have to be assessed whether the measures meet the conditions of Article 32(4)(d)(i), (ii) or (iii) of the BRRD. Thus, if these

[55] See M Bodellini, 'Greek and Italian 'Lessons' on Bank Restructuring: Is Precautionary Recapitalisation the Way Forward?' (2017) 19 *Cambridge Yearbook of European Legal Studies* 144, *passim*.

[56] See n 25, 8.

[57] ibid, 35–37, also stating that precautionary recapitalisation can be any combination of 'recapitalisation aid (injected into the bank to recapitalise it) and impaired asset aid (as a price contribution to a higher price at which the bank transfers impaired assets to the AMC to help the bank avoid bearing the full extent of losses that would stem from the sale of the impaired assets in the market)'.

[58] See European Commission (2020), Communication from the Commission, Temporary Framework for State aid measures to support the economy in the current Covid-19 outbreak [2020] OJ CI91/1.

[59] On this, see C Gortsos, M Siri and M Bodellini, 'A proposal for a temporarily amended version of precautionary recapitalisation under the Single Resolution Mechanism Regulation involving the European Stability Mechanism' 73 EBI Working Paper Series (2020), *passim*.

conditions are fulfilled, the credit institution receiving extraordinary public financial support would not be deemed to be FOLF.[60]

Importantly, if these measures are implemented with a view to addressing problems linked to the COVID-19 pandemic, they would be deemed to fall under point (45) of the 2013 Banking Communication, which provides for an exception to the requirement of applying the burden-sharing mechanism to shareholders and subordinated creditors.[61] This exception is key since it empowers the Commission to exclude the application of the burden-sharing mechanism when this could endanger financial stability or lead to disproportionate results. As a result, notwithstanding the use of public resources, the burden-sharing mechanism, affecting both shareholders and subordinated creditors, does not necessarily have to apply. Against this backdrop, the Temporary Framework could pave the way for an increased number of precautionary recapitalisations taking place, as both shareholders and subordinated creditors could be exempted from the application of the burden-sharing requirement should the COVID-19 pandemic be deemed to have provoked the need for such a public support.[62] In this vein, the purchase of NPLs in the context of a precautionary recapitalisation with a view to tackling the increase of NPLs caused by the COVID-19 pandemic is also mentioned by the Commission in its Action Plan of December 2020.[63]

On these grounds, we advanced the proposal to design a temporarily revised and standardised form of privately and publicly funded precautionary recapitalisation, planned beforehand and operating on a quasi-automatic basis.[64] Accordingly, we advocated a temporary amendment of the precautionary recapitalisation regime under the Single Resolution Mechanism Regulation, also calling for the involvement of the European Stability Mechanism and building on the Commission's Temporary Framework on State Aid.[65] Particularly, we proposed that for a limited period of time (to be determined on the basis of the evolution of the pandemic and its economic impact), some of the conditions currently required by the SRMR for the precautionary recapitalisation of credit institutions should be amended in line with the recent measures adopted by the Commission with a view to facilitating public intervention to support the economy.[66] This should be combined with the

[60] See n 58, para 7.
[61] ibid, para 7, third sentence.
[62] See n 3, 209.
[63] See n 26.
[64] See n 59, 8.
[65] ibid, 9.
[66] ibid, 11, arguing that the requirements of banks being solvent and not FOLF for being eligible for precautionary recapitalisation might soon become an issue. 'Indeed, depending on the amount of NPLs accumulated by credit institutions and due to the regulatory requirement to write them off, several institutions will likely end up being balance sheet insolvent, and thus FOLF, in the forthcoming future. To face this obstacle, there might be some alternative solutions to consider, i.e.: first, a more lenient approach of supervisory authorities and regulators allowing credit institutions to phase-in, over a reasonably long period of time, the write off of NPLs; and second, a narrower application (just for the purposes of the proposed temporarily amended precautionary recapitalisation) of the concepts

creation of a new ESM facility which would allow it to buy hybrid instruments issued by those credit institutions facing the need to be recapitalised. The ESM could raise the resources to invest by issuing senior bonds on the market. Such resources could be then used to buy contingent convertibles (CoCos) issued by banks with characteristics that would allow them to be accounted in the Common Equity Tier 1 (CET1) capital, as was the case in Greece in 2015 with regard to Piraeus Bank and National Bank of Greece.[67] CoCos could be particularly suitable for these purposes as they are expected to allow for a faster divestment when market conditions would allow for it. This type of intervention could, in turn, be placed within a broader framework enabling the ESM to monitor the credit institutions' activity against some targets designed to allow them to repay over time the issued CoCos.[68]

VI. Capital and Funding Structure and Governance Arrangements

The effectiveness of AMCs critically depends also on their capital and funding structure. In this respect, several alternatives can be taken into consideration; it

of insolvency and FOLF limited only to situations relating to institutions whose assets were already less than their liabilities before that recently accumulated stocks of NPLs will be written off. In this regard, a practically feasible way to enable such a mechanism to work could be the introduction of a timeline (i.e. the World Health Organisation's (WHO) pandemic declaration on 11 March 2020). For the purposes of the proposed revised precautionary recapitalisation, only loans which have become non-performing due to repayment defaults occurred after the WHO declaration will be relevant. Accordingly, credit institutions which already had less assets than liabilities before 11 March 2020 will not be considered solvent, while the ones whose liabilities have exceeded the assets as a consequence of their requalification as NPLs due to defaults occurred after the WHO declaration will keep on being considered solvent for the purposes of the proposed temporarily amended precautionary recapitalisation. Both solutions would in fact enable credit institutions to continue being considered solvent, hence not FOLF, and therefore potentially eligible for precautionary recapitalisation'. The second condition to amend according to the proposal relates to the requirement that the measure should not be used to offset losses that the institution has incurred or is likely to incur in the near future. 'This requirement might represent an issue since the proposal conceives the amended precautionary recapitalisation tool as the instrument to prevent the bank from becoming FOLF and insolvent as a consequence of the Covid-19 provoked crisis. As previously discussed, the impact of such crisis on credit institutions will cause a significant increase of NPLs that, at some point, will have to be accounted and subsequently written off, thereby leading the institutions to record losses. Whether it can be argued that these losses are not previous losses already incurred by the institution to recapitalise, it seems more difficult to claim that they are not to be considered as losses that the institution 'is likely to incur in the near future', according to the language of Article 18(4) SRMR. As a consequence, in order to make the proposal operational, this requirement should be either temporarily removed or reformulated with a view to excluding from its scope losses resulting from the Covid-19 provoked crisis. A possible reformulation of this requirement could be based on the same time-line previously discussed. In other words, losses arising from loans which have become NPLs due to repayment defaults occurred after the WHO declaration on 11 March 2020 would not be considered likely future losses relevant to rule out the application of such tool'.

[67] See n 55, *passim*.

[68] See n 59, 16.

seems desirable, nonetheless, to rely upon public-private partnerships and thus on a mix of private and public funding. In this regard, and on the basis of the Asian financial crisis experience, it has been argued that government-supported AMCs are a better way to restore banking sector stability and strengthen national economies than internal loan restructurings accompanied by bank closures and/or mergers.[69] Similarly, in a broad study examining more than 190 countries over a period of 27 years it was found that the combined use of AMCs with public funds injected to recapitalise banks is a very effective way to resolve the NPL problem.[70]

Even though AMCs should be, at least partially, owned by the transferring banks in order to reduce moral hazard, they can be either privately or publicly funded.[71] And according to past experiences all over the world it appears that some sort of public support has often been a key element for their success.[72] Adequate and timely funding gives time to maximise asset value by avoiding fire sales while preventing permanent warehousing of bad loans.[73] The acquisition of NPLs can also be financed with the issuance of CoCos to be bought by market investors. CoCos could contain put and call options, respectively, to write down losses and write up profits arising from liquidation and restructuring procedures.[74] The protection mechanism provided by debt write-downs included in CoCos and the incentives given to investors by debt write-ups are expected to help close the gap between banks' NPL bid prices and ask prices.[75]

While the effectiveness of AMCs critically depends on access to public funding, in the EU this aspect needs to reconcile with the state aid framework. Public funding does not constitute state aid per se. The relevant factor in this regard is

[69] See DW Arner, E Avgouleas, and E Gibson, 'Financial Stability, Resolution of Systemic Banking Crises and COVID-19: Toward an Appropriate Role for Public Support and Bailouts' 2020/044 University of Hong Kong Faculty of Law Research Paper (2020), which, in analysing the experience in Indonesia, South Korea and Thailand, argues that AMCs helped the banking sector to tackle NPLs and restore profitability without serious long-term losses affecting the state budgets.

[70] See M Balgova, A Plekhanov and M Skrzypinska, 'Reducing non-performing loans: Stylized facts and economic impact' (2017); American Economic Association, '2018 Annual Meeting: Non-Performing Loans: Causes, Effects and Remedies' (2018); similar results are reached by M Brei, L Gambacorta, M Lucchetta and BM Parigi, 'Bad bank resolutions and bank lending' 837 BIS Working Paper (2020), who also found that also find that bad banks are more effective when: asset purchases are funded privately; smaller shares of the originating bank's assets are segregated; and they are located in countries with more efficient legal systems.

[71] Publicly funded AMCs typically issue senior unsecured bonds, which are bought by those banks that intend to transfer their NPLs to the AMCs. Such senior bonds usually carry a full and irrevocable guarantee of the national Treasury and would thus be eligible as collateral in refinancing transactions with the central bank. They often also have a call option available to the issuer.

[72] See n 69, discussing the use of AMCs during the Asian financial crisis in Thailand, Indonesia, South Korea and Malaysia and during the eurozone debt crisis in Spain, Ireland, Italy and Greece.

[73] See n 31, *passim*.

[74] See n 22, 23.

[75] See MAO Santos, 'Can Contingent Convertibles Help Private Asset Managers Fund Their Acquisition of Non-Performing Loans from Portuguese Banks?' (Washington, International Monetary Fund, 2019), *passim*.

the result of a comparative assessment against what a private market economy operator would do in a similar situation. Public funding would not be considered state aid if a private market operator would act in an equivalent way in similar circumstances. For this to occur, arguably the purchase of NPLs should take place at market prices (or at the estimated market value[76] when the former is not available) and the other conditions laid down in the European Commission's Crisis Communications would also need to be met.[77]

Yet, the Commission immediately stated that 'The option of an AMC involving State aid should not be seen as the default solution since AMCs can take multiple forms and can be structured and financed in several ways'[78] and that the use of AMCs should not prevent FOLF banks 'from being liquidated or resolved under the BRRD, which provides for an efficient framework enabling market exit of troubled banks while minimising costs to the taxpayer and negative repercussions to the economy'.[79]

Governance and control arrangements are also key factors and should protect AMCs from political intrusion. Such arrangements should establish AMCs duration *ex ante* and allow them to rely upon the most efficient work-out and loan-enforcement schemes. AMCs should also have strong commercial focus in order to be successful.[80]

AMCs should be able to benefit from professional distressed asset management, strong governance practices, robust transparency requirements as well as strong internal controls. Independent boards with private sector knowledge and

[76] See n 25, 50, stating that 'In circumstances where there is no liquid market and no directly comparable transaction taking place at the same moment, the Commission may, in order to establish the market value, use adjusted benchmarking to correct the price observed for the sale of assets that have some similarities with the assets in question. The adjustment is based on the difference of the characteristics and quality of the two sets of assets'.

[77] 'Crisis Communications' are: Communication from the Commission of 25 October 2008 on the application of State aid rules to measures taken in relation to financial institutions in the context of the current global financial crisis ('2008 Banking Communication') [2008] OJ C270/8; Communication from the Commission of 15 January 2009 on the recapitalization of financial institutions in the current financial crisis: limitation of aid to the minimum necessary and safeguards against undue distortions of competition ('Recapitalisation Communication') [2009] OJ C10/2; Communication from the Commission of 26 March 2009 on the treatment of impaired assets in the Community financial sector ('Impaired Assets Communication') [2009] OJ C72/1; Communication of the Commission of 19 August 2009 on the return to viability and the assessment of restructuring measures in the financial sector in the current crisis under the State aid rules ('Restructuring Communication') [2009] OJ C195/9; Communication from the Commission of 7 December 2010 on the application, from 1 January 2011, of State aid rules to support measures in favour of financial institutions in the context of the financial crisis ('2010 Prolongation Communication') [2010] OJ C329/7; Communication from the Commission of 6 December 2011 on the application, from 1 January 2012, of State aid rules to support measures in favour of financial institutions in the context of the financial crisis ('2011 Prolongation Communication') [2011] OJ C356/7; Communication from the Commission of 30 July 2013 on the application, from 1 August 2013, of State aid rules to support measures in favour of banks in the context of the financial crisis ('Banking Communication') [2013] OJ C216/1.

[78] See n 26, 11.

[79] See n 25, 23–24.

[80] See n 22, 24.

international presence, documentation of key decisions, internal staff policies and codes of conduct, key performance indicators and periodic progress evaluations conducted by external auditors are all important elements for an effective governance structure.

AMCs also need to adopt strategic and operating plans aligned with their mandate. Asset purchases should be made on the basis of a clear rationale and all assets should have well-defined resolution plans and exit strategies.

VII. Concluding Remarks

The COVID-19 pandemic and the ensuing crisis are bound to cause a sharp increase of NPL stocks, thereby further depressing their market prices. In the current economic environment, buyers are unlikely to be willing to pay a price reflecting the real economic value of NPLs, possibly also exploiting the new rules mandating credit institutions to progressively increase loan loss provisioning.[81]

Against this backdrop, the use of publicly supported AMCs, of publicly supported pan-European AMCs or of a network of publicly supported national AMCs can help overcome these market failure(s) and their broader consequences on both the economy and society. Nevertheless, several legal shortcomings and structural obstacles might hinder the ability of AMCs to effectively contribute tackling the expected surge in NPLs provoked by the COVID-19 pandemic.

This results from a certain amount of public support likely being needed for AMCs to be able to successfully operate. Although this seems to be also the view of the Commission,[82] the main issue in this respect is that every purchase of NPLs made by publicly supported AMCs at a price exceeding the estimated market value would qualify as state aid.[83] Qualifying these purchases as state aid in turn would cause the beneficiary bank(s) to be determined as FOLF, thereby paving the way for the initiation of a crisis management procedure, unless the intervention took place in the form of a precautionary recapitalisation. This entails that the only

[81] Regulation (EU) 2019/630 of the European Parliament and of the Council of 17 April 2019 amending Regulation (EU) No 575/2013 as regards minimum loss coverage for non-performing exposures [2019] OJ L111/4.

[82] See n 25, 15, highlighting that 'Market funding without a guarantee should be explored as part of the national AMC design process and, if feasible, may be preferred over the government-guaranteed funding. However, historical experience indicates that such market-based solutions prove difficult to implement and may require a significantly larger equity contributions'; even more explicitly n 26, 11, states that 'even if private capital and funding could be attracted, sizeable public funding would probably be needed in most cases, which would necessitate a State Aid assessment'.

[83] Article 107 TFEU provides that any state aid is incompatible with the internal market, unless it qualifies as one of the narrow exceptions set out in Art 107(2) TFEU or unless it has been approved by the Commission for one of the reasons set out in Art 107(3) TFEU. In relation to public support given to banks, the reason mostly adopted so far to authorise the aid has been, according to Art 107(3)(b) TFEU, 'to remedy a serious disturbance in the economy of a Member State'.

way for publicly supported AMCs to buy NPLs from banks at a price reflecting their real economic value would currently be through a precautionary recapitalisation. Despite the Commission's decision to relax the rules on public support and to extend the exception under point 45 of the 2013 Banking Communication as a consequence of the COVID-19 pandemic, it is arguable whether precautionary recapitalisation would be a suitable tool to handle the widely predicted increase of NPLs possibly impacting several banks.[84] This results from precautionary recapitalisation being primarily a measure to tackle single (or a limited number of) idiosyncratic crises through the injection of public funds in the form of fresh capital. It might then fall short if several institutions had the need to offload large portfolios of NPLs at the same time.[85]

On these grounds, we argued that the Commission could rethink the way state aid rules apply to the purchase of NPLs. Accordingly, it could prove helpful to reconsider the treatment of NPL purchases at prices reflecting their real economic value. Yet, even though developing criteria and a valuation methodology that would make the real economic value a more concrete concept is a key objective to reach, this might result a difficult task nearly impossible to achieve in the short term. Still, NPLs purchases carried out at prices reflecting their real economic value should not automatically qualify as an illegitimate state aid, on the basis that no financial loss for the state would be expected. A Treaty-compliant interpretation could be then advanced on the grounds that in the current situation, public support would be used, not only to the benefit of single banks, but primarily to address a system-wide market failure affecting the price formation of NPLs.[86] Such a market failure seems to be caused by the negative macroeconomic scenario provoked by the pandemic, along with a number of other structural factors (ie lack of information and illiquidity) and could only be properly tackled over time through a host of measures, such as the ones that the Commission has included in its Action Plan.[87] Such an argument could be at least supported in the case of a pan-European system-wide AMC whose mandate would be to help clean up the banking system from the burden of NPLs generated by the COVID-19 crisis.

Nevertheless, some structural issues would still remain and might affect the ability of publicly supported AMCs to contribute to resolving the NPL problem. The most relevant obstacles in this regard relate to: long recovery times and

[84] See n 22, 33.

[85] The Commission has already stated that if a transfer of NPLs to an AMC is to be (partially) financed with a precautionary recapitalisation, that bank should first participate in a national or EU-wide AQR, stress testing or similar exercise; see n 25, 8.

[86] See n 22, 34.

[87] The Treaty legal basis could be either: Art 107(2)(b): 'The following shall be compatible with the internal market: … aid to make good the damage caused by natural disasters or exceptional occurrences'; or Art 107(3)(b): 'The following may be considered to be compatible with the internal market: … aid … to remedy a serious disturbance in the economy of a Member State'.

consequent high costs that diverge from country to country; low and different levels of transparency, which create 'market for lemons'[88] conditions in the secondary market and increase bid-ask price discrepancies; significant differences between net book value and market value; and low profitability of banks.[89] Thus, for publicly supported AMCs to be effective tools, such structural obstacles also need to be removed. From this perspective, the Commission Action Plan of December 2020 has put forward a number of effective measures that should be able to contribute to solve the NPL problem and therefore the envisaged legislative reforms should be quickly passed.[90]

[88] See n 37, 488.
[89] See E Avgouleas and C Goodhart, 'Utilizing AMCs to tackle Eurozone's legacy non-performing loans' (2017) 1 European Economy – Banks Regulation and the Real Sector 99.
[90] See n 22, 34.

8

Conclusions

In discussing bank crisis management, this work has taken a clear stance emphasising the importance of specific procedures tailored to banks on the grounds of their special nature.

While with regard to systemic banks, special regimes have been implemented in many countries on the basis of the FSB Key Attributes of Effective Resolution Regimes for Financial Institutions[1] and are, therefore, already in place, this is not always the case for non-systemic banks (typically small and medium-sized institutions), which are in several jurisdictions still handled in the context of normal corporate insolvency proceedings.[2] However, irrespective of their more limited size, as systemic banks, if they end up in a crisis, they should be managed within special procedures, where the authorities involved can apply specific tools with a view to minimising value destruction, providing depositors' protection and keeping financial stability.[3] In the view of many, the lack of specific regimes to deal with such banks represents a key issue which can possibly be further exacerbated by the expected serious economic consequences resulting from the COVID-19 pandemic.[4] To this end, the pandemic-provoked crisis is expected to cause a significant increase of the stock of non-performing loans (NPLs) held by banks.[5] Reclassifying such assets as non-performing will in turn lead banks to record losses, which will negatively impact on their capital requirements, thereby causing, in the most serious cases, institutions to fail. Against this background, effective bank crisis management regimes will be key to tackling all those issues,

[1] See Financial Stability Board, 'Key Attributes of Effective Resolution Regimes for Financial Institutions' (15 October 2014).

[2] See P Baudino, A Gagliano, E Rulli and R Walters, 'FSI insights on policy implementation no 10 Why do we need bank-specific insolvency regimes? A review of country practices' (2018) *passim*, listing inter alia France, Spain and Germany.

[3] See M Bodellini, 'Alternative forms of deposit insurance and the quest for European harmonised deposit guarantee scheme-centred special administrative regimes to handle troubled banks' (2020) 2–3 *The Uniform Law Review* 213.

[4] See European Forum of Deposit Insurers, 'EFDI State of Play and Non-Binding Guidance Paper, Guarantee Schemes' Alternative Measures to Pay-out for Effective Banking Crisis Solution' (7 November 2019) 27; see also A De Aldisio, G Aloia, A Bentivegna, A Gagliano, E Giorgiantonio, C Lanfranchi and M Maltese, 'Towards a framework for orderly liquidation of banks in the EU' 15 Notes on Financial Stability and Supervision of Banca d'Italia (2019) 9.

[5] See M Bodellini and P Lintner, 'The impact of the Covid-19 pandemic on credit institutions and the importance of effective bank crisis management regimes' (2020) 9 *Law and Economics Yearly Review* 182.

thereby limiting spillover effects. Accordingly, a number of initiatives are currently ongoing to try to address the lack of such special regimes. Prominent among them are the efforts of the European Commission to design a harmonised Union-wide bank crisis management regime for institutions that do not meet the public interest test for resolution[6] as well as the global bank insolvency project launched by UNIDROIT with a view to drafting general principles, standards and guidelines to be considered by jurisdictions around the world once designing the crisis management regimes for their non-systemic banks.[7]

Focusing on these issues, after defining a number of key terms, this study has analysed the bank supervisory and crisis management architecture in the EU, UK and US, the first lines of defence in front of a crisis, namely bank capital and early intervention measures, the regimes of some key countries to handle the crisis of non-systemic banks vis-à-vis their regimes to manage the crisis of systemic banks, the role of deposit guarantee schemes in bank crises and the NPL problem potentially resulting from the COVID-19 crisis.

Based on these considerations, in dealing with international bank crisis management, this work contributes to the debate currently taking place between policy-makers, scholars and law practitioners, with a view to critically discussing some of the most controversial issues at stake, while advancing policy remarks and exploring ideas for reform proposals.

In this regard, while the US and UK systems have developed special regimes for both systemic and non-systemic institutions, the situation in the EU is more fragmented. Whilst the resolution procedure to manage the crisis of systemic institutions has been harmonised through the adoption of the BRRD, which has implemented the FSB Key Attributes of Effective Resolution Regimes for Financial Institutions, this is not the case for the procedures with regard to the crisis of non-systemic banks. Such procedures diverge from country to country, with some jurisdictions providing for administrative procedures and others providing for judicial procedures. In several countries, the procedures adopted to handle FOLF non-systemic banks are the same that apply to non-financial institutions.[8] However, this solution is considered to be suboptimal and potentially unable to reach the resolution objectives.[9]

[6] See European Commission, 'Targeted Consultation Review of the Crisis Management and Deposit Insurance Framework', available at ec.europa.eu/info/consultations/finance-2021-crisis-management-deposit-insurance-review-targeted_en.

[7] See UNIDROIT, 'Project on Bank Liquidation Work Programme 2020-2022', available at www.unidroit.org/work-in-progress/bank-insolvency/#1631778452950-20a21187-49af.

[8] See n 2, *passim*, arguing that the insolvency regimes for troubled banks can be grouped as follows: corporate insolvency law (adopted by France, Spain and Germany); modified corporate insolvency law (adopted by the UK and Ireland); free-standing bank insolvency regime (adopted by Italy, Greece, Luxembourg, Switzerland, the US, Canada and many others outside Europe).

[9] See WG Ringe, 'Bail-in between Liquidity and Solvency' University of Oxford Legal Research Paper Series (2016) 6; see also F Restoy, 'How to improve crisis management in the banking union: a European FDIC?' CIRSF Annual International Conference 2019 on 'Financial supervision and financial stability 10 years after the crisis: achievements and next steps' (Lisbon, 4 July 2019), available at www.bis.org.

On these grounds, a number of policy considerations have been put forward and some reform proposals have been discussed with regard to the design of a Union-wide harmonised special administrative regime for FOLF non-systemic banks. For the design of such a regime, the frameworks in place to handle both systemic and non-systemic institutions in Italy, UK and US might be relevant in many respects. Such frameworks have been accordingly analysed with a view to identifying their main strengths and weaknesses in order to explore whether the former can be, to a certain extent, imported.

Thus, a strong position in favour of providing the authorities with resolution-like tools (particularly the transfer tools) has been taken and an enhanced role for DGSs in crisis management has been advocated. In particular, the main features of such a regime have been sketched out. On these grounds, its objectives should include, along with value maximisation of the insolvency estate, depositor protection and financial stability. From the institutional perspective, such a regime should have an administrative nature and, accordingly, empower the resolution authorities to run the proceedings as this would provide expertise, sophisticated skills and access to bank-related information. The triggers applied to initiate these proceedings should have a forward-looking approach, as the ones which apply in resolution; such triggers could accordingly also be linked to serious regulatory breaches concerning capital requirements as well as other violations of laws and regulations causing the authorisation to be withdrawn. Relatedly, using the same triggers as in resolution, except for the public interest, would have a number of advantages, on the grounds that the EU framework has a dual-track regime, where two different crisis management procedures are available and the authorities are given the power to choose resolution according to EU law or liquidation according to national law (depending on what is in the public interest). As a consequence, a risk always exists for banks to end up in a limbo situation. Such risk, on the other hand, would be effectively addressed with the application of the same triggers, apart from public interest, used for initiating resolution. Also, these proceedings should be treated as a last resort measure, and therefore their activation should be based on the clear lack of alternatives, such as supervisory measures and market solutions. The legal effects arising from the submission of a bank to this procedure should include the authorisation withdrawal on the basis that the bank concerned should, as a result, exit the market. Yet, the continuation of the banking activity for a short period of time (typically some days or weeks) after the withdrawal should also be allowed according to the authorities' decision, as this might enable to achieve value maximisation and depositors' protection, thereby maintaining financial stability. As to the instruments to apply, this regime should ensure that the authorities have the power to transfer assets and liabilities from the FOLF bank to another institution at market prices. In addition, a bridge bank-like tool and an asset separation-like tool should be available as well. The availability of these tools is particularly important to maintain the stability of the system, protect depositors and reduce the destruction of value, as shown by the Italian, UK and US experiences. As to funding, while public support should be avoided as far as possible, the resources provided by deposit guarantee schemes are crucial. Accordingly, the latter should be empowered to also implement measures other than depositor payouts, through the so-called optional interventions. In particular, the provision of their resources at the early stage of a crisis or in the context of a liquidation should be made possible. At EU level, in this regard, a number of provisions might need to be amended, but this seems to be in line with the overall framework as well as with the main rationale behind the FSB Key Attributes of Effective Resolution Regimes for Financial Institutions.

To conclude, bank crisis management will continue for long time to be a key part of banking both from the perspective of the banking activity and the internal organisation of banks, and from the perspective of the public controls exercised by the authorities over them. The COVID-19-provoked economic crisis as well as the first effects of the war in Ukraine, which are materialising as I write, provide a clear confirmation of this.[10] On these grounds, effective bank crisis management

[10] On 27 February 2022, a few days after the start of the war in Ukraine, the 'European Central Bank has assessed that Sberbank Europe AG and its two subsidiaries in the Banking Union, Sberbank d.d. in Croatia and Sberbank banka d.d. in Slovenia, are failing or likely to fail owing to a deterioration of their liquidity situation. The Austrian parent bank Sberbank Europe AG is fully owned by Public Joint-Stock Company Sberbank of Russia, whose majority shareholder is the Russian Federation (50% plus one voting share). The ECB took the decision after determining that, in the near future, the bank is likely to be unable to pay its debts or other liabilities as they fall due. Sberbank Europe AG and its subsidiaries experienced significant deposit outflows as a result of the reputational impact of geopolitical tensions. This led to a deterioration of its liquidity position. And there are no available measures with a realistic chance of restoring this position at group level and in each of its subsidiaries within the banking union'; see European Central Bank, 'ECB assesses that Sberbank Europe AG and its subsidiaries in Croatia and Slovenia are failing or likely to fail', Press release (28 February 2022), available at www.bankingsupervision.europa.eu/press/pr/date/2022/html/ssm.pr220228~3121b6aec1.en.html; 'Following the European Central Bank's assessment, the Single Resolution Board has today decided that Sberbank Europe AG in Austria and its subsidiaries in Croatia (Sberbank d.d.) and Slovenia (Sberbank banka d.d.) are failing or likely to fail. The decision follows a rapid and significant deterioration of the banking group's liquidity situation. The SRB has applied a suspension of payments, enforcement and termination rights, known as a moratorium, to the three banks, Sberbank Europe AG (Austria), Sberbank d.d. (Croatia) and Sberbank banka d.d. (Slovenia). Depositors will be able to withdraw a daily allowance amount, determined by the respective national resolution authorities. The SRB is the resolution authority for Sberbank Europe AG and its subsidiaries in the Banking Union (Croatia and Slovenia) and responsible for determining failing or likely to fail following the ECB's assessment. The SRB is now considering the next steps for the banks with the aim of preserving financial stability in the Banking Union, in line with its mandate, i.e. whether resolution action in respect of any of the entities within the Banking Union would be in the public interest. In any case, eligible deposits up to €100,000 are protected by law'. The moratorium determines that until 1 March at 23:59:59: a) all payment or delivery obligations pursuant to any contract to which Sberbank Europe AG, Sberbank d.d. (Croatia) or Sberbank banka d.d. (Slovenia) are parties, including eligible deposits, are suspended, with the exception of payment or delivery obligations to the following: i) systems and operators of systems designated in accordance with Directive 98/26/EC; ii) CCPs authorised in the Union pursuant to Art 14 of Regulation (EU) No 648/2012 and third-country CCPs recognised by ESMA pursuant to Art 25 of that Regulation; iii) central banks; b) all secured creditors of Sberbank Europe AG, Sberbank d.d. (Croatia) or Sberbank banka d.d. (Slovenia) are restricted from enforcing security interests in relation to any of the assets of those institutions; and c) all the termination rights of any party to a contract with Sberbank Europe

regimes for both systemic and non-systemic institutions will be crucial to minimise the negative effects of bank failures. Having in force effective and well-functioning regimes, tailored to the special nature of banks, is therefore a key priority for every jurisdiction around the globe. While some jurisdictions already have in place such regimes, their frameworks and experiences should be used as a reference point by those countries that do not yet have special procedures in force to apply to their banks. Taking such a comparative approach, this study also offers a contribution in terms of legal analysis to those legislators and regulators who in the next future will be developing special crisis management regimes to apply to both systemic and non-systemic banks.

AG, Sberbank d.d. (Croatia) or Sberbank banka d.d. (Slovenia) are suspended. 'During the moratorium, depositors will be able to withdraw a daily allowance amount, determined by the respective national resolution authorities. Please see the notices published by the respective national authorities'; see Single Resolution Board, 'SRB determines Sberbank Europe AG in Austria, and its subsidiaries in Croatia and Slovenia as failing or likely to fail', Press release (28 February 2022), available at www.srb.europa.eu/en/content/srb-determines-sberbank-europe-ag-austria-and-its-subsidiaries-croatia-and-slovenia-failing. On 1 March 2022, the Single Resolution Board decided to resolve Sberbank d.d. and Sberbank banka d.d. while determining that resolution is not necessary for the Austrian parent bank Sberbank Europe AG. On these grounds, the 'Single Resolution Board has decided to transfer all shares of the group's Croatian subsidiary Sberbank d.d. to Hrvatska Poštanska Banka d.d. (Croatian Postbank) and all shares of the group's Slovenian subsidiary Sberbank banka d.d. to Nova ljubljanska banka d.d. (NLB d.d.). The banks will open on Wednesday, 2 March, as normal with no disruption to depositors or clients. They are now part of well-established, robust and stable banking groups. The SRB has also decided that resolution is not necessary for the Austrian parent of Sberbank Europe AG. Insolvency procedures will be carried out according to national law. Eligible deposits up to €100,000 are protected by the Austrian deposit guarantee system'; see Single Resolution Board, 'Sberbank Europe AG: Croatian and Slovenian subsidiaries resume operations after being sold while no resolution action is required for Austrian parent company' Press release (1 March 2022), available at www.srb.europa.eu/en/content/sberbank-europe-ag-croatian-and-slovenian-subsidiaries-resume-operations-after-being-sold.

BIBLIOGRAPHY

Abley, R and Goulding, S, *Relationship management in banking* (London, Kogan Page, 2018).
Akerlof, GA, 'The Market for "Lemons": Quality Uncertainty and the Market Mechanism' (1970) 84 *The Quarterly Journal of Economics* 488.
Alexander, K, *Principles of Banking Regulation* (Cambridge, University of Cambridge Press, 2019).
American Economic Association, 'Annual Meeting: Non-Performing Loans: Causes, Effects and Remedies' (2018).
Andenas, M and Chiu, I, 'Financial Stability and Legal Integration in Financial Regulation' (2013) 38 *European Law Review*.
Armour, J, 'Making Bank Resolution Credible' *Oxford Handbook of Financial Regulation* (2015) 453.
Arner, DW, *Financial Stability, Economic Growth, and the Role of Law* (Cambridge, Cambridge University Press, 2007).
Arner, DW, Avgouleas, E and Gibson, E, 'Financial Stability, Resolution of Systemic Banking Crises and COVID-19: Toward an Appropriate Role for Public Support and Bailouts' University of Hong Kong Faculty of Law Research Paper (2020).
Arnold, M and Espinoza, J, 'ECB pushes for Euro Zone bad bank to clean up soured loans' *Financial Times*, 19 April 2020.
Avgouleas, E, *Governance of Global Financial Markets: The Law, the Economics, the Politics* (Cambridge, Cambridge University Press, 2012).
Avgouleas, E and Goodhart, C, 'Critical Reflections on Bank Bail-ins' (2015) I *Journal of Financial Regulation 3*.
—— 'Utilizing AMCs to Tackle the Eurozone's Legacy Non-Performing Loans' European Economy - Banks, Regulation, and the Real Sector (2017).
—— 'Bank resolution 10 years from the global financial crisis: a systematic reappraisal' LUISS University School of European Political Economy, Working Paper (2019).
Avgouleas, E et al, *Principles of Banking Law*, 3rd edn (Oxford, Oxford University Press, 2017).
Avgouleas, E et al, 'Non-performing loans – new risks and policies? What factors drive the performance of national asset management companies?' Policy Paper drafted for the European Parliament (2021).
Avraham, D, Selvaggi, P and Veckery, J, 'A Structural View of U.S. Bank Holding Companies' (2012) 7 *FRBNY Economic Policy Review* 65.
Baldi, F, Bredice, M and Di Salvo, R, 'Bank-Crisis Management Practices in Italy (1978–2015) and their perspectives on the Italian Cooperative Credit Network' (2015) 44 *The Journal of European Economic History* 115.
Balgova, M, Plekhanov, A and Skrzypinska, M, 'Reducing non-performing loans: Stylized facts and economic impact' (2017).
Balthazar, L, *From Basel 1 to Basel 3: The Integration of State of Art Risk Modelling in Banking Regulation* (New York, Palgrave Macmillan, 2006).
Banca d'Italia, 'Banca Tercas – Cassa di Risparmio della Provincia di Teramo. Nomina degli organi dell'amministrazione straordinaria' *Italian Official Gazzette* (2012).
—— 'Provvedimenti rilevanti di carattere particolare delle autorità creditizie. Sezione XI Provvedimenti straordinari. Banca Network Investimenti S.p.A.', *Bollettino di Vigilanza* (2012).
—— 'Information on the resolution of Banca Marche, Banca Popolare dell'Etruria e del Lazio, CariChieti and Cassa di Risparmio di Ferrara crisis' (2015).
—— 'Annual Report of the National Resolution Fund' (2016).
—— 'Questions and answers on the solution of the crisis at the four banks under resolution' (2016).

—— 'Informazioni sulla Soluzione della Crisi di Veneto Banca S.p.A. e Banca Popolare di Vicenza S.p.A.' Memoria per la VI Commissione Finanze della Camera dei Deputati (2017).
—— '*La Crisi di Veneto Banca S.p.A. e Banca Popolare di Vicenza S.p.A.: Domande e risposte*' (2017).
Banco Popular, 'Group resolution plan' (2016).
Bank for International Settlements, 'History of the Basel Committee'.
Bank for International Settlements, 'Governors and Heads of Supervision Finalise Basel III Reforms' (2017).
Bank for International Settlements, 'Effects of Covid-19 on the banking sector: the market's assessment' *BIS Bulletin* (2020).
Bank of England, 'The Bank of England's approach to setting a minimum requirement for own funds and eligible liabilities (MREL)' Responses to Consultation and Statement of Policy (2016).
Barr, M, Jackson, H and Tahyar, M, *Financial Regulation: Law and Policy* (Eagan, Foundation Press, 2016).
Basel Committee on Banking Supervision, 'International Convergence of Capital Measurement and Capital Standards' (1988).
—— 'Basel II: International Convergence of Capital Measurement and Capital Standards: A Revised Framework' (2006).
—— 'Basel III: A Global Regulatory Framework for More Resilient Banks and Banking Systems' (2011).
—— 'A Framework for Dealing with Domestic Systemically Important Banks' (2012).
—— 'Core Principles for Effective Banking Supervision' (2012).
—— 'Global Systemically Important Banks: Updated Assessment Methodology and the Higher Loss Absorbency Requirement' (2013).
—— 'Finalising Post-Crisis Reforms' (2017).
—— 'High Level Summary of Basel III Reforms' (2017).
Bates, C and Gleeson S, 'Legal Aspects of Bank Bail-ins' (2011) 5 *Law and Financial Markets Review* 264.
Baudino, P et al, 'FSI insights on policy implementation no 10 Why do we need bank-specific insolvency regimes? A review of country practices' (2018).
Baudino, P, Orlandi, J, and Zamil R, 'FSI Insights on Policy Implementation The identification and measurement of non- performing assets: a cross-country comparison' (2018).
Belratti, A and Paladino, G, 'Basel and Regulatory Arbitrage. Evidence from Financial Crises' (2016) 39 *Journal of Empirical Finance* 180.
Belviso, U, 'Il trasferimento dell'azienda bancaria nella liquidazione coatta amministrativa' (1972) I *Banca Borsa Titoli di Credito*.
—— 'La liquidazione coatta nel quadro di una riforma delle procedure concorsual' (1979) I *Giurisprudenza Commerciale* 274.
—— 'La liquidazione coatta amministrativa e il caso Banco di Napoli (1998) I *Banca Borsa Titoli di Credito* 1.
Biljanovska, B, 'Aligning Market Discipline and Financial Stability: a More Gradual Shift from Contingent Convertible Capital to Bail-in Measures' (2016) 17 *European Business Organization Law Review* 105.
Binder, JH, 'The Banking Union and the Governance of Credit Institutions: A Legal Perspective' (2015) 16 *European Business Organization Law Review* 467.
Binder, JH et al, 'The choice between judicial and administrative sanctioned procedures to manage liquidation of banks: a transatlantic perspective' (2019) 14 *Capital Markets Law Journal* 178.
Boccuzzi, G, 'Towards a new framework for banking crisis management. The international debate and the Italian model' (2011) *Quaderni di Ricerca Giuridica della Consulenza Legale della Banca d'Italia* 193.
Boccuzzi, G and De Lisa R, 'The Changing Face of Deposit Insurance in Europe: from the DGSD to the EDIS Proposal' in G Bracchi, U Filotto and D Masciandaro (eds), *The Italian banks: which will be the 'new normal'?* (Rome, Edibank, 2006).
Bodellini, M, 'From Systemic Risk to Financial Scandals: the Shortcomings of U.S. Hedge Fund Regulation' (2017) 11 *Brooklyn Journal of Corporate Financial & Commercial Law* 417.
—— *Attività Bancaria e Impresa Cooperativa* (Bari, Cacucci Editore, 2017).

—— 'Greek and Italian "Lessons" on Bank Restructuring: Is Precautionary Recapitalisation the Way Forward?' (2017) *Cambridge Yearbook of European Legal Studies* 144.

—— 'Corporate Governance of Banks and Financial Stability: Critical Issues and Challenges Ahead' (2018) 39 *Business Law Review* 160.

—— 'To Bail-In, or to Bail-Out, that is the Question' (2018) 19 *European Business Organization Law Review* 373.

—— 'Impediments to resolvability: critical issues and challenges ahead' *Open Review of Management, Banking and Finance*, 20 December 2019.

—— 'The long "journey" of banks from Basel I to Basel IV: has the banking system become more sound and resilient than it used to be?' (2019) 20 *ERA Forum* 81.

—— 'The Quest for European Harmonised Deposit Guarantee Scheme-Centred Special Administrative Regimes to Handle Troubled Banks' (2020) 25 *The Uniform Law Review*.

—— 'Old Ways and New Ways to Handle Failing Banks across the Atlantic' (2021) *Journal of Comparative Law*.

—— 'The Optional Measures of Deposit Guarantee Schemes: Towards a New Bank Crisis Management Paradigm?' (2021) 13 *European Journal of Legal Studies* 341.

Bodellini, M and De Groen, WP, 'Impediments to resolvability – what is the status quo?' Policy Paper drafted for the European Parliament (2021).

Bodellini, M, and Lastra, R, 'Soft Law and Sovereign Debt' Intergovernmental Group of Experts on Financing for Development, United Nations (2018).

Bodellini, M and Lintner, P, 'The impact of the Covid-19 pandemic on credit institutions and the importance of effective bank crisis management regimes' (2020) 9 *Law and Economics Yearly Review* 182.

Bodellini, M and Singh, D, 'Monetary policy in the face of the covid-19 crisis: the interesting case of the United Kingdom' (2020) 2 *Open Review of Management, Banking and Finance* 48.

Bodellini, M, Gortsos, C and Siri M, 'A proposal for a temporarily amended version of precautionary recapitalisation under the Single Resolution Mechanism Regulation involving the European Stability Mechanism' EBI Working Paper Series (2020).

Bolognesi, E, Stucchi, P and Miani, S, 'Are NPL-backed securities an investment opportunity?' (2020) 77 *The Quarterly Review of Economics and Finance* 327.

Bracchi, G, Filotto, H and Masciandaro, D, *The Italian banks: which will be the 'new normal'?* (Rome, Edibank, 2016).

Brei M et al, 'Bad bank resolutions and bank lending' 837 BIS Working Paper (2020).

Brescia Morra C, 'Crisi bancarie e disciplina degli aiuti di Stato: un chiarimento importante dalla Corte di Giustizia' II *Banca Borsa Titoli di Credito* (2019).

—— 'Crisi bancarie e disciplina degli aiuti di Stato: un chiarimento importante dalla Corte di Giustizia' II *Banca Borsa Titoli di Credito* (2019).

—— 'The New European Union Framework for Banking Crisis Management: Rules versus Discretion' (2019) 16 *European Company and Financial Law Review* 365.

—— 'Lending activity in the time of coronavirus' in C Gortsos and WG Ringe 'Pandemic Crisis and Financial Stability' European Banking Institute (2020) 392.

Brierley, P, 'Ending Too-Big-To-Fail: Progress Since the Crisis, the Importance of Loss-Absorbing Capacity and the UK Approach to Resolution' (2017) 18 *European Business Organization Law Review* 457.

Bruno, EA and Nicholson, C, *Global Financial Crisis: Navigating and Understanding the Legal and Regulatory Aspects* (New York, Globe Law and Business, 2009).

Calello P and Erwin, W, 'From Bail-Out to Bail-In' *The Economist*, 30 January 2010.

Calomiris, CW et al, 'Seven Ways to Deal with a Financial Crisis: Cross-Country Experience and Policy Implications' (2012) 24 *Journal of Applied Corporate Finance* 8.

Cannata, F and Quagliariello, M, *Basel III and Beyond: A Guide to Banking Regulation After the Crisis* (London, Risk Books, 2011).

Capriglione, F, 'Discrezionalità del provvedimento amministrativo di messa in liquidazione coatta di un'azienda di credito e pretesa risarcitoria del socio' (1978) II *Banca Borsa Titoli di Credito*.

—— 'Banking crises and systemic crises. The Italian case' (2019) II *Law and Economics Yearly Review*.
Carnell, RS, Macey, JR and Miller, GP, *The Law of Financial Institutions* (New York, Wolters Kluwer, 2017).
Carney, M. 'To G20 Leaders, Financial Stability Board (FSB) Chairman's Memo to G20 Leaders' (2017).
Carstens, A, 'Deposit insurance and financial stability: old and new challenges' Keynote address. 17th IADI Annual General Meeting and Annual Conference on Deposit insurance and financial stability: recent financial topics, Basel (2018).
Cerruti, C and Neyens, R, 'Public asset management companies: a toolkit' World Bank (2016).
Cochrane, JH, 'Toward a run-free financial system' in M Neil-Baily and JB Taylor (eds), *Across the great divide: new perspectives on the financial crisis* (Stanford, Hoover Institution Press, 2014).
Colavolpe, A, 'Decreto EUROSIM: le modifiche al T.U. bancario' (1996) 15 *Le società* 1068.
Committee on Economic and Monetary Affairs, 'Public Hearing with Andrea Enria' Chair of the Supervisory Board of the European Central Bank (2020).
Communication from the Commission, Temporary Framework for State aid measures to support the economy in the current Covid-19 outbreak [2020] OJ C 191/1.
Conference of State Bank Regulators, 'State Bank Supervisors Annual Report 2018' (2018).
Conlon, T and Cotter, J, 'Anatomy of a bail-in' (2014) 15 *Journal of Financial Stability* 257.
Consob, 'Incontro Annuale con il Mercato Finanziario, Discorso del Presidente al Mercato Finanziario' (2017).
Cornford, A, 'Basel II: The Revised Framework of 2004' United Nations Conference on Trade and Development (UNCTD) (2005).
Curry, TJ et al, 'Financially Distressed Banks: How Effective Are Enforcement Actions in the Supervision Process?' FDIC Banking Review (1999).
De Aldisio, A et al, 'Towards a framework for orderly liquidation of banks in the EU' 15 Notes on Financial Stability and Supervision of Banca d'Italia (2019).
De Groen, WP, 'Impediments to resolvability of banks?' In-depth analysis requested by the ECON committee of the European Parliament (2019).
Della Negra F and Smith R, 'The Banking Union and Union Courts: overview of cases as at 11 February 2019', available at www.ebi-europa.eu/publications/eu-cases-or-jurisprudence.
Deloitte, 'Hippocrates – Provisional Valuation Report' (2017).
Desiderio, L, 'La liquidazione coatta amministrativa delle aziende di credito (Milano, Giuffrè, 1981).
Deslandes, J, Dias, C and Magnus, M, 'Liquidation of Banks: Towards an "FDIC" for the Banking Union?' In-depth analysis (2019), available at www.europarl.europa.eu/RegData/etudes/IDAN/2019/634385/IPOL_IDA(2019)634385_EN.pdf.
Deslandes JJP, Dias, CS, Magnus, M, 'Recent measures for Banca Carige from a BRRD and State Aid perspective', European Parliament Briefing (2019).
Dewatripont, M, 'European Banking: Bailout, Bail-in and State Aid Control' (2014) 34 *International Journal of Industrial Organization* 37.
Douglas JL and Guynn, RD, 'Resolution and Liquidation of US Financial Institutions' (2009).
Draghi, M, 'We face a war against coronavirus and must mobilise accordingly', *Financial Times*, 25 March 2020.
Enria, A, 'ECB: the EU needs a regional "bad bank"' *Financial Times*, 26 October 2020.
European Central Bank, 'ECB deemed Veneto Banca and Banca Popolare di Vicenza failing or likely to fail', Press release (2017).
—— 'The Fiscal Impact of Financial Sector Support During the Crisis' ECB Economic Bulletin (2018).
—— 'ECB Banking Supervision provides temporary capital and operational relief in reaction to coronavirus', Press release (2020).
—— 'ECB Banking Supervision provides temporary relief for capital requirements for market risk', Press release (2020).
—— 'ECB contribution to the European Commission's targeted consultation on the review of the crisis management and deposit insurance framework' (2021).
—— 'Targeted Consultation Review of the Crisis Management and Deposit Insurance Framework' (2021).

European Court of Auditors, 'Special report no 23/2017: Single Resolution Board: Work on a challenging Banking Union task started, but still a long way to go' (2017).
European Forum of Deposit Insurers, 'EFDI State of Play and Non-Binding Guidance Paper, Guarantee Schemes Alternative Measures to Pay-out for Effective Banking Crisis Solution' (2019).
—— 'Cost-Benefit Analysis and Least-Cost Calculation for Decision Making Process of Deposit Guarantee Schemes', State of Play and Non-Binding Guidance Paper (2021).
Fauceglia, G, 'L'esercizio provvisorio nella liquidazione coatta amministrativa delle banche' (1996) *Giurisprudenza Commerciale* 711.
—— 'La cessione di attività e passività nella liquidazione coatta amministrativa delle banche e la successione nei rapporti contrattuali' (1997) 50 *Banca Borsa Titoli di Credito* 453.
Federal Deposit Insurance Corporation, 'The First Fifty Years: A History of the FDIC 1933–1983' (1984).
—— 'Managing the Crisis: The FDIC and RTC Experience 1980–1994' (1998).
—— 'Cross Guaranty Program', Press release (2009).
—— 'Crisis and Response: An FDIC History, 2008–2013' (2017).
—— 'Insured Bank Deposits are Safe; Beware of Potential Scams Using the Agency's Name' Press release (2017).
—— 'FDIC Annual Report 2018' (2018).
—— 'Resolutions Handbook' (2019).
Federal Financial Institutions Examination Council, 'Annual Report' (2018).
Ferran, E, 'European Banking Union: Imperfect but It Can Work' Legal Studies Research, Paper Series, University of Cambridge (2014).
Ferrarini, G, 'Single Supervision and the Governance of Banking Markets: Will the SSM Deliver the Expected Benefits?' (2015) 16 *European Business Organization Law Review* 513.
Financial Stability Board, 'Policy Measures to Address Systemically Important Financial Institutions' (2011).
—— 'Key Attributes of Effective Resolution Regimes for Financial Institutions' (2014).
—— 'Principles on Loss-Absorbing and Recapitalisation Capacity for G-SIBs in Resolution' (2015).
—— 'Implementation and Effects of the G20 Financial Regulatory Reforms' 3rd Annual Report (2017).
—— Public disclosures on resolution planning and resolvability, Discussion paper for public consultation, 3 June 2019, 2.
Fondo Interbancario di Tutela dei Depositi, 'FIDT's Interventions' Interventions Report (2020).
Fortunato, S, 'Sulla liquidazione coatta delle imprese bancarie' (1991) I *Banca Borsa Titoli di Credito* 715.
—— 'La liquidazione coatta delle Banche dopo il Testo Unico: lineamenti generali e finalità' (1995) I *Banca Borsa Titoli di Credito* 761.
—— 'La liquidazione coatta amministrativa delle società del gruppo bancario' (1997) I *Banca Borsa Titoli di Credito* 317.
Gardella, A, 'Bail-in and the Financing of Resolution within the SRM Framework' in Busch, D and Ferrarini, G, *European Banking Union* (Oxford, Oxford University Press, 2015).
Gelpern, A and Véron, N, 'The Long Road to a US Banking Union: Lessons for Europe' in Kirkegaard, JF and Posen, AS, *Lessons for EU Integration from US History* (Washington, Peterson Institute for International Economicsm 2018).
—— 'An Effective Regime for Non-viable Banks: US Experience and Considerations for EU Reform' Study Requested by the ECON committee of the European Parliament, Economic Governance Support Unit (EGOV) – Directorate-General for Internal Policies of the Union (2019).
Giglio, V and Setola Roberto, 'La disciplina degli aiuti di Stato e le crisi bancarie italiane' (2002) 1 *Mercato Concorrenza Regole* 230.
Gleeson, S, 'Bank Capital Regulation and Sovereign Debt restructuring' (2018) 13 *Capital Markets Law Journal* 467.
Gleeson, S and Guynn, R, *Bank Resolution and Crisis Management: Law and Practice* (Oxford, Oxford University Press, 2016).
Goodhart, C, 'Multiple Regulators and Resolutions', Paper presented at the Federal Reserve Bank of Chicago Conference on Systemic Financial Crisis: Resolving Large Bank Insolvencies (2004).

Gordon, JN and Ringe, WG, 'Bank Resolution in the European: a Transatlantic Perspective on What It Would Take' (2015) 115 *Columbia Law Review* 1354.
Gortsos, C, 'The role of deposit guarantee schemes (DGSs) in resolution Financing' (2019) 37 European Banking Institute Working Paper Series 67.
—— 'The application of the EU banking resolution framework amidst the pandemic crisis' in Gortsos, C and Ringe, WG, 'Pandemic Crisis and Financial Stability', European Banking Institute (2020).
Gortsos, C and Ringe, WG, 'Pandemic Crisis and Financial Stability', European Banking Institute (2020).
Government Accountability Office, '1992 Bank Resolutions: FDIC Chose Methods Determined Least Costly, but Needs to Improve Process' GGD-94-107, May 1994, 10.
Grande, M, 'Resolution planning in practice', Presentation delivered at the Florence School of Banking and Finance (2017).
Greenspan, A, Speech given at the Federal Reserve of Chicago Bank Structure Conferences (2010).
Guynn, RD, 'Are Bailouts Inevitable?' (2012) 29 *Yale Journal on Regulation* 121.
Hadjiemmanuil, C, 'European economic governance and the pandemic: Fiscal crisis management under a flawed policy process' in Ringe, WG 'Pandemic Crisis and Financial Stability' European Banking Institute (2020).
Heffernan, S, *Modern Banking* (New York, Wiley, 2004).
Huertas, T, 'The case for bail-ins' in Dombret, A and Kenadjian, S (eds), *The Bank Recovery and Resolution Directive* (Philadelphia, Institute for Law and Finance Series, 2013) 167.
Hull, JC, *Risk management and financial institutions* (Hoboken, Wiley, 2018).
Ingves, S, 'Remarks Given at IADI Conference on Designing an Optimal Deposit Insurance System' (2017).
International Association of Deposit Insurers, 'IADI Core Principles for Effective Deposit Insurance Systems' (2014).
International Monetary Fund, 'Orderly and Effective Insolvency Procedures: Key Issues' (1999).
—— From Bail-out to Bail-in: Mandatory Debt Restructuring of Systemic Financial Institutions', Staff Discussion Notes (2012) '.
—— 'A strategy for resolving Europe's problem loans', Staff Discussion Notes (2015).
—— 'Euro Area Policies, Financial System Stability Assessment', IMF Country Report No 18/226 (2018).
—— 'Global Financial Stability Report October 2018: A Decade after the Global Financial Crisis: Are We Safer?' (2018).
Jassaud, N and Kang, K, 'A strategy for developing a market for nonperforming loans in Italy' (2015) 15 International Monetary Fund Working Paper.
Jones, E, and Zeitz, A, 'The Limits of Globalizing Basel Banking Standards' (2017) 3 *Journal of Financial Regulation* 89.
Klingebiel, D, 'The use of asset management companies in the resolution of banking crises: cross-country experience' World Bank (2000).
Kokkoris, I, 'State Aid Law v Single Resolution Mechanism: David v Goliath or vice versa' (2013) 10 *International Corporate Rescue* 392.
Kokkoris, I and Olivares-Caminal, 'The Operation of the Single Resolution Mechanism in the Context of the EU State Aid Regime' in Binder, JH and Singh D, *Bank Resolution: The European Regime* (Oxford, Oxford University Press, 2016).
Krugman, P, *The Return of Depression Economics and the Crisis of 2008* (New York, WW Norton, 2009).
LaBrosse, JR, *Financial Crisis Management and Bank Resolution* (London, Informa Law/Routledge, 2009).
Lannoo, K, 'Bank State Aid under BRRD and SRM' (2014) 13 *European State Aid Law Quarterly* 630.
Lastra, R, *Legal Foundations of International Monetary Stability* (Oxford, Oxford University Press, 2006).
—— 'Banking Union and Single Market: Conflict or Companionship?' (2013) 36 *Fordham International Law Journal* 5.

——*International Financial and Monetary Law* (Oxford, Oxford University Press, 2015).
—— 'Accountability mechanisms of the Bank of England and of the European Central Bank' Study for the Committee on Economic and Monetary Affairs, Policy Department for Economic, Scientific and Quality of Life Policies (2020).
Lastra, R and Alexander, K, 'The ECB Mandate: Perspectives on Sustainability and Solidarity', In-depth analysis requested by the ECON committee of the European Parliament (2020).
Lastra, R, Russo, C and Bodellini, M, 'Stock Take of the SRB's activities over the past years: What to Improve and Focus On?' Policy Paper drafted for the European Parliament (2019).
Laviola, S, 'SRB's new heat-map approach enhances resolvability assessment' (2021).
Leckow, R, Gullo, A and Emre, E, 'Bank Resolution Frameworks: Key Legal Design Issues' in Brodie, S (ed), *Bank Resolution Key Issues and Local Perspectives* (London, INSOL International, 2019).
Lehmann, M, 'Impediments to resolvability of banks' In-depth analysis requested by the ECON committee of the European Parliament (2019).
Libonati, B, *Contratto bancario e attività bancaria* (Milano, A. Giuffrè Editore, 1965).
Lo Schiavo, G, 'State Aids and Credit Institutions in Europe: What Way Forward?' (2014) 24 *European Business Law Review* 427.
Lubben SJ and Wilmarth AE, 'Too Big and Unable to Fail' (2017) 69 *Florida Law Review* 1205.
Lupo-Pasini, F and Buckley, RP, 'International Coordination in Cross-Border Bank Bail-ins: Problems and Prospects' (2015) 16 *European Business Organization Law Review* 208.
Maccarone, S, 'Il ruolo e l'ambito di intervento dei fondi di risoluzione e dei DGS nelle crisi bancarie' (2015) 2 *Diritto della Banca e del Mercato* Finanziario 177.
—— 'La sentenza del Tribunale europeo sul caso Tercas' (2019) 3 *Bancaria.*
Magnus, M et al, 'Upgrading the Basel Standards: From Basel III to Basel IV?' Economic Governance Support Unit, European Parliament Briefing Paper (2017).
Malek, H, Potts, P and Dzwig, S, *Bank Resolution – Key Issues and Local Perspectives* (London, Insol International, 2019).
McHenry, P, 'Letter sent to the Chair of the Board of Governors of the Federal Reserve System' (2017).
Micossi, S, Bruzzone, G and Casella, M, 'Bail-in Provisions in State Aid and Resolution Procedures: Are They Consistent with Systemic Stability?' (2014) 318 *CEPS Policy Brief.*
—— 'Fine-Tuning the Use of Bail-in to Promote a Stronger EU Financial System' CEPS Special Report (2016).
Miles, D, Yang, J and Marcheggiano, G, (2011) 'Optimal Bank Capital. External MPC Unit Discussion Paper No. 31' Bank of England (2011).
Minervini, G, 'Il "ristoro" ex d.m. 27 settembre 1974 e il fondo interbancario di tutela dei depositi' (1996) I *Giurisprudenza Commerciale.*
Mitts, J, 'Systemic Risk and Managerial Incentives in the Dodd-Frank Orderly Liquidation Authority' (2015) 1 *Journal of Financial Regulation* 51.
Moloney, N, 'European Banking Union: Assessing its Risks and resilience' (2014) 51 *Common Market Law Review* 1609.
Morais, LS, 'The EU fiscal response to the COVID-19 crisis and the Banking sector: risks and opportunities'.
Nielsen BS, 'Main Features of the European Banking Union' (2015) 26 *European Business Law Review* 805.
Nieto, M, 'Banking on Single Supervision in the Eurozone: Scepticism and a Reform Proposal' (2015) 16 *European Business Organization Law Review* 539.
Nigro, A, 'La disciplina delle crisi bancarie: la liquidazione coatta amministrativa' (1996) I *Giurisprudenza Commerciale* 144.
Pratis, CM, *La disciplina giuridica delle aziende di credito* (Milano, Giuffrè, 1972).
Price Waterhouse Coopers, '"Basel IV": Big Bang – or the Endgame of Basel III?. BCBS finalises on Risk Weighted Assets (RWA)' (2017).
Restoy, F, How to improve crisis management in the banking union: a European FDIC?' CIRSF Annual International Conference 2019 on 'Financial supervision and financial stability 10 years after the crisis: achievements and next steps' (Lisbon, 4 July 2019).

Reuters, 'JPMorgan ends WaMu disputes with FDIC, to receive $645 million', 19 August 2016.
—— 'Bank of Italy sells last of four small rescued banks to BPER', 2 March 2017.
—— 'Italy's UBI to buy rescued banks, raise cash in latest clean-up', 11 January 2017.
—— 'Italy in talks with EU over Popolare Bari rescue', 9 January 2020.
Ringe, WG, 'Bail-in between Liquidity and Solvency' University of Oxford Legal Research Paper Series (2016).
—— 'COVID-19 and European banks: no time for lawyers' in Ringe, WG, 'Pandemic Crisis and Financial Stability' European Banking Institute (2020).
Rulli, E, *Contributo allo studio della risoluzione bancaria* (Torino, Diritto dell'economia, 2017).
Russo, C, 'Resolution plans and resolution strategies: do they make G-SIBs resolvable and avoid ring fence?' (2019) *European Business Organization Law Review* 1.
Salanitro, N, 'La cessione dei crediti anomali ad una società di gestione (c.d. bad bank)' (1997) I *Banca, Borsa Titoli di Credito.*
Sands, P, Liao, G and Ma Y, 'Rethinking Operational Risk Capital Requirements' (2018) 4 *Journal of Financial Regulation* 1.
Santos, MAO, 'Can Contingent Convertibles Help Private Asset Managers Fund Their Acquisition of Non-Performing Loans from Portuguese Banks?' (Washington, International Monetary Fund, 2019).
Schillig, M, 'Bank Resolution Regimes in Europe – Part I. Recovery and Resolution Planning, Early Intervention' (2013) 24 *European Business Law Review* 751.
Schneider, S et al, 'Basel "IV": What's Next for Banks?: Implications of Intermediate Results of New Regulatory Rules for European Banks' McKinsey Global Risk Practice Paper (2017).
Schoenmaker, D, 'The financial trilemma' (2011) 111 *Economics Letters* 57.
Scott, H and Gelpern A, *International Finance: Transactions, Policy, and Regulation* (New York, University Casebook Series, 2018).
Sepe, M, 'La vecchia e la nuova socializzazione delle perdite: elementi di continuità e di discontinuità' (2017) 4 *Rivista Trimestrale di Diritto dell'Economia* 22.
Shakdwippe, P and Mehta, M, 'From Basel I to Basel II to Basel III' (2017) 3 *International Journal of New Technology and Research* 66.
Shleifer, A and Vishny R, 'Fire Sales in Finance and Macroeconomics' (2011) 25 *Journal of Economic Perspectives* 29.
Singh, D, *European Cross-Border Banking and Banking Supervision* (Oxford, Oxford University Press, 2020).
Single Resolution Board, 'Introduction to resolution planning' (2016).
—— 'Decision concerning the adoption of a resolution scheme in respect of Banco Popular Español S.A.', 7 June 2017.
—— 'The SRB will not take resolution action in relation to Banca Popolare di Vicenza and Veneto Banca' (2017).
—— 'Single Resolution Board work programme 2017' (2018).
—— 'Single Resolution Board work programme 2019' (2018).
—— 'SRB Multi-Annual Planning and Work Programme' (2018).
—— 'Public Interest Assessment: SRB Approach' (2019).
—— Reply to written question Z-038/2019 by MEP Sven Giegold, 20 August 2019, 3, available at www.srb.europa.eu.
—— 'Single Resolution Board work programme 2020' (2019).
—— 'Expectations for banks' (2020).
—— 'Multi-Annual Work Programme 2021–2023' (2020).
Single Resolution Board, 'SRB replies to consultation on Review of the Crisis Management and Deposit Insurance Framework' (2021).
Sommer, JH, 'Why bail-in? And how?' (2014) 20 *Economic Policy Review* 207.
Svoronos, JP, 'FSI Insights on policy implementation No 6 Early intervention regimes for weak banks' (2018).

Tröger, TH, 'Regulatory Influence on Market Conditions in the Banking Union: the Cases of Macro-Prudential Instruments and the Bail-in Tool' (2015) 16 *European Business Organization Law Review* 575.
UNCITRAL, Model Law on Cross-border Insolvency (1997).
—— 'Legislative Guide on Insolvency Law' (2005).
—— Convention on Substantive Rules for Intermediated Securities (Geneva Convention) (2009).
—— Model Law on Recognition and Enforcement of Insolvency-Related Judgments (2019).
—— UNCITRAL Model Law on Enterprise Group Insolvency (2019).
Unidroit, 'Principles on the Operation of Close-out Netting Provisions' (2013) 18 *Uniform Law Review* 330.
US Treasury, 'Orderly Liquidation Authority and Bankruptcy Reform' Report to the President of the United States (2018).
Vignini, A, 'State Aid and Deposit Guarantee Schemes. The CJEU Decision on Tercas and the role of DGSs in banking crises. The role of the CJEU in shaping the Banking Union: notes on Tercas (T-98/16) and Fininvest' (2019) 85 *Quaderni di Ricerca Giuridica della Consulenza Legale della Banca d'Italia.*
Walker, G, 'Basel III Market and Regulatory Compromise' (2011) 12 *Journal of Banking Regulation* 95.
Walker, G and Purves, R, *Financial Services Law* (Oxford, Oxford University Press 2018).
Wojcik, KP, 'Bail-in in the Banking Union' (2016) 53 *Common Market Law Review* 92.
World Bank, 'Out-of-Court Debt Restructuring' World Bank study (2012).
Yeoh, P, 'Basel IV: International Bank Capital Regulation Solution or the Beginning of a Solution?' (2018) 39 *Business Law Review* 176.

INDEX

www.ingramcontent.com/pod-product-compliance
Ingram Content Group UK Ltd.
Pitfield, Milton Keynes, MK11 3LW, UK
UKHW021030041026
15470UKWH00013B/1108

9 781509 961306